D0944978

WITHDRAWN

CRIME AND THE MAN

CRIME AND THE MAN

BY

EARNEST ALBERT HOOTON

GREENWOOD PRESS, PUBLISHERS
NEW YORK   1968

PREFACE

IN this volume I have tried to epitomize the results of a twelve years' survey of the anthropology of the American criminal in a way which will be tolerable for intelligent and determined readers who are interested in human behavior but not in statistics. I am entirely sympathetic with persons who find arrays of tabular material revolting, because I feel that way myself. However, I have to grapple with the raw material of statistics, with their analysis, and compilation into tables, and finally with the interpretation of those tables, simply because there is no other way of elucidating information pertaining to large groups of men or things. In the course of time I have become so thoroughly inured to statistics that I prefer to scan tables rather than to read the accompanying interpretative text. This is probably because I am of a suspicious nature. I have steadfastly refused to publish any of my criminal data until I could beguile some publisher into printing all of the grim statistical facts upon which I base my contentions. That formidable task has been undertaken by the Harvard University Press, which is bringing out three ponderous volumes, each positively bristling with statistical documentation. I think that the first volume has 480 pages of tables, or some such appalling number. But this present book contains not a single statistical table, practically no footnotes, and not even a bibliography. It is written primarily for persons who are willing to accept on faith my conclusions from statistics, without taking the trouble to wade through the statistics themselves. However, I have a sneaking hope that many of them will have their anthropological and criminological appetites so whetted by this gentle little primer that they will tackle the really scientific monographs, thus rewarding the Harvard University Press for its manifestation of an incredibly non-commercial policy. Of course, I shall be quite as well satisfied if some of the readers of this book resort to the larger work through sheer unbelief and with the malicious intent of "showing me up."

I planned this non-technical summary partly to "temper the wind to the shorn lambs," by which I mean my publishers and the general reading public, but when I was beginning to put it together, I received an opportune invitation to deliver a course of Lowell Institute lectures. So I have been able to kill two birds with one stone, or slay two lambs with one blast, or what will you? Not all of the contents of this book were delivered before the lecture audience, but only as much of it as I thought they could sit through. I figured it pretty closely.

I originally intended to illustrate the lectures and the book with diagrams and graphs, but decided that ordinary graphs are hardly less depressing than tables. So I began to embellish or deface the graphs with nasty little human figures. Beginning thus innocently, I gradually relapsed into an adolescent vice of which I have been free for a quarter of a century — drawing bad pictures. These are supposed to illustrate the text, but I suppose that a psychologist would say that I perpetrated them "as a way of escape."

However, there are also in this book some professionally drawn and admirably executed heads, which were made by Mr. Elmer Rising. Now I want to say this "very loud and clear," in fact "to shout it in your ear": these drawings of heads are not portraits of criminals, real or imaginary. They are not portraits at all, nor even composites, but only mosaics of facial features and proportions. If my data show, for example, that first degree murderers, as a group, have more square chins and more long noses than total criminals, I have arbitrarily put together a facial mosaic representing a person who has a square chin, a long nose, and every other delineable facial feature found to characterize the group. I did this because it is impossible for an audience or a reader to visualize anything from a long list of anatomical peculiarities, unless they, or he, are, or is, versed in physical anthropology. So you must not imagine that any single criminal of a given classification resembles the drawing made to illustrate the anatomical peculiarities of that class. Some of the criminals in each class have none of these variations which are found in excess in the entire class, and none have all of them. It is even possible that no one, criminal or noncriminal, looks like any of these drawings. I hope so. I had the drawings redone by Mr. Rising from original rough sketches, because I wanted these mosaics of criminal features to be handsome rather than ugly. I wanted the criminals to be as good-looking as is compatible with the prescribed combination of features. My own mosaics are altogether too villainous in appearance. We try to be fair.

In the preparation of the text of this volume, as in the analysis of the results of the entire criminal survey, I have had the inestimable advantage of the suggestions, corrections, and criticisms of my junior colleague and friend, Dr. Carl C. Seltzer. In fact, a full acknowledgment of my indebtedness to him would protract this preface to an altogether unpardonable length, and it is too long already.

Misses Charity Mason and Elizabeth Warren, of the staff of the Division of Anthropology of Harvard University, have had to read, type, and otherwise deal with the stuff of this book *ad nauseam*. I have often been sorry for them, although they have cheerfully dissembled their fatigue and boredom. Miss Mason, especially, has borne the brunt of the work. She abundantly merits her Christian name, because she "suffereth long and is kind."

EARNEST A. HOOTON

Peabody Museum of
Harvard University,
Cambridge, Massachusetts,
November 16, 1938

CONTENTS

ILLUSTRATIONS

CRIME AND THE MAN

CHAPTER I

THE ORGANIC BASIS OF CRIME: THEORIES, METHODS, MATERIALS, HEADACHES

ORGANIC BEHAVIOR

THE anthropologist who obtrudes himself into the study of crime is an obvious ugly duckling and is likely to be greeted by the lords of the criminological dung-hill with cries of "Quack! quack! quack!" Such a raucous reception is not strange, when one considers the nefarious activities of palm readers, physiognomists, and misguided persons who have sought to localize mental faculties by groping for bumps on the bony skull. The latter pseudo-science — phrenology — is hardly more sensible than the efforts of the diviner whose pathetic forked wand led him to the mountain tops in search of water. Distrust of anatomical guides through the maze of human conduct has resulted in a flat denial of the relationship of the body to the mind and to behavior, loudly voiced by bigoted social scientists and feebly echoed by timorous students of human biology.

The democratic principle of human equality, torn from its political context, has been used as a moral sanction for declarations of psycho-physical independence. The mere proposal to investigate seriously the racial anatomical characters which are the outward signs of inheritance, in their relation to psychological or sociological phenomena, is regarded as a sin against the Holy Ghost of Science. For this state of affairs we have to thank principally the Fascist prostitution of anthropology to political and economic oppression. Such a perversion of the science of race puts the anthropologist into a worse position than that of Caesar's wife. For he must be above suspicion of having anything to do even with Caesar. He is free to study environmental factors, but concern for his good repute makes him afraid to tackle heredity. He may work around the kitchen, but has to stay out of the bedroom. This enforced vestal virginity has sterilized human biology. I protest that he who investigates the human organism itself and the relation of its gross morphology to the putatively higher functions of the mind and to the noble phenomena of behavior, is not "living in sin." It is convenient for social scientists to ignore the organism and heredity, as Victorian prudery pretended to be unaware of organs and sex. The traditional rôle of the spinster is devotion to good works of a strictly sterile and even inorganic type. Anyone may attempt to manipulate institutions and even to save souls, but he *must believe* in the incorruptible body. Man is comparatively callous about his institutions and his behavior, moderately insensitive on the subject of his intelligence, but excessively touchy about his organic equipment and his heredity.

The social scientist seeks to better the environment of the human organism, either upon the assumption that the environment makes the organism and its conduct, or that, whatever may be wrong with human institutions, there is nothing the matter with man. He can conceive of no situation in which "Nature shows a smiling face, and only man is vile." Now it is far from my intention to belittle the efforts of the sincere, intelligent, and conscientious workers who have poured out their blood and other people's treasure in investigating the causes of crime and in devising methods of preventing delinquency and of reclaiming the criminal. Prison reform, probation, the juvenile court, the cleansing of the Augean stables of the city slums, the draining of familial and neighborhood cesspools which spawn criminality — all of these are notable achievements which must not be decried. Yet, it cannot be claimed that the sociologists have succeeded where the jurists and the police have failed.

The sociological approach may have been near enough to the crime problem to grapple with it, but it has not been able to put it down.

Psychiatry has shed some light upon the causation of crime, but it is baffled by the intangibility of psychological processes. If one could put his finger upon a mental defect as upon a wart, or could measure a subnormal mentality with a clinical thermometer, the task of the psychiatrist would, at least, be simplified. At present the diagnosis of mental disease and the determination of mental defect remain somewhat fuzzy, and subject to personal equation. An unkind critic has suggested that in the field of criminology psychiatrists have often based their diagnoses of mental disease upon the antisocial acts which they attribute to the aforesaid psychopathic states. Certainly there is no logical validity in a judgment that a man is crazy because he has committed a murder and that he has committed the murder because he is crazy. The absence of norms for mental states is partially due to the abstract quality of psychological processes. Nevertheless, a great merit of the psychiatric approach lies in its primary concern with the organism of the criminal. At the same time it does not neglect the influence of environmental factors upon that organism.

It is no part of this research to examine the extent to which the criminal's behavior is determined by his mental deficiency or sufficiency, or by the state of his mental health. Nor is it incumbent upon us to ascertain to what precise degree the career of the delinquent is an effect of his social environment. Our task is to study the physical characteristics of criminals for the purpose of discovering whether or not these are related to antisocial conduct.

We may first examine the *a priori* basis for an assumption that the behavioristic tendencies of man may be associated in some fashion with his physical characteristics. It can hardly be denied that, in a general way, the behavior of different kinds of animals is an expression or function of their respective organisms. Thus the behavior of chimpanzees, although varying individually, is typically chimpanzee behavior and arises from the morphology, physiology, and psychology of that particular animal genus. We cannot assert that the chimpanzee pattern of behavior is caused by the chimpanzee type of ear, of dentition, of prehensile foot, or even of cerebral convolution, but we do maintain that an animal whose details of structure are those of a chimpanzee will inevitably conduct itself in a manner befitting that ape. Similarly, an animal of gorilla morphology will behave like a gorilla, and the evidence thus far gathered indicates that gorillas and chimpanzees differ as markedly in respect of behavior as in their anatomy. Since, then, the behavior of an animal arises from its specific bodily organization, or, at any rate, is characteristic of the latter, it follows that the physical characteristics of any animal should afford some clue to the type and quality of his mental and emotional responses, always allowing for individual variation and differentiating environmental influences. But this, of course, does not imply that any particular morphological variation of a bodily part, or any combination of such variations, is causally related to the generic, specific, or individual behavior of the animal. They are merely bound together in an indissoluble organic association, such that one may be predicted, to some extent, from the other.

Human mental processes and human behavior are sharply distinct from those of the anthropoid apes, and the differences are inherent in the organisms of the zoological families, and not merely the effects of divergent environmental forces. These differences are, moreover, qualitative as well as quantitative, just as are their respective physical differences. Within the human species there are hereditary physical differences which divide mankind into distinct physical types which we call races. These differences, like those which distinguish man from any ape, are both qualitative and quantitative, although by no means so great as those which separate the human family as a whole from that of the apes. It may, therefore, be postulated that different physical racial types of man will display mental and emotional qualities diverging one from another, in conformity to their respective peculiarities of physical organization which are of hereditary origin. Even if one is so wrong-headed as to insist that all racial physical variations should be ascribed to environmental molding, it, nevertheless, follows that the psycho-biological processes of the animal, and ultimately what we call its "behavior," will be modified in correlation with changes in its physical attributes. But this does not mean that there exists a direct causal relationship between the physical minutiae of an animal and its psychological processes — much less its behavior. All of these are varied expressions of the organism, arising from heredity, and modified in their several directions by environment.

Thus, it would appear that racial physical differences should naturally be associated with racial psychological differences, and that the social behavior of distinct racial stocks should vary in accordance with their physiological and psychological divergences. But neither racial psychological differences nor racial differences in social behavior have been demonstrated hitherto in any adequately scientific manner. The lack of demonstration does not, however, imply a *de facto* absence of such racial differences. On the contrary, it may be ascribed, in all probability, to the crudity and general inadequacy not only of methods of measuring psychological differences, but also of the anthropological techniques employed for the determination of racial physical types. Differences in racial psychology cannot be ascertained until we are able to select for psychological examination racial physical types. Before you can pick fleas off a dog, you must catch your dog. Slipshod thinking, faulty techniques, and general pusillanimity are responsible for the meager anthropological achievements which fail to provide the sound basis for a psychological examination of races. But the psychologist has, nevertheless, rushed in where the anthropologist has feared to tread, and has attempted to discover racial differences and to measure them, without knowing or caring what a race may be. Thus the blind has led the blind and both have fallen into the ditch and got all wet. But let us not be content to leave them there.

The physical anthropologist must provide a scientific classification and definition of races which will enable the psychologist and the sociologist to eliminate from their data the confusing and complicating factors of racial, physical heterogeneity.

I shall now attempt to justify the contention that the relation of social behavior to the physical characteristics of the human organism can be studied advantageously in criminals. A criminal, for our present purpose, is a person who is under sentence in a penal institution, having been convicted for an antisocial act punishable by imprisonment. Here is no presupposition that a criminal is a biologically or psychologically abnormal being, or that he is the victim of a malign environment. There is no assumption whatsoever as to the nature of crime, except that it is an act which in the society under observation is punishable by commitment to a penal institution. Crimes are obviously infractions of more or less arbitrary social rules, and whether an act is or is not accounted a crime depends not only upon the nature of that act, but also upon the attitude of society toward it, which may differ radically from time to time and in various political, social, and ethnic groups.

There is, however, one constant element in all conceptions of crime — one immutable feature in a Protean form — the criminal act is always an offense against society sufficiently heinous to actuate a large proportion of the society to demand its punishment through processes of law and to secure such legislation and some measure of its enforcement. Therefore, the criminal is a person distinguished by the commission of an overt act against society, and he exemplifies for us an extreme of human conduct, thus making himself an excellent subject for the investigation of the relation of physique to behavior.

The identification and apprehension of a criminal are most frequently accomplished by utilizing the unique combinations of his physical characteristics — anthropometric features, fingerprints, et cetera. The use of such methods merely helps to ascertain what individual is responsible for a given act. It simply distinguishes him from the rest of mankind who are innocent of that particular offense. It does not imply that the physical features which describe and identify the criminal are causally related to his antisocial conduct. Similarly, it may be worth while to examine the physical characteristics of large groups of criminals to discover whether they are in any sense physically homogeneous, and, if so, whether they are distinguishable from noncriminals. Here, again, there is no necessary implication of causality — at least in the sense of a direct relationship between the physical characteristics of criminals and their antisocial conduct. If, however, it were demonstrated that criminals do indeed differ physically in a significant degree and in a constant direction from law-abiding citizens, the question would be raised as to the meaning of such differences. It is conceivable that the linkage of bodily features with mental processes may be such that the latter may be predicted from the former. Whether the association of physical and psychological characters is due to hereditary influences or to environmental influences, or to both, it is none the less important if, in reality, it exists.

Again, since different types of criminal acts are obviously the results of diverse motives and widely different psychological states, it is clear that any physical or mental differentiation of the criminal should manifest itself amongst criminals classified according to their types of offense, as well as between criminals as a group and non-criminals. None of these ideas is novel, but they must be restated here because they have never been demonstrated to be true, nor have they been refuted finally by any adequate body of scientific evidence.

It has been the fashion among certain criminologists to insist upon dealing with the "individual delinquent," on the ground that the nexus of hereditary and environmental influences in each case is so different that any profitable analysis of groups of delinquents is impossible. Certainly the behavior of any individual is an individual problem, and corrective treatment and preventive measures must be suited to the individual case. But, unfortunately, society has not time to concern itself with the heredity of each criminal, with his particular environment, and with the intricate web of circumstance which enmeshes him in crime. Such an individual method is too costly and too time-consuming, because of the vast numbers of potential and actual delinquents.

"If seven maids with seven mops swept it for half a year,
  Do you suppose," the Walrus said, "that they could get it clear?"
"I doubt it," said the Carpenter, and shed a bitter tear.

Just as the experimental zoologist must keep his genera, species, and varieties distinct in his genetic or physiological studies, so must the criminologist discriminate between the different races and nationalities involved in his investigations, so that he will not further complicate an already involved problem by utilizing organically heterogeneous material. No one supposes that the work of the classificationist explains the individual variations within any stated zoological group. Similarly, the description and analysis of different races and nationalities in the United States, with especial reference to their antisocial behavior, does not presuppose that their differences in criminal propensities (if there are any) are directly related to their racial characteristics. Such processes of selection merely insure the homogeneity of the experimental groups, just as the zoologist separates the different strains of his laboratory animals before subjecting them to experiments involving the effects of diet, heat, light, et cetera.

Nationalities, as well as races, should be separated in criminological investigations. Races are physical groupings of mankind established on the basis of inherited morphological and metric features. A nation is a large body of people under a central government, usually inhabiting a geographical area within defined boundaries, and further possessing certain cultural traits in common, such as customs, historical traditions, and often language. While nationality does not connote race, it is by no means devoid of biological significance. For nations are, almost invariably, great inbred groups, and as such present certain recurrent physical types which are the result of the hereditary perpetuation of specific racial blends. These national physical types are often as easily recognizable as the so-called racial types, and show much more definite patterns of behavior. They exhibit not only a restricted range of physical characters, but also some degree of social and psychological solidarity. United by heredity, nativity, education, and existence within the same state, nationals are likely to manifest also similar criminal proclivities. Hence, in an anthropological study of the criminal it is essential to deal with each nationality separately, because each has in some degree its own physical and cultural individuality.

When the relation of crime to physique within a specified nationality has been ascertained, we may proceed further to pool the different nationalities and to attempt studies of the relation to crime of the larger racial physical types within our combined international series.

Before embarking upon an historical summary and criticism of earlier work in criminal anthropology it is necessary to deal with one stupid, perennial objection advanced against the study of criminals. This objection is that prisoners represent only the failures of the criminal population. It further implies that the inferior physical, mental, or sociological qualities of incarcerated felons are not shared by the more clever criminals who escape arrest and conviction. But more than half of the criminals now in jail have been there before, and most of them will be there again. Hence a large, but indeterminate, proportion of the crimes presently to be committed will be due to the activities of the convicts who are going to be paroled or released. Again, the presumption that successful criminals are rarely or never convicted is almost certainly incorrect. I doubt that any considerable part of the crimes committed in the United States is perpetrated by persons who steadily pursue anti-social careers without ever falling into the clutches of the law. I do not believe that many clever men commit crimes, and that only a few of the stupid are caught. Even if this were the case, it would be no more sensible to neglect the study of convicted criminals because some criminals escape conviction than to give up the study of hospitalized victims of infantile paralysis, because the majority of children exposed to this disease escape it, or having contracted it, fail to enter the clinics where their ailment may be diagnosed and treated, and where preventive measures for the non-infected are being sought.

HISTORICAL SUMMARY OF CRIMINAL ANTHROPOLOGY

LOMBROSO

Although unconcerned with the vociferous objections of penologists, sociologists, and sentimental humanitarians to the invasion of the criminological field by a biological anthropologist, and quite unperturbed by the cries of "Scab!" which have greeted me as I have labored without a union card, I find it necessary to agree with much of the adverse criticism which has been directed against previous anthropological studies of the criminal. The methods and results of such investigations must be discussed here.

The central idea of the great Italian criminologist, Cesare Lombroso, was that criminals differ from law-abiding citizens in showing many physical anomalies which are of atavistic or degenerative origin. The theory of atavism postulates a reversion to a primitive or subhuman type of man, characterized physically by inferior morphological features reminiscent of apes and lower primates, which occur in the more simian fossil men, and are to some extent retained in modern savages. There is a further implication that the mentality of such atavistic individuals is also that of the primitive man or the savage, and that, consequently, the behavior of these "throw-backs" is contrary to the rules of civilized society. The degenerative theory is at the opposite pole from the atavistic and almost incompatible with it. The degenerate is the product of diseased ancestral stocks which have ceased to evolve progressively and are well along in the process of devolution — simulating frequently in their pathological offspring the rudimentary physical and mental attributes of primitive man.

Both of these theories, held successively or simultaneously by Lombroso and his followers, emphasize the hereditary basis of antisocial conduct and stress the organism of the criminal to the exclusion of his environment. Underlying these conceptions is the conviction that the criminal is a biological anomaly and that crime is, to some extent, an abnormal biological phenomenon.

Lombroso's first contention was that the skulls of criminals show larger percentages of primitive and pathological features than do those of the non-criminal population. He supported it by a profusion of metric and morphological data, presented however in such a faulty way and in so partisan a spirit, that his alleged results were easily demolished by exposure of his weakness in technique and by citation of contradictory conclusions reached by his equally biased opponents. No impartial and accurate investigator has taken the trouble to go into the question with sufficient thoroughness either to refute or to confirm Lombroso's claims. A completely new survey of all documented crania, carefully distinguished as to race and nationality and compared with adequate samples of the crania of civilians of the same ethnic and racial origin, will provide the only solution of the problem.

Serious objections must also be raised against Lombroso's evidence of criminal anomaly in living delinquents. These are: inadequate size of the samples studied, the mixing up of diverse ethnic and racial strains in the material investigated, and the lack of a scientific method of statistical analysis. The Lombrosians seem to have assumed that criminals are more or less of the same type the world over, irrespective of race and nationality, and that characteristics demonstrated, for example, in Italian criminals, will be found to occur with equal frequency in German or French offenders. The conception that there are but two types of men, normal and criminal, and that these types transcend the physical differences which distinguish the various races of men, is almost too fantastic for serious consideration. If one is disposed to admit that criminals do, indeed, differ from "normal" persons, they must diverge from their own particular racial patterns. But it is hardly conceivable that such divergence is always in the same direction and of such extent as to make one unified criminal type, irrespective of race. Then if there are criminal types, there must be multiplicity of them, just as there are numerous racial types. Consequently, it is utterly futile to investigate the differences between criminals and civilians without first making sure that both belong to the same racial group and are thus physically comparable.

Certainly no blame can be attached to the Lombrosians for not utilizing the modern methods of statistical analysis which have been developed by Karl Pearson and the biometricians, since these tools had not yet been invented at the time when most of the work in criminal anthropology was done. These statistical devices, unknown to Lombroso, make it possible to analyze biometric data with sufficient precision to dispel the cloud of uncertainty and suspicion which hangs so heavily over the raw material and dubious findings of the early criminal anthropologists.

The central thesis that the criminal deviates psychologically and anatomically from the normal law-abiding citizen was not proved by Lombroso and the criminal anthropologists, but it has never been refuted. The same is true of the conception of distinct types of criminals differentiated according to the nature of their offenses. Such notions as that of the born or instinctive criminal, of the moral imbecile, and of the epileptoid criminal may be left for the consideration of the psychiatrist, after the physical anthropologist has settled the question of the anatomical distinctiveness of the criminal. The psychological characteristics and etiology of hypothetical physical types of criminals must await the demonstration of such types. Questions of ultimate causation cannot be settled on grounds of inherent probability or improbability.

Charles Goring was a medical officer in the English prison service, who published in 1913 a work entitled "The English Convict." This book has been commonly regarded as a final refutation of Lombroso's theories pertaining to criminal type — especially by criminologists who have not read it, or have been unable to understand it.

Goring was a statistical genius and an evangelistic humanitarian. I entertain the most profound admiration for him in the former capacity, since I believe that his volume represents a more substantial contribution to methods of anthropometric analysis than anyone had made previously. Although I have learned more from him than from any other single anthropological source, it is unavoidable that I express certain adverse and even harsh criticisms of his great work.

Goring was frankly and violently prejudiced against Lombroso and all of his theories. Here is his own plain statement of bias made at the outset of his work:

This, then, is our contention: admitting the criminal does possess all the characters that have been attributed to him; admitting, even, that he is marked by a "dome-shaped" head, and by a face like a "bird of prey"; admitting that he is drunken, impulsive, obstinate, dirty, and without control — despite all this, we maintain that he is not an abnormal man. He may represent a selected class of normal man; many of his qualities may present extreme degrees from the normal average: yet the fact remains that, in the pattern of his mind and body, in his feelings, thoughts, desires, and recognition of right and wrong, and in his behaviour, however outrageous it may be, he exists by the same nature, and is moved by the same springs of action, that affect the conduct, and constitute the quality, of normal human beings.[1]

However much one may admire the fervid humanitarianism of this dictum, it can scarcely be claimed that such an

---

[1] Charles Goring, *The English Convict*, London, 1913, pp. 24–25.

attitude is consistent with the objective examination of facts which is indispensable to scientific method. Sentimentality must be removed from social science, if it is to produce anything more constructive than emotional orgies. If criminology must be the sloppy science, let us hope, at least, for a few investigators of the Walrus variety, who will mingle their tears with a little scientific discrimination:

"I weep for you," the Walrus said: "I deeply sympathize."
With sobs and tears he sorted out those of the largest size,
Holding his pocket-handkerchief before his streaming eyes.

Impelled by his moral convictions, Goring used his statistical genius to distort the results of his investigation to conformity with his bias. He was quite unable to emulate the Walrus in divorcing his scientific procedure from his social sentiments. The following are his principal methods of perverting evidence: a specious and unjustifiable use of statistical devices for the purpose of reducing and minimizing physical differences actually observed between different classes of criminals or between criminals and non-criminals; the practise of impugning the accuracy and validity of his original data only when the results fail to conform to his bias; the use of comparative data which are really not comparable at all, having been derived from populations which are ethnically diverse from his criminals and which have been studied by different techniques; his selection of anthropometric measurements and observations which have never been considered criminologically important, and his neglect of those which have been regarded by criminal anthropologists as the most significant; his disregard of the ethnic and even racial heterogeneity of his series, which consists not only of English, Welsh, and Scotch, but even of a smattering of other races and nationalities.

Elsewhere I have explained in detail the objectionable and illegitimate use of statistical processes which Goring makes in his attempts to nullify the evidence of criminal physical differentiation which his materials exhibit.[2] I cannot embark here upon the lengthy technical discussion which the matter entails. One simple illustration of his procedure must suffice. Let us suppose that murderers and thieves differ in average stature, and that they also differ in average intelligence, estimated upon some crude scale. By a device known as correlation it is then possible to obtain a mathematical quantity purporting to denote the extent to which mean stature is altered when mean intelligence is raised or lowered. From this figure one may make a mathematical guess at the average statures which murderers and thieves might exhibit if they were reduced to the same hypothetical level of intelligence. Supposing further that murderers and thieves differ both in average stature and in estimation of average intelligence, Goring subtracts from their crude statural differences the amount which he thinks may be due to their differences in intelligence, and then appraises the residual difference in stature, if there is any, as the sole deviation of criminological significance. Such a procedure involves the fallacious assumption that if stature and intelligence vary together, a change in one is causally related to a change in the other, that, for instance, an increase in stature causes an increase in intelligence, or *vice versa*.

The entire work of Goring bristles with statistical sophistries, all devoted to his purpose of proving that criminals, although they differ from each other, or from non-criminals, physically, would not so differ if they were all of the same age, the same stature, the same intelligence, et cetera — in short, a triumphant demonstration that if due allowance be made for all of the physical and mental differences between criminals and non-criminals, the former do not differ from the latter. By dubious statistical methods, he succeeds in

[2] Earnest A. Hooton, *The American Criminal*, vol. I, pp. 18–31.

reducing the problem to a series of quasi-philosophical abstractions, which are completely removed from reality and serve only to confuse the issues in the minds of persons whose unacquaintance with mathematical statistics renders them unduly suggestible to formidable arrays of coefficients and formulae.

Nevertheless, there are many portions of Goring's work which are of great value. His notable contributions are in the study of criminal physique (which he finds definitely inferior, thus confirming the conclusions of Lombroso), in the influence of age upon crime, in the vital statistics of the criminal, in the mental differentiation of the criminal (which again agrees with Lombrosian ideas), and in his investigation of "force of circumstances," fertility, and heredity. He also merits abundant praise for the variety of delicate and ingenious statistical devices which he employs, although his use of them is frequently culpable.

Actually, Goring left the problem of the relation of the criminal's physique to his offense unsolved. Mathematical formulae and verbal sophistry may befuddle lay readers, but no one who reads and understands Goring's *English Convict* can accept his conclusions, unless he shares the prejudice of that author. Humanitarian motives should not palliate a disingenuous use of statistics. Disraeli is alleged to have said of Gladstone that he did not mind his playing the political game with an ace up his sleeve, but he did object to his claiming that God had put it there. That is the way I feel about Goring.

HISTORY, MATERIAL, AND METHODS OF THE HARVARD SURVEY OF THE RELATION OF RACE AND NATIONALITY TO CRIME IN THE UNITED STATES

These lectures are intended to provide a non-technical summary of the results of the Harvard Survey of the Relation of Crime to Race and Nationality in the United States, begun in 1926 and now thankfully terminated. The detailed presentation of statistical data, upon which the validity of this summary depends, is in process of publication elsewhere.[3] The critical student must satisfy himself as to the correctness of the methods employed and the conclusions drawn from the mass of material tabulated in the larger work. I do not wish to describe the present lectures as a "popular" summary, because the adjective "popular" implies that the material and manner of presentation are such that the populace likes them, a supposition contrary to fact in the case of my writings. However, palatable or not, these conclusions represent the closest approximation to the truth which I am able to make from the largest body of data on criminal anthropology heretofore collected and analyzed. They will be neither sugared with the sentiments of social uplift nor salted with the cynicism of misanthropy.

The materials for the study were collected over a period of three years by graduate students trained by me in physical anthropology. The raw data have been analyzed under my direction in the Statistical Laboratory of the Division of Anthropology of Harvard University. I cannot catalogue here the names of the many individuals to whose support and cooperation I owe the completion of this research. I can only request that you accord to these inarticulate workers, advisers, and patrons whatever meed of approbation may be due to this work. Like Arnold von Winkelried, I wish to gather to my own breast all of the hostile spears of my critics — not because I am heroic, but because my hide is tough, indurated by the scar tissue of many previous wounds.

This survey began with a study of some 2000 county jail prisoners of Massachusetts, carried out under the aegis of the State Department of Mental Diseases. It was then ex-

[3] Earnest A. Hooton, *The American Criminal*, Harvard University Press.

tended to the adult male inmates of Massachusetts prisons and reformatories, and to those of the states of North Carolina, Tennessee, Kentucky, Wisconsin, Missouri, Texas, Colorado, Arizona, and New Mexico. The choice of states was dictated partially by the ambition to secure adequate samples of criminals of every race and nationality represented in the country, and was limited to some extent by the impermeability of certain states to the type of investigation undertaken. North Carolina, Kentucky, and Tennessee were selected because of the high representation of Old American and Negro stocks, the states of the Southwest because of their copious infusion of criminalistic Mexicans. Wisconsin yielded samples of German and Scandinavian stocks, and Missouri a large series of Negroes and Negroids. It was thought that Massachusetts would provide samples of virtually all of the immigrant stocks from Europe, and the anticipation was amply fulfilled. The only considerable portion of the country omitted from the survey was the Pacific coast, partly because this salubrious area contains no racial or ethnic elements unrepresented elsewhere, with the exception of the Hollywood breed and a larger proportion of Chinese and Japanese. Very few of these latter appear to get into jail,[4] a fact which seems to reflect the difficulty of Americanizing the Oriental.

If one aspires to find out whether criminals differ from civilians, the latter must be studied also in order to provide a basis of comparison. In Massachusetts and Colorado criminal insane were matched with a series of civil insane, and a similar procedure was followed in the case of criminal insane Negroes in North Carolina. (I take no little satisfaction from the beautiful justice of these comparisons.) Check samples for sane Negro criminals were obtained in Tennessee and in North Carolina. Series of civilians for

---

[4] Only 368 Chinese and Japanese of both sexes were present in the prisons, jails, reformatories and workhouses of the United States on January 1, 1923.

comparison with Whites were secured in Tennessee and in Massachusetts. In the latter state the civilians measured were members of the state militia and out-patients from hospitals in Boston.

The totals of subjects measured and observed in the survey were: prison and reformatory inmates 10,953; county jail prisoners 2,004; criminal insane 743; defective delinquents 173; insane civilians 1,227; sane civilians 1,976. The grand total was 17,680, but of these some 604 were omitted in analysis, largely because of unknown parentage or because they belonged to racial and ethnic groups too small in the prison population to furnish samples adequate for study.

Some 22 standard anthropometric measurements on head and body were taken in the case of each individual, and from these measurements were calculated 13 indices or percental relations of one measurement to another, such as the relation of head breadth to head length. Sociological items pertaining to each person included name, age, birthplace, birthplace of parents, occupation, education, previous convictions, length of sentence, marital status, nature of offense, religious affiliation, racial and ethnic extraction. Where reliable data were available, intelligence quotients, mental classification, and pathologies noted in medical examinations were recorded. There were also 33 main categories and 72 subcategories of morphological features which were visually graded and appraised in the case of each subject. These items include hair color, hair form, eye color, and other traits which do not lend themselves to measurement. The total number of anthropological facts available for the study of each individual was 107, and of sociological items 13, exclusive of sundry medical and psychological information.

In the case of each individual record sheet, thirteen indices were calculated and checked, and all of the data were coded and then transferred to Hollerith punch cards. These cards have 80 columns, each column containing numbers and spaces for twelve possible punch holes. Every fact relating to a single individual is represented by a hole punched at a specified place in one of the 80 columns. Often a column is subdivided to accommodate two or more classes of items. The punched cards are then fed (at the rate of 400 per minute) through an electrical sorter, which separates them into 12 pockets, corresponding to the 12 numbered holes punched in any one of the 80 columns selected for sorting. The sorter is connected with a three-bank printing card counter, which counts, prints, and totalizes the numbers of cards in each position in the column which is being sorted, and simultaneously counts, prints, and totalizes upon two other columns. It is thus possible by repeated sortings and tabulations not only to secure mechanically the total counts of single items, but also to determine the occurrences of any required combination of items, however intricate. Thus it might be possible (although not necessarily desirable) to ascertain how many men of Irish parentage, tall stature, long heads, red hair, and blue eyes were convicted of assault, what were the educational attainments of such individuals, and whether they were single, married, divorced, separated, or widowers. The tabulations of facts printed by the card counter are copied upon appropriate forms and then go to the statisticians who compute averages, percentages, and mathematical constants of various kinds, utilizing for this purpose electric calculators which perform automatically the processes of addition, subtraction, multiplication, and division. After these have been rechecked, the data are compiled into typewritten tables. All that then remains is for the anthropologist to make sense out of them. This, of course, is very easy.

You will now understand that the credit which may accrue from the results of such a survey as I have described belongs first to the field workers who collect the data, secondly, to the clerks who prepare it, thirdly, to the super-human but inanimate machines which sort it and tabulate it, fourthly, to the statisticians who reduce it by endless calculations, and last but not least, to the persons and organizations which have supplied the necessary funds. Conversely, the blame for any failure or shortcoming belongs to the individual who analyzes and interprets, in this case to me.

There are a few grim and tedious statistical processes to which we must devote a brief and reluctant attention. Statistics are merely quantitative or qualitative data, and statistical methods are those adapted for the elucidation of such data affected, as Yule says, "by a multiplicity of causes." There are two classes of data which may be treated statistically. First of all, there are variables which have in themselves a quantitative measurable value, as, for example, the length of the human head in millimeters. Secondly, there are attributes, which are subject to qualitative appraisal and gradations, and presence or absence of which in the individuals or objects of a series may be counted. We grade these attributes subjectively, because we cannot measure them easily or at all, but we treat our counting of these observations by statistical methods.

In dealing with series of measurements we apply to them certain elementary processes which extract from the data the principal items of the general information required. Firstly, the individual measurements are arranged in classes or groups of ascending numerical value, the class limits taken at equal intervals so that each class represents one, three or five, or some other number of units used in measurement. Thus in stature seriation, or arrangement, we might establish the class interval at two centimeters, and we should then ascertain how many of the individuals measured fell into the class 165–166 centimeters, how many in the class 167–168 centimeters, and so on through the series.

When we have finished this process of seriating, we know the range of our data — the maximum and minimum values — how many individuals fall into each class of the series, and in which classes the frequencies or numbers of observations are greatest. By adding the class totals we secure the grand total of the individual observations taken. Having thus learned the range and the distribution of individual measurements by classes, we proceed to ascertain the ordinary average value of the individual observations — the arithmetic mean with which we have all been painfully familiar from childhood. The next step is to obtain some measure of the dispersion of the series — the average extent to which individuals in the whole series deviate from the arithmetic mean. If we know, for example, that the average weight of a series of men is 150 pounds, but that the mean extent to which individuals in the series deviate from the average of the series is 15 pounds, we have then acquired a measure of the variability of the series — we know to what extent it may be considered homogeneous. We now know the range, the distribution of individual observations in equal classes through that range, the central value in terms of the arithmetic mean, and the average or standard deviation of individuals from that mean.

In most scientific studies it is impossible to measure or to observe the entire universe of animals, plants, or things, concerning which we desire to deduce valid generalizations. We are compelled to confine our attention to samples of greater or lesser size drawn from that universe. These samples, even when selected at random, are likely to be unrepresentative — i.e. they may not reflect accurately the characteristics of the population or universe from which they are drawn. Thus, if I were to attempt to gauge the intelligence of Greater Boston by securing the intelligence quotients of a Lowell Lecture audience, I should certainly commit a grievous error; firstly, because the audience would be selected, not at random, but on the basis of their common interest in the possibly superior mental pabulum which lectures under the Lowell Institute purport to offer, or perhaps on the basis of their common desire to spend an hour in a warm place on a cold night. There is no mathematical means of correcting such an error in the selection of a scientific sample, because the error is based upon bad judgment. Even if this hypothetical sample of Boston intelligence were representative in respect of selection, it would be unreliable because of its numerical inadequacy. There are not enough individuals in the group to provide an adequate basis for generalizing concerning the entire population from which it is drawn. This sort of error, due to the insufficient size of small random samples, can be estimated, and the margin of leeway for inaccuracy due to this cause can be appraised.

The method of calculating the sampling error is based upon the laws of probability. It is a matter of observation and experience that most human measurements, when recorded upon very large samples of individuals, fall into a so-called normal distribution. On a piece of squared paper a horizontal line is ruled, and marked off at regular intervals which are given the ascending values of the individual observations in the series. A vertical is erected at the left extremity of the base line and is graduated to represent, by its equal intervals, the number of individual observations. Then the number of observations of a given value determine the height from the base line, and the value of the observation the horizontal distance from the left extremity of the base line, so that dots made upon the squared paper at the points so determined give a graphic picture of the distribution in two-dimensional form. Now if the sample is large enough, it is possible, by joining the dots with lines, to construct what is called a frequency polygon which can be smoothed into a curve — the so-called normal curve of error. Such a curve has its highest point at the arithmetic mean of the series and drops off rapidly and symmetrically on both sides of the mean until it approaches the base line, when it is again inflected. The curve is approximately bell-shaped; it may be expressed as an equation, and the properties of its areas, and the values of its ordinates or verticals at any given point, are accurately known. These mathematical properties of the normal curve of distribution may be utilized for the estimation of the probable amount of error which may be expected in small samples which cannot realize the ideal normal distribution because of their numerical inadequacy. In the case of the arithmetic mean of a sample, for instance, its so-called probable error is a quantity such that the odds are even that the true value of the observed mean will fall somewhere between ordinates drawn on either side of the mean at distances equal to the probable error. The probable error of the mean thus enables us to estimate the limits of its reliability. When the means of two samples are compared it is possible to estimate the significance of their differences on the basis of probable errors. As a rough measure of the significance of differences we use three times the probable error of the differences in means, since differences of such a magnitude are to be expected to occur in only four out of 100 cases, if the samples are drawn at random from the same population.

This use of the probable error thus enables us to distinguish those differences between samples which may be due merely to accidents of the sampling process and inadequate numbers of observations, from those which may be of some real validity and assignable to anthropological or other causes. A device of this character is of inestimable value in biometric analysis.

In studying the statistics of attributes or qualitatively observed characters, it is possible to use similar means of estimating the extent to which pairs of them, as, for example, blue eyes and blond hair, are associated in groups of individuals over and above what may be expected on the basis of chance. The theory of probability and the application of its laws enable us to avoid falling into the error of confusing fortuitous differences, due to sampling, with those which may be of real anthropological or sociological, or other significance. Consequently, we are enabled to conclude, for instance, that murderers are really anthropologically different from thieves, when, in the sum totals of the arrays of their respective means of indices and measurements, and in their proportions of observed morphological observations, they differ from each other to an extent which corresponds to heavy odds against their having been derived from the same population or universe.

All of this sounds very complicated, and it is complicated. These statistical devices and tricks are used, however, merely to prevent the student from making a fool of himself by confusing fictitious and accidental differences with those which are real and significant. They should not be used to fool gullible auditors or readers.

The student who is attempting to analyze data collected by two or more different observers has also to be on his guard against the particularly misleading and generally malign influence of an anti-scientific goblin called the Personal Equation. This spirit of evil operates persistently and insidiously to corrupt and pervert the honest labors of the scientific observer. Two anthropologists, for example, may have been rigorously trained to take all of their measurements in exactly the same way, with identical instruments, so that their results will be strictly comparable. As time goes on these observers unconsciously diverge slightly in their techniques. Perhaps one of them compresses the soft parts slightly in applying the arms of the calipers to the subject's body. Possibly another tends to go off a wee bit in locating some particular anatomical point of measurement.

Then their series will, upon analysis, exhibit differences which are specious and misleading.

In the present survey the bulk of the data was collected by two men. The demon Personal Equation was not exorcised with bell, book, and candle, but by laborious multiple sortings, comparisons, and scrutiny of the differences shown in the subseries of the different observers working upon comparable human material. Take, for example, ten pairs of offense subgroups, each pair consisting of a series of men convicted of the same offense and each pair consisting of native Whites of native parentage, but in every case one of the paired subgroups measured by Observer A in Kentucky and the other by Observer B in North Carolina. If, for instance, in head length Observer A's first degree murderers, robbers, thieves, forgers, et cetera show consistently lower or higher averages than do the comparable groups of Observer B, we suspect that Personal Equation is at work. Otherwise, the small deviations between means of the respective subgroups measured by the two observers would not be consistent in the same direction. In the Harvard Criminal Survey an enormous amount of computation was performed in order to search out these possibilities of error. It turned out that only three of 20 measurements gave evidence of incomparability because of personal equations in technique of measuring. The difficulty was resolved in these measurements and the indices derived from them, by keeping the respective series of the two observers separate, dealing with them as if they were entirely distinct measurements, and accepting as valid only inter-group differences confirmed by both observers, each using his own technique on his own series. Thus, if we found that Observer A always recorded longer measurements of ear length than Observer B, and we found further that A's first degree murderers had significantly longer ears than his burglars and thieves, we then proceeded to examine separately Observer B's first degree murderers and his burglars and thieves. If he then also found the former to have longer ears than the latter, we accepted, as valid, the difference in ear length between the offense subgroups under examination.

Personal equation is even more diabolically troublesome in subjective morphological observations, when each observer has to depend upon his own ideal standard of judging immensurable attributes, as, for example, whether the hair of a subject is absolutely straight in form or has low waves, whether his eyes are blue or blue-gray. In the 70 classes of such graded subjective morphological observations protracted scrutiny and comparison resulted in their classification into four grades of reliability: Class A observations which show no evidences of divergence between the two main observers (27 per cent of all observations); Class B in which there was some small personal equation, but, on the whole, a fair agreement (19 per cent); Class C with marked discrepancy (23 per cent); and Class D, radical divergence (31 per cent).

Thus, Class A results of the two observers could be combined and interpreted with full confidence, Class B observations with only slight reservations, and Class C observations only with the greatest caution. In the case of Class D observations only the data of the one observer, judged to be the more accurate and reliable, were accepted in the few cases where they were utilized at all. Most of them went down the drain. There is but one scientific method of dealing with really bad data: throw them away!

In the exhaustive and long-drawn-out struggle with these difficulties there came a belated and horrid recognition of a new and unexpected complication, which ultimately turned out to be a blessing in disguise. All native White prisoners of native parentage were at first combined in a single series, on the apparently justifiable assumption that they were representatives of the same or nearly the same ethnic and racial blends, irrespective of their state of birth and incarceration. Gradually there grew up in my mind a nasty and ineradicable conviction of something wrong, since, for example, first degree murderers, in their differences from other offense groups, showed characteristics which reflected an excess of the Kentucky hill-billy physique rather than any combination of characters which would be of general anthropological and criminological significance.

Therefore, with maledictions and moans we tore the whole Old American series to pieces and analyzed each state group separately. There resulted the discovery that in the case of these old stocks, native Whites of native parentage, and probably of many generations' residence in the United States, local inbred physical types had differentiated, so that the criminals of each state differed from those of every other, presumably because of slightly different original mixtures of ethnic strains and subsequent divergence through inbreeding.

This dark and gruesome dawn was then illuminated by a simple little invention christened State Prediction. From the total of criminals of a given descent observed in any one state we know the average of stature or the proportion of blue eyes to be expected from that state. Hence, if we have murderers combined in an offense subgroup with representation from nine states, we are able to predict the mean stature and the proportion of blue eyes to be expected in combined first degree murderers by taking the averages of the several states, weighted by their numerical contributions to the combined offense subgroup. The quite simple arithmetical process of subtraction enables us to make allowance for the effect of diversity of state composition in judging the physical and other differences which may be manifested between first degree murderers and total criminals, or between any offense subgroup and the entire series of criminals of a given descent.

The same method happily takes care of personal equations of the observers, since each of the two principal workers was responsible for separate total state groups. Hence, a prediction, based upon state composition of an offense subgroup, is a mathematical estimate of the value of the character to be expected, not only as a result of the diversity of state physical types, but also because of the observers' variations in technique manifested in combination, arising from their personal idiosyncrasies in their exclusive states. Again, this process sounds complicated, but this time it is not. It enables us, in appraising criminological differences, to discount such quantity of a given divergence as may be attributable to factors irrelevant to our anthropological purpose.

CONCLUSION

Statistics are not flowery meads, through which one may trip the light fantastic. They are, rather, treacherous jungles, concealing many a slough of despond. To thread a safe and successful way through such difficult ground requires of the guide ample experience, some little knowledge, and a steadfast orientation toward the goal of truth, which recedes as one advances. It is possible to conduct a party of tourists over this route, but it is hardly a blithesome journey. A street car conductor inquired of a woman who boarded his conveyance with a huge bevy of youngsters, "Madam, are these all your children or is it a picnic?" She replied: "Sir, these *are* my children, and it is *no* picnic." This little parable has a twofold application: to the director of a research and his hapless but devoted assistants; to the deliverer of this lecture and his bored but patient audience.

In future lectures those of us who persist will pluck

the fruit of the trees of knowledge which we encounter in this journey; we shall taste them, and some of us will find them sour, some will adjudge them rotten, and many will acquire stomach-aches. Most will probably drop by the wayside.

Man is an organism, and his behavior arises from his organic constitution, as it responds and reacts to environmental stimuli. The variations of the individual organism, as well as the nature of the stimuli, determine the nature of the response. Specifically, we are undertaking to examine the physical characteristics of a large series of antisocial individuals in order to find out whether their varied types of delinquency are associated with their anthropological characters, and whether they are physically distinguished from those of us who are, perhaps temporarily, at large, and at least putatively, law-abiding.

CHAPTER II

OLD AMERICAN CRIMINALS: SOCIOLOGICAL GLEANINGS, PHYSICAL DIFFERENCES BY STATE AND BY OFFENSE

ALL human beings of any single generation have lineage of equal length; all spring from Adam or some Adamitic ape. Yet, some of us are said to belong to "old families" for no other reason than that of ancestral immobility. It is accounted a virtue to come of a strain which has abode for generations in a single spot, stuck like a limpet to a rock. Men and women born in the United States, who can claim parents and grandparents of similar nativity, have been called "Old Americans" by our most distinguished government anthropologist.[1] They constitute the backbone of our nation, not only of its law-abiding citizens, but also of its criminals. However, for criminological purposes it is necessary to scale down the definition of an Old American to a native born White of native parentage — from three to two generations of American nativity — largely because criminals seem less addicted to genealogy than to certain other vices. In deference, then, to priority of settlement as well as superiority of numbers, we may begin with a consideration of the Old American Criminal.

SOCIOLOGY

It is essential to deal with the social statistics of our criminal series, since criminals form a social class, distinguished by antisocial behavior. Under social statistics I include all data that are not primarily biological, such as the facts pertaining to geographical distribution and state nativity.

---

[1] Aleš Hrdlička, *The Old Americans*, Baltimore, 1925.

The logic of classification is thus brutally subordinated to convenience of treatment. Because this investigation *is* primarily biological, it is limited, for the most part, sociologically, to the analysis of a few bare and basic facts, copied from the records, and sparsely supplemented by personal interrogation. Some of these data, doubtless, include items which are incorrect, but lack of precision is inherent in social science. I have been compelled to omit from analysis the details of case histories, nor do I propose to titillate your criminological fancies with juicy anecdotes.

PARENTAGE AND DISTRIBUTION

Comparative data from the census indicate that our total prison and reformatory series of males represented between 10 and 12 per cent of all of the male prisoners then incarcerated in such institutions through the United States. The composition in parentage and race is closely similar to that of the total prison population of 1928, but with a slight excess of Negroes and Negroids. The 4212 native Whites of native parentage, our so-called Old Americans, constitute 38.46 per cent of our prison series. The nine states represented in this Old American criminal series are Massachusetts, Tennessee, Kentucky, Texas, North Carolina, Wisconsin, Arizona, Colorado, and New Mexico. (The last three have been combined in a single group.) The series is heavily overloaded with southerners, since it includes 28.18 per cent of Kentuckians and 21.72 per cent of Texans. Such a sectional overweighting is inevitable, simply because the Old American stock is concentrated in the south and we have gathered it where it grows. Much more important is the fact that the several states contribute markedly disproportionate numbers to the various offense groups. Thus, first degree murder contains an unduly large number of Kentuckians; second degree murder is overloaded with persons from Kentucky, Tennessee, and North Carolina; forgery and fraud, and offenses against public welfare include altogether too many Texans; while, finally, Wisconsin appears to overindulge in rape. Some of these inequalities of state representation in offenses are attributable to differences in penal codes. For example, a state which hangs or electrocutes first degree murderers is unlikely to keep many in stock. Other variations are probably ascribable to local differences in *mores* and to restriction or diversification of criminal opportunity. In some states, the honor of the family may still demand an occasional homicide committed upon some equally honorable neighboring family. In another state, natural resources may encourage the sale of worthless oil stocks. In industrialized states, the weekly pay roll offers temptation to the slum gangster, and so on. States have favorite crimes as well as favorite sons. It is perfectly evident, then, that if the state contributions to the ten offense groups are disproportionate to their total contributions to the series, an allowance for state composition must be made when any offense group is compared with the total series of which it is itself a part.

EXTRACTION

In about half of this series it was possible to obtain information as to the extraction, or national descent, of parents' families, although all parents were native born Americans. Approximately 37 per cent of extractions other than straight American were recorded. In Kentucky and Tennessee very few European extractions were reported, whereas in Wisconsin and North Carolina, more or less remote European descents were described in 84 and 75 per cent respectively. Such information is often more easily obtainable in populations which have grown through fairly recent European immigration. Of course in a criminal group there are many individuals who do not even know their parentage, and are thus hampered in effort to trace

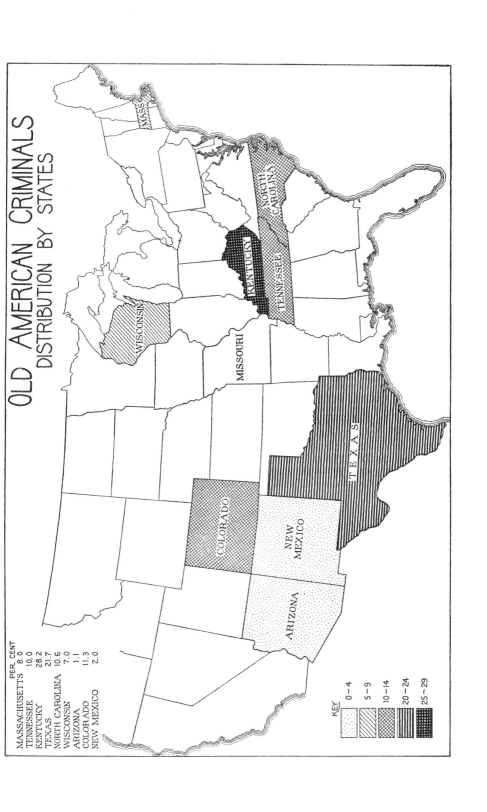

OLD AMERICAN CRIMINALS
DISTRIBUTION BY STATES

	PER CENT
MASSACHUSETTS	8.0
TENNESSEE	10.0
KENTUCKY	28.2
TEXAS	21.7
NORTH CAROLINA	10.6
WISCONSIN	7.0
ARIZONA	1.1
COLORADO	11.3
NEW MEXICO	2.0

KEY

0 – 4
5 – 9
10 – 14
20 – 24
25 – 29

their genealogy back to Brian Boru or William the Conqueror.

In every state except North Carolina the leading extraction reported is Irish, a finding consonant with the claims of certain historians as to the ethnic composition of the American Revolutionary Army. This strain comprises 36 per cent of all foreign extractions reported. Next comes English with 21 per cent, then German with 12 per cent, Scotch-Irish with 9 per cent, and French with 7 per cent. Pure Scotch is in sixth place with 6 per cent and there are insignificant scatterings of other European strains. Our Old American criminals are, then, of predominantly British and Irish descent and may boast of a purely Aryan, if not Nordic, heritage.

RELIGIOUS AFFILIATION

The data upon religious affiliation were analyzed without enthusiasm, since it was anticipated that they would not be highly relevant and might be invidious. First of all, we tried to get some inkling of the northern or southern Irish origins of our Old American criminals of Irish extraction by tabulating their religious affiliations, Catholic or Protestant. It was found that 43 per cent were Catholic, 41 per cent Protestant, and the rest had no religion at all. Thus, if we split the pagans nearly equally, with a 2 per cent bonus to the Protestants, it comes out even, with half of the Irish descendants green and the other half orange. However, I am not inclined to have much confidence in such an inference.

The whole Old American series, taken by ethnic extractions, shows 60 per cent of Protestants, 15 per cent of Catholics, and 25 per cent with no religious affiliation. It is rather remarkable that Tennessee, a fundamentalist state, reports 65 per cent of the irreligious, while Massachusetts can lay claim to but 4 per cent. Texas has 46 per cent of Old Ameri-

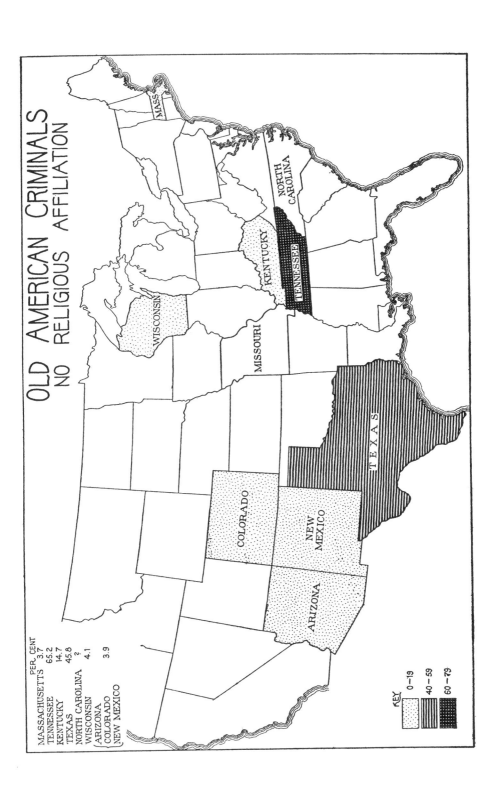

OLD AMERICAN CRIMINALS
NO RELIGIOUS AFFILIATION

	PER CENT
MASSACHUSETTS	3.7
TENNESSEE	65.2
KENTUCKY	14.7
TEXAS	45.8
NORTH CAROLINA	?
WISCONSIN	4.1
ARIZONA	
COLORADO	3.9
NEW MEXICO	

KEY

0—19

40—59

60—79

can criminals without church connections, but Wisconsin only 4 per cent. The criminals who are such Old Americans that they have forgotten their European extraction seem also to have lost their religious affiliations oftenest, since the straight American group leads the unchurched with 32 per cent. One suspects that length of residence in the United States and the level of education within the state of residence both affect the reports of religious affiliation. Ignorance and ungodliness are prison cell mates in benighted districts. Massachusetts is our only state in which more Old Americans are Catholic than are Protestant, with 91 per cent of the Irish Old Americans professing Catholicism. In many of the other states the criminals of Irish extraction are predominantly Protestant. These few extracts from the complete analysis suggest that the longer a person's ancestors have been in this country, the less likely he is to "belong to a church," at any rate, if he is a criminal.

CRIMINAL MIGRATION

A study of the birthplaces of men imprisoned in each of our nine states indicates the migrations of Old American criminals and affords a means of comparing the nativities of the criminals in each state with those of the total state population. Only 30.5 per cent of our Old Americans are in jail outside of their native states. The lowest proportion of extra-state born inmates is found in Kentucky with 13.6 per cent. This fact reminds me of the reason given by Tacitus for his contention that the Germans are an indigenous people. He said that no one who was not born there would go there. The maximum of extra-state inmates occurs in Arizona, with 72 per cent. Evidently some states grow their own crops of delinquents and some import them. The Old American criminals in Kentucky, when not born there, are nearly all natives of adjacent states. The situations in

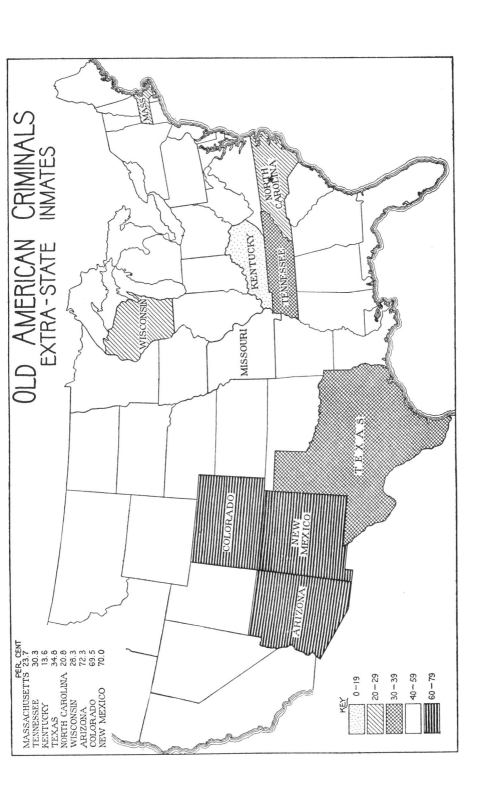

OLD AMERICAN CRIMINALS
EXTRA-STATE INMATES

PER CENT
MASSACHUSETTS 23.7
TENNESSEE 30.3
KENTUCKY 13.6
TEXAS 34.8
NORTH CAROLINA 20.8
WISCONSIN 28.3
ARIZONA 72.3
COLORADO 69.5
NEW MEXICO 70.0

KEY
0 – 19
20 – 29
30 – 39
40 – 59
60 – 79

North Carolina, Tennessee, and Massachusetts are closely similar.

The further west the state, the higher its proportion of Old American criminals born to the eastward, as compared with its home-grown products and those of its immediate neighbors. Thus, Wisconsin has natives of 28 outside states in its prison; Texas has representatives of 33 other states; and Colorado is most cosmopolitan of all, with Old American criminals born in 37 outside states. Here one regrets the absence of data from California, which might be expected to show that all of its Old American criminals have been imported, and from at least 47 other states, or, alternatively, that there are no criminals there at all.

The leading contributors of their native sons to the prison population of Wisconsin are New York and Michigan, whereas Texas draws mainly from Tennessee and the Southeastern states. New Mexico and Arizona are victimized principally by Texas, and Colorado receives similarly undesirable elements from Missouri, Kansas, and the Middle Western states.

By comparing the Old American extra-state inmates of prisons and reformatories with the proportions and states of nativity of the total population of native born in each state, it is possible to discern whether the Old American criminals come from the same states and in similar proportions as the more welcome residents. Every state has relatively more non-native criminals than non-native lawabiding Old Americans, partly because the latter include women and children, who are not so migratory as are the adult males. Then, too, it seems probable that a spell in prison does not enhance one's love for one's native state. Upon release the jailbird is likely to flit elsewhere.

When we attempt to fit the nativity composition of the prisoners to the total population makeup of the same state, with respect to proportions of native and extra-state place of

birth, we find that Kentucky shows the closest correspondence, with only 2.2 per cent more of extra-state inmates in
the prison series, and with the same outside states con-
tributing in the same order of importance to both criminal
and total population. Tennessee obtrudes its native sons
into the prisons of other states more than it contributes to
the law-abiding populations of those states. It may be that
the natives of Tennessee prefer even the penitentiaries of
other states to residence in their natal area. On the whole,
however, the Old American criminal population, in any
state, seems to correspond quite closely in nativity to the
composition of its total population. There is little indication that this criminal series consists of migratory delinquents. It is, rather, drawn in each state from the indigenous
or resident criminalistic strains.

PREVIOUS CONVICTIONS

We have seen that the majority of our Old American
criminals are in jail at home. We next discover that many
of them are also at home in jail. Records of the previous
convictions of the criminals were available in all of the
states studied except North Carolina. These records show
that 39 per cent of our Old American criminals have been
previously convicted. The figure is certainly far below the
correct proportion, because the records are of varying fullness in the several states. Massachusetts and Wisconsin show
the highest proportions of recidivists, probably not because
they harbor the most incorrigibles, but because they keep
the best records. In order to have complete files of previous
convictions of prison inmates, the administrators of justice
must be able to read and write.

Before we can determine the significance of differences
in recidivism among the ten offense subgroups, it is necessary to make a correction for state sampling, in order to
eliminate the confusing effect of the unequal values of state

prison records. We then find that persons with records of previous convictions are disproportionately few among first and second degree murderers, sex offenders, and the group committed for offenses against public welfare (principally bootleggers and violators of automobile laws). On the other hand, burglars and thieves include very large excesses of persons with previous convictions. Burglary and larceny is always the largest crime category and it includes the most habitual criminals, irrespective of variations in the state records.

MARITAL STATUS

It is simple enough to classify criminals according to marital status, in four categories: single, married, divorced or separated, and widowers. It is not so easy to interpret these findings, especially when it is noted that bachelors are unduly frequent in Massachusetts and the Southwest, husbands in Texas, and divorcés and widowers in Wisconsin. Thus before we can reach a conclusion in regard to the offense differences in matrimonial state, we must again clear away the effects of state sampling. These turn out to be unimportant, except an excess of divorced men among rapists, which proves to be due to the preponderating activity of Wisconsin in that illegal pastime. There remains clear evidence that high proportions of single men are characteristic of robbers, burglars, and thieves; that married men are excessively frequent among those convicted of sex offenses other than rape, of offenses against public welfare, and of arson and miscellaneous crimes. Finally, widowers, divorced, and separated men are disproportionately numerous among first degree murderers, rapists, and other sex offenders. However, we must also consider the fact that age affects marital status. Very young men are likely to be bachelors; somewhat older men, married; men still older, divorced; and the oldest, widowers. It is also a fact, hereto-

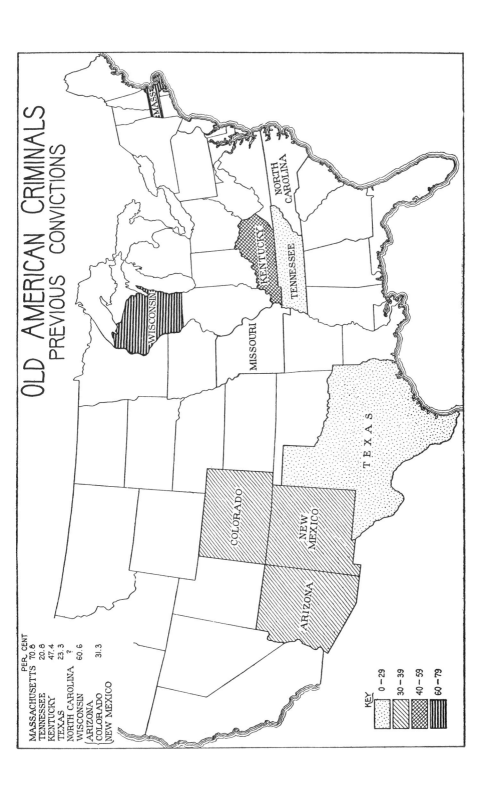

OLD AMERICAN CRIMINALS
PREVIOUS CONVICTIONS

	PER CENT
MASSACHUSETTS	70.8
TENNESSEE	20.8
KENTUCKY	47.4
TEXAS	23.3
NORTH CAROLINA	?
WISCONSIN	60.6
(ARIZONA	
(COLORADO	31.3
(NEW MEXICO	

KEY
0 – 29
30 – 39
40 – 59
60 – 79

fore unmentioned, that our criminal offense subgroups vary considerably in mean age. For example, first degree murderers are likely to be very old, because they have to serve the balance of their lives, or a good share of it, in prison. It is, therefore, necessary to introduce a correction for age in order to discover whether differences which are independent of state sampling are also free from the effects of inequalities in mean age of the offense subgroups.

When this process has been carried out, first degree murderers lose their excesses of married men, but still retain their unduly high proportion of widowers. This fact raises the suggestion that these superfluous widowers convicted of first degree homicide may have murdered their wives. However, since there are only 22 of them altogether, and since, in fact, we do not know whom they killed, the matter must rest in this intriguing uncertainty. It may be noted, also, that excesses of married men among the second degree murderers, although not of widowers, survive the corrections for state sampling and age. We are inclined to agree with Goring that marriage appears to be an incentive to murder. Bootleggers and incendiaries, who compose the majority of two offense subgroups — versus public welfare and arson and all other offenses — also display independent excesses of married men and deficiencies of celibates, quite apart from age and state sampling. Perhaps the economic stress of married life may contribute also to these types of delinquency, and possibly these criminals are unusually good "providers."

In strong contrast are the robbers, thieves, and burglars, who remain unmarried much oftener than would be expected from their ages. Of course these men are the most persistent recidivists and frequent imprisonments may tend to disqualify them for the responsibilities of family life. At any rate, one cannot assume the bonds of matrimony while wearing those of penal servitude. If we may conjecture that these most habitual criminals are least likely to have progeny, we have at last uncovered one cheering possibility. However, one suspects that many of these individuals do not take the trouble of stealing marriage licenses, but live in sin, without benefit of Marie Stopes.

OCCUPATION

The crude data on the alleged occupations of our criminals are influenced by the predominantly rural character of all of the nine states studied, except Massachusetts. Thus, in the total Old American series nearly 32 per cent belong to the so-called extractive occupations (of a legitimate nature), which include agriculture, mining, stock raising, lumbering, forestry, and fishing. In the ten categories of occupations listed, the extractive category is almost twice as numerous as any other, and is followed in ranking by factory workers, unskilled laborers, skilled trades, transportation, personal service, trades, clerks, semi-professional, the professions (law, medicine, education, religion), and, finally, public service.

State inequalities in criminal occupations are so great that the true relationship of offense to civil occupation claimed can be ascertained only after the application of the usual state predictions and corrections. It then emerges that the most striking association of type of crime with occupation is that of murder with extractive pursuits (principally farming). There are many more murderers in this occupational category than there should be, even when due allowance is made for the rural character of certain states. There is also a marked deficiency in this extractive group of robbers, burglars, thieves, and fraudulent offenders. On the other hand, factory workers include an excessive number of robbers; skilled trades are disproportionately high in bodily assault; trade and clerical work in forgery and fraud; personal service in burglary and larceny; and the professions in fraudulent offenses. When an occupational group seems to specialize in some type of offense, it naturally is deficient in others. These marked relationships of occupation to type of offense will be subjected to further examination at a later stage of this survey. It is futile to discuss them until we have satisfied ourselves that the legitimate occupations claimed by criminals are not largely fictitious. Incidentally, at this point it may be stated that a study of the age distribution of alleged criminal occupations shows a reasonable correspondence of physical requirements in strength, age, and vigor to vocation, and, also, the expected relationship of pursuits which require extensive training, experience, and maturity, with advanced age. Subsequently, we shall see whether criminals are physically differentiated in conformity with their alleged occupations.

EDUCATION

Naturally, we have investigated in some detail the educational attainments of our Old American criminals. They are, in general, very meager. The raw statistics show 10 per cent who are illiterate and another 4.5 per cent who claim to be able to read and write but have not attended school. Here we need not labor through the tabulations of each state and each offense group, which indicate how many and what percentage have reached each grade of education, all the way from the primary class to college. We may use, instead, a short-cut method of educational ranking, which contrasts the proportion of the well educated in each group with those who are almost, or quite, illiterate. Specifically, the percentages of men who have reached the last two years of high school, or have attended professional school or college, are divided by the percentages of the illiterates plus those who read and write but have never gone to school. I call this the educational ratio, and it is, in effect, a comparison of the extremes, with the intermediates neglected.

OLD AMERICAN CRIMINALS

Educational Ratios by Offense

$$\frac{3rd - 4th \ yr \ high + college}{illiterate + read \ and \ write}$$

Offense	Ratio
FORGERY FRAUD	2.31
ROBBERY	2.00
BURGLARY LARCENY	.65
ASSAULT	.56
SEX	.47
ARSON	.43
BOOTLEGGING	.37
RAPE	.25
2nd DEGREE MURDER	.11
1st DEGREE MURDER	.10

The highest ranking offense group is forgery and fraud, which has an educational ratio of 2.30. This signifies that it contains 2.3 times as many highly educated as crassly ignorant. Next in rank come successively: robbery, 2.00; burglary and larceny, 0.65; assault, 0.56; sex offenses other than rape, 0.47; arson, 0.43; versus public welfare, 0.37; rape, 0.25; second degree murder, 0.11; first degree murder, 0.10. Thus, there are nearly 23 times as high a proportion of well educated to ignorant men among fraudulent criminals as among murders of either degree, while burglars and thieves include approximately six and one-half times as many educated persons in proportion to the ignorant as are found among the first degree murderers. However, we may not conclude that amount of education determines type of offense. The reverse may be true, or neither.

We must first consider state rankings of prisoners in this same educational ratio. These are: first, Massachusetts (there she stands) with 11.91; next, Wisconsin, 2.43; the three combined Southwestern states (Arizona, New Mexico, Colorado), 2.16; Texas, 1.01; Tennessee, 0.46; North Carolina, 0.30; and Kentucky, a very poor last with 0.08. On this rating Massachusetts has nearly 149 times the ratio of well educated to ignorant as has Kentucky, and Wisconsin criminals of high academic attainment are 81 times as numerous with respect to their unlearned brethren as are well educated felons from North Carolina. Whether or not these states should congratulate themselves on the high educational attainment of their criminals is a question you may debate for yourselves.

When the huge differences in educational status of the nine state groups have been duly corrected, it is possible to distinguish the offense group relationships which are independent of varying opportunities for education in the several states. Both classes of murderers are definitely stigmatized by excessive illiteracy and generally poor educational

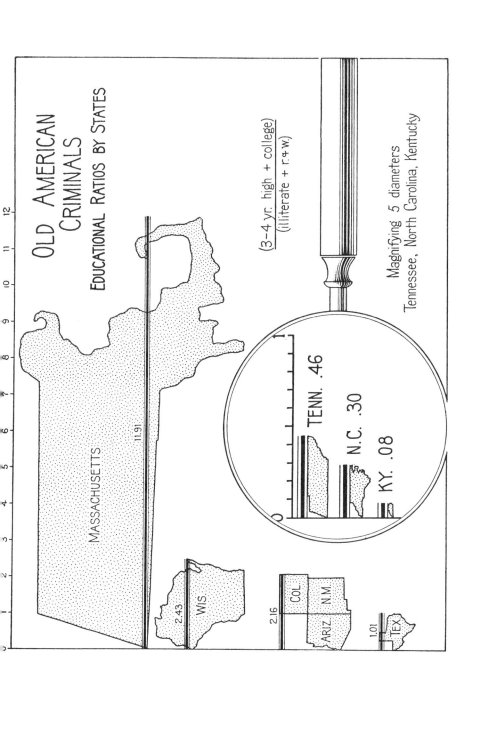

OLD AMERICAN
CRIMINALS
EDUCATIONAL RATIOS BY STATES

MASSACHUSETTS 11.91

WIS 2.43

COL 2.16
ARIZ
N M

TEX 1.01

$$\frac{(3\text{–}4 \text{ yr. high} + \text{college})}{(\text{illiterate} + \text{r.} \& \text{w.})}$$

Magnifying 5 diameters
Tennessee, North Carolina, Kentucky

TENN. .46
N.C. .30
KY. .08

attainment, while rapists are to a lesser degree distinguished by deficiencies of well educated persons. Quite as outstanding is the educational preëminence of the robbery, and the forgery and fraud groups, which presumably constitute the criminal intelligentsia. Burglars and thieves are remarkable for their intermediate position, since they are deficient in persons who are illiterate or have had no formal education, but show excesses of individuals who have reached the seventh grade and the first two years of high school. One supposes that they have learned to subtract, at any rate. Evidently, then, educational differentiation in the several offense groups of delinquents is by no means wholly dependent upon state sampling. There is, further, no consistent relationship of the age of the criminal to his educational status. Perhaps the strongest criminological argument in favor of a protracted education is that it keeps adolescents and near-adults less heinously occupied than they might otherwise be, during the ages of high criminalistic susceptibility.

SUMMARY

We may now assemble and summarize the sociological peculiarities of the ten offense groups which survive corrections for age and for state sampling. First degree murderers are distinct from total Old American criminals in their infrequency of recorded previous convictions, in their high proportions of widowers, in their excessive representation of the extractive occupations, and in their abysmal ignorance. Second degree murderers are distinguished from the entire series in a similar manner, except that their marital deviation is deficiency of bachelors and excess of husbands. The small offense group convicted of assault is high in married men and in skilled trades workers. Apparently in skilled trades, short tempers and short hours, strikes and personal violence, go together. Robbers are notable for their unmarried status, for their excess of factory operatives and deficiency of extractive workers, and for their unduly large numbers of men who have reached the eighth grade or attended high school. Burglars and thieves are again overloaded with celibates, and also with laborers, factory operatives, and personal service workers. They are low in illiterates and high in individuals with moderate educations, and above all they include great excesses of persons with records of previous criminal convictions. The fraudulent criminals are outstanding in representation of the clerical, trade, and professional occupations with corresponding deficiencies in laborers and extractives. Highly educated men are most numerous in this category of delinquents, and the illiterate are disproportionately rare. The rape group, apart from state complications, is notable only for deficiencies of the highly educated, for generally poor scholastic status, and for a dearth of men previously convicted. Offenders committed for sex crimes other than rape are independently differentiated by fewness of unmarried men, and excess of persons claiming to belong to the professional occupations (law, medicine, teaching, and the church). Versus public welfare convicts (guilty of violation of liquor laws, of automobile laws, of peddling drugs, carrying concealed weapons, and the like) differ from the whole series, apart from accidents of state sampling, in their greater proportions of married men and of those engaged in the extractive occupations. The small residual offense subgroup which includes arson and some miscellaneous offenses is finally distinguished only by a deficiency of the unmarried and an excess of the married.

When the sociological deviations of the ten offense groups are compared in number and significance with those expected in purely random samples, it is clear that every single category of criminal displays differences in social statistics from the total series which cannot be ascribed to chance and which supervene the effects of state composition. Such sociological differentiation of offenders convicted of different types of crime will scarcely evoke surprise. However, there is no inevitable implication of causality in the demonstration of the sociological separateness of various classes of criminals. Only if these social differentiae were unaccompanied by evidence of physical distinction in the subgroups, might it be assumed that environment is more potent than heredity in crime causation.

PHYSICAL DIFFERENTIATION BY STATES

If the Old American criminals of the nine states studied constitute nine distinct physical types, the finding is of great anthropological importance. However, our concern in this investigation is with the relation of crime to physique. We must isolate these state types of physique, if they exist, solely in order that they may not cause misinterpretation of the observed relationship of nature of offense to bodily characters. For it is all too clear that overloading of any offense group with the natives of a certain state would lead to wrong conclusions if that state were physically distinct in its population. Actually, first degree murder is packed with Kentuckians, versus public welfare with Texans, rape with the indigenes of my own natal state, Wisconsin, et cetera. Our aim is not merely to discover that this or that state physical type has a preference for some particular form of crime. We desire, rather, to study the general relation of physique to crime. Then as a necessary preliminary, we must undertake the irksome, though interesting task, of comparing the physical characters of each state series of Old American criminals with the total series of which it is a part.

CONCLUSIONS ON METRIC AND INDICIAL FEATURES

No audience or circle of voluntary readers in a comparatively free country would endure the detailed presentation of the amount and statistical significance of the mean deviations of nine state groups in each of 20 anthropometric measurements, 13 indices, and 70 morphological observations. It is inexpedient to strain the quality of mercy. Hence, I proceed directly to the briefest possible summary of results. Every state differs from the total series in such number of metric features and to such degree in each, that it must be concluded that its prison series of Old Americans is drawn from a population anthropologically distinct from that of the nine state aggregate.

Massachusetts differs significantly from the total Old American criminals in 25 of 33 characters. It is the youngest, the second shortest, lightest, narrowest in shoulder and chest, smallest in sitting height and in face breadth, of all the state groups. It has relatively the longest and narrowest face form, and the narrowest jaws.

Tennessee diverges least of all state groups from the combined series, but has, nevertheless, 17 significant deviations out of the total of 33 measurements and indices. It has the shortest head length, the largest head circumference, second largest forehead breadth, relatively shortest and broadest nose, and broadest forehead relative to face breadth.

Kentucky has 26 significant deviations, but most of them are not extreme. It is a little below mean age and mean weight, and a little above mean height; is markedly narrow in shoulder and forehead, and short in ear length. The narrow forehead is also notable in its extremely exiguous relation to head breadth and face breadth.

Texas presents 28 dependable divergences from the total series. The Texans are the tallest and heaviest of the state groups. They approach the maximum in breadth of face and nose, and present the assemblage of relatively shortest and broadest countenances.

North Carolina has 26 of 33 distinctive metric differences. Stature and weight are above the average, age well below (2.30 years). The North Carolinians have the longest and narrowest heads, the smallest cranial circumferences, the shortest noses, and very narrow jaws.

Wisconsin has 22 metric differentiae. Notably these men are oldest, shortest, second lightest, and greatest in head breadth. They have the second longest upper faces, the longest and relatively narrowest noses, and the greatest sitting height relative to stature.

Colorado, Arizona, and New Mexico are combined in a single group which is differentiated in 23 of 33 metric features. The most important of these involve absolutely long faces and relatively long noses.

Texas is the most strongly deviating state from the total group and Tennessee departs least from the metric means of the Old American criminals. It is, perhaps, a coincidence that Tennessee contributes more than twice as many of its native sons to the prisons of the other states than does any other state here studied. It is, in a sense, both the focus and the center of distribution of the most nearly typical Old American criminal. It is possibly atypical only in that it included (as of 1928) a Hooton among its penitentiary inmates. However, I have been assured by an anonymous female correspondent that I am the double of a man recently hanged for murder in Michigan. Certainly, if he was my double, he was not hanged for his beauty.

CONCLUSIONS ON MORPHOLOGICAL FEATURES

While it would be impracticable to enumerate here all of the morphological minutiae which distinguish the various state groups, some of the outstanding features of each may be mentioned.

Massachusetts criminals are notable for thick beards, red-brown hair, dark brown, green-brown and blue-gray eyes, whites of eyes discolored with yellow or brown pigment flecks, rayed pattern of the iris of the eye, external and

OLD AMERICAN CRIMINALS
MOSAIC OF CRANIAL, FACIAL, METRIC AND MORPHOLOGICAL FEATURES
MASSACHUSETTS

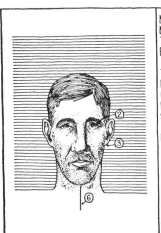

Narrowest face
Narrowest jaw
Thick beards
Broad, high nasal roots and
  bridges
Thick nasal tips
Right deflections of nasal septum
Concave profiles ①
External and Median eyefolds ②
Small, attached ear lobes ③
Thin integumental lips ④
Membranous lips – upper thin,
  lower thick
Lip seams absent
Undershot jaw
Facial prognathism ⑤
Right facial asymmetry ⑥
Median chins

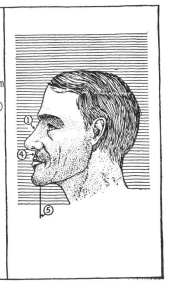

OLD AMERICAN CRIMINALS
MOSAIC OF CRANIAL, FACIAL, METRIC AND MORPHOLOGICAL FEATURES
TENNESSEE

Beard sparse
Shortest head length
Largest head circumference
Second largest forehead breadth
Broadest forehead relative to
  face breadth
Relatively shortest and broadest
  nose
Foreheads with little or no slope
Downward inclined septum ①
No deflection of septum
Compressed jaw angles
Median or pointed chins
Left facial asymmetry ②
Hollow temples
Long thin necks

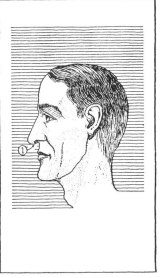

median folds of the upper eyelids, broad, high nasal roots and bridges, concave nasal profiles, thick nasal tips, right deflections of the nasal septum, thin integumental lips, thin upper membranous lip and thick lower lip, absence of lip seam, some facial prognathism or protrusion of the jaws, pointed or median chins, much dental decay but few teeth lost, small and soldered or attached ear lobes, and right facial asymmetries.

Tennessee criminals are outstanding in the following features: thin beards and scanty body hair, light brown shade of hair, blue-brown eyes with speckled or diffused irides, foreheads with little or no slope, nasal septum inclined downward, absence of deflected nasal septa, median or pointed chins, narrow or compressed jaw angles, many dental caries, prevalence of edge-to-edge bite of the incisor teeth, hollow temples, left facial asymmetries, and long, thin necks.

Kentucky Old American convicts show the following characters in excess: thick head hair and body hair, both dark brown and ash-blond hair color, gray-brown and blue eyes, homogeneous irides and those with rayed pattern, internal or Mongoloid and median folds of the upper eyelids, thin eyebrows, low foreheads, receding foreheads, low height of the nasal root but high nasal bridge, concavo-convex nasal profile, thin nasal tip with upward inclined septum, nasal septa skewed both to right and left, thin integumental but thick membranous lips, pronounced lip seams, slight and medium alveolar and facial prognathism (protrusion of jaws and face), square or bilateral chins, compressed cheek bones or malars, incisor teeth with edge-to-edge bite, small ear lobes, slight roll of the helix or outer rim of the ear, pronounced Darwin's point (vestige of the free tip of the mammalian ear), marked protrusion of the ears, both hollow and bulging temples, right asymmetry, and both long and thin and short, thick necks.

OLD AMERICAN CRIMINALS
MOSAIC OF CRANIAL, FACIAL, METRIC AND MORPHOLOGICAL FEATURES
KENTUCKY

Forehead absolutely narrow
Forehead narrow relative to
  head and face breadth
Forehead low, receding
Short ears, small lobes,
  slight roll of helix,
  marked Darwin's point,
  marked ear protrusion
Thin eyebrows
Median and Mongoloid eyefolds
Low nasal root ②   ①
High nasal bridge
Concave and convex profile
Thin tip
Upward inclined septum ③
Deflected septum
Compressed cheek-bones
Compressed jaw angles
Thin integumental lips
Thick membranous lips
Pronounced lip seams ④
Alveolar and facial prognathism
Square or bilateral chins
Right facial asymmetry ⑤

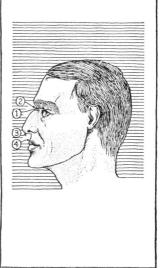

OLD AMERICAN CRIMINALS
MOSAIC OF CRANIAL, FACIAL, METRIC AND MORPHOLOGICAL FEATURES
TEXAS

Wavy hair
Heavy beard
Maximum face breadth
Very pronounced cheek-bones
Hollow temples
Relatively shortest and broadest
  faces
Nasal profile straight
Broad noses
Thick nasal tips
Downward inclined septum ①
Membranous lips - upper thin,
  lower thick
Full cheeks
Pronounced jaw angles
Bilateral chins
Slight alveolar prognathism
Long ear lobes ②
Pronounced Darwin's point ③
Slight antihelix

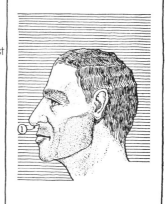

Notable features of the Texan criminals include, excesses of both scant and abundant head hair, heavy beard and body hair, wavy hair, frequent red hair, red-brown hair and black hair, prevalence of gray-brown eye color, thick nasal tips and downward inclined septa, absence of nasal septum deflections, thin upper and thick lower membranous lips, absence of lip seam, slight alveolar prognathism, bilateral or square chins, very pronounced malars (cheek bones), full cheeks, pronounced jaw (gonial) angles, many carious teeth but few lost, marked dental overbite (overlapping), long ear lobes, pronounced Darwin's point, slight prominence of the antihelix of the ear, hollow temples.

Next we come to North Carolina with distinguishing features as follow: sparse beard and body hair, excess of dark brown hair and of green-brown and blue-gray eyes with clear whites and frequently speckled irides, pronounced eyebrow thickness, low foreheads with extreme variations in forehead slope, high narrow nasal roots and high nasal bridges, excess of both convex and concave noses, thin nasal tips, nasal septa directed upward, frequency of septal deflection both to right and to left, thin membranous lips, with sometimes a thick lower lip, bilateral chins, compressed cheek bones, thin cheeks, jaw angles lacking prominence, large proportion of persons who have lost no teeth, absence of Darwin's point on the ear and prominence of the antihelix (the inner ridge), pronounced ear protrusion, full temples, right facial asymmetry, long, thin necks, and sloping shoulders.

Our Wisconsin criminals have the highest mean age, are distinguished also by thick beards but sparse body hair, straight hair in excess with frequency of dark brown and gray or white shades, many blue-gray and dark brown eyes with clear sclerae (whites), the iris frequently patterned in concentric zones, both low and high foreheads in excess but a tendency for the brow to be vertical, narrow nasal root and

OLD AMERICAN CRIMINALS
MOSAIC OF CRANIAL, FACIAL, METRIC AND MORPHOLOGICAL FEATURES
NORTH CAROLINA

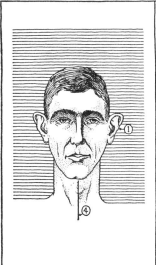
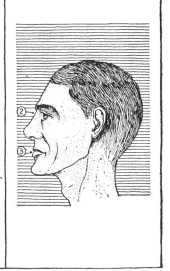

Longest and narrowest heads
Smallest cranial circumference
Thick eyebrows
Sparse beards
Pronounced ear protrusion
Darwins point absent
Prominent antihelix ①
Low foreheads
Extreme variation in slope
Shortest noses
High, narrow nasal roots and
 bridges ②
Concave and convex profiles
Thin nasal tips
Upward inclined septum
Frequent deflection
Thin membranous lips, but lower
 often thick ③
Compressed cheekbones
Compressed jaw angles
Bilateral chins
Full temples
Right facial asymmetry ④
Long, thin necks

OLD AMERICAN CRIMINALS
MOSAIC OF CRANIAL, FACIAL, METRIC AND MORPHOLOGICAL FEATURES
WISCONSIN

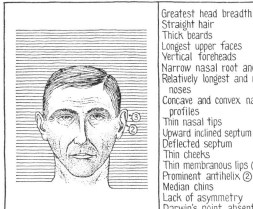
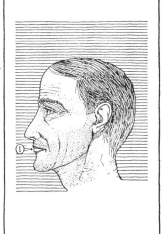

Greatest head breadth
Straight hair
Thick beards
Longest upper faces
Vertical foreheads
Narrow nasal root and bridge
Relatively longest and narrowest
 noses
Concave and convex nasal
 profiles
Thin nasal tips
Upward inclined septum
Deflected septum
Thin cheeks
Thin membranous lips ①
Prominent antihelix ②
Median chins
Lack of asymmetry
Darwin's point absent ③

bridge, undue frequency of both convex and concave nasal profiles, thin nasal tips, nasal septa inclined upward and frequently deflected to one side or other, thin membranous lips, median chins, many teeth lost, presence of Darwin's point on the ear and prominent antihelix, lack of facial asymmetry.

The Southwestern series, composed of criminals from Arizona, Colorado, and New Mexico, has finally its own distinguishing morphological features. These are: sparse beard and body hair, but also a slight excess of heavy beards, abundance of straight hair, reddish-brown, light brown, and golden hair, light brown, green-brown, and blue-gray eyes, clear whites or sclerae, rayed irides, median eye fold of the upper lids, thick eyebrows, high foreheads, broad nasal roots and nasal bridges, convex nasal profiles, thick nasal tips, absence of deflected septa, thick integumental lips, bilateral chins, thin cheeks, many persons who have lost no teeth, excess of undershot jaws (underbites), small ear lobes, pronounced antihelices, and frequent absence of any facial asymmetry.

Some of the outstanding positive morphological characteristics of the state series have been described. There are also, corresponding to these excess characters, deficiencies in certain complementary variations of the different parts of the head and face. It must be stated as emphatically as possible that the excesses of characters found in the various states are not found singly or in combination in all criminals of that state. In fact, the chances are that no one criminal from any state would exhibit all of the excess features which distinguish the state group. You might as well enumerate all of the cardinal virtues with the expectation of finding individuals who possess them *in toto.*

Taking the morphological variations of the state series singly, the statistical deviations of significance range from 82.98 per cent of all complete characters in Wisconsin and

OLD AMERICAN CRIMINALS

MOSAIC OF CRANIAL, FACIAL, METRIC AND MORPHOLOGICAL FEATURES

ARIZONA, NEW MEXICO, COLORADO

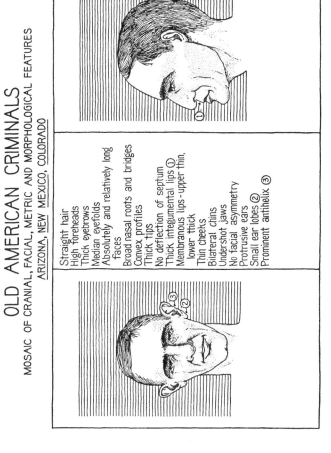

Straight hair
High foreheads
Thick eyebrows
Median eyefolds
Absolutely and relatively long
    faces
Broad nasal roots and bridges
Convex profiles
Thick tips
No deflection of septum
Thick integumental lips ①
Membranous lips - upper thin,
    lower thick
Thin cheeks
Bilateral chins
Undershot jaws
No facial asymmetry
Protrusive ears
Small ear lobes ②
Prominent antihelix ③

Massachusetts to 68.09 per cent in Tennessee. From the total series the mean morphological deviation of state series is 79.33 per cent and of metric features 72 per cent. Every state group is physically different from the total of which it forms a part. There is also a general consistency in the rankings of each state in its morphological and metric deviations, with the single exception of Wisconsin, which is one of the two most aberrant series in the observed morphological features, but does not deviate strongly from total criminals in measurements. The rather high mean age of the Wisconsin criminals causes them to diverge in certain manifestations of senility not found so often in the younger groups. Taking together both classes of features (metric and morphological) the Texans and North Carolinians are the most strongly differentiated state series. At the opposite extreme is Tennessee with the fewest of either class of differences from the total series and the largest number of its native sons in prison in the other states.

Massachusetts and Wisconsin criminals curiously resemble each other, although they exhibit the greatest disparity in mean ages. They are the only northern states; they have the narrowest noses — an interesting fact in the light of theories that pinched noses are adapted for breathing cold air. They also include the strongest French Canadian strains. It may be significant that Wisconsin is in the direct westerly path of Massachusetts migrations, although the direction of migration is occasionally reversed.

The remarkable differences in the Old American criminals of the several states indicate that types localized in geographical areas are being evolved in the stocks of long residence in the United States. The facts presented raise many anthropological questions which are worthy of intensive examination. Here, however, our sole business is to isolate these state physical peculiarities in order that they may not be confused with physical variations that may be related to type of criminal offense. These state types furnish the basis for the predictions which must be made before the effect of state sampling can be eliminated from our findings of the relation of physique to offense. In the analysis of the data of our survey, the recognition of these state complications, and the contrivance and application of a method of eliminating them, added more than one year of statistical labor and probably subtracted several years from the expectation of life of at least one individual.

PHYSICAL DIFFERENTIATION BY OFFENSE GROUPS

METRIC DIFFERENTIATION OF OFFENSE GROUPS

Now, at length, we can sift out the physical differences between each offense group and the total series which persist after due allowance has been made for state sampling, age variations, and other confusing factors. The crude differences between any single offense group of criminals and a random sample of the whole series of the same size as the subgroup are usually numerous and striking, although not so overwhelming as the differences between the total state series. These differences are considerably reduced when allowances are made for state preponderance in this or that offense series, and when, for example, the excess of gray hair in first degree murderers is corrected by a prediction of the amount which would occur if these "lifers" were reduced to the mean age of other criminals.

At this point we are not concerned with the causation of these independent and valid differences, but only with the question as to whether they are of a sufficient number and magnitude to establish the probability that the criminals of each offense group are anthropologically distinct from the total series and may be considered to have been derived from a population which is physically peculiar.

Let us begin by considering the metric and indicial deviations of first degree murderers from a random sample of the whole series of identical size. After crude differences have been scaled down by age and state sampling corrections — a process which obliterates or reduces to statistical insignificance a large number of raw divergences — we are left with 10, or 25.6 per cent, of a total of 39 measurements and indices in which this type of criminal remains deviant. These differences include an excess of seven years in mean age, excesses of weight, stature, chest diameters, and jaw breadth. Further, these first degree murderers as compared with total Old American criminals have smaller shoulder breadth relative to stature, inferior sitting height relative to stature, foreheads narrower relative to facial breadth, and jaws broader in relation to the same dimension. These differences are vastly greater and more numerous than would be expected to occur in samples drawn at random from the same population.

Second degree murderers display 5, or 12.8 per cent, of residually independent metric differences, including excesses of age and chest depth, deficiencies of head height and of the proportional or indicial relation of head height to head length and head breadth. These are amply sufficient to distinguish the second degree murderers from a random sample of total criminals.

The group of criminals committed for bodily assault is extremely small. It includes only 80 men. The margin of leeway which must be allowed in appraising the accuracy of averages increases as the size of the sample diminishes. Consequently, deviations of small groups are likely to be statistically insignificant, which simply means that we cannot be at all certain that they are not accidental. In the case of this assault group, initially numerous deviations from the entire group are pared down by corrections to two differences — an excess of age and a superior shoulder breadth. These two differences comprise 5.1 per cent of the metric data and are barely more than might occur in any random sample of the same size.

Robbers exhibit 12.8 per cent of independent excesses. They are younger, have narrower chests, higher heads, broader faces, shorter ears, and relatively broader noses than would be expected in a random sample of the series. If we discard the shortness of ear, which may be due to their comparatively tender age, we are still left with enough differences in hand to make this group anthropometrically distinct.

Burglars and thieves are overwhelmingly differentiated from total series, in part because this offense group is so large (39.2 per cent of the entire series) that its deviations are statistically valid, even when small. Actually, after due allowance has been made for age, state sampling, observational equation, et cetera, the burglars and thieves still show 28 per cent of distinctive metric differences. They are: deficiencies in age, weight, chest depth and chest breadth, head length, head circumference, face breadth, jaw breadth, and an excessive breadth of the forehead relative to breadth of the face (zygo-frontal index).

The forgery and fraud group is heavily weighted with Texans, and many crude differences between the group and the total series are eliminated when allowance is made for state sampling. Nevertheless, these fraudulent criminals retain a superiority in sitting height, in head length, in head circumference, and in total height of the face — none of which is ascribable to state sampling or the effect of age. They deviate in 10.26 per cent of metric features, whereas only about 4 per cent of deviations of such magnitude would be expected in random samples drawn from the same population.

Rapists have 12.8 per cent of ultimately valid differentiae, including greater mean age, deficient stature and sitting height, and superior chest depth and breadth. More independent differences would have survived, had it not been for the overloading of this offense group with inmates of the Wisconsin penitentiary.

Men who have committed sex offenses other than rape have no metric features which distinguish them from total Old American criminals, with the exception of greater mean age and several differences in measurement which are suspected to be due to superior age.

Versus public welfare offenders have too many Texans among them who tend to overweight the subgroup with their state characteristics. When these have been taken into account, this criminal group still has 15.4 per cent of differentiating metric features. It has an excess age, an excess of chest depth and of face breadth, nose breadth, jaw breadth, and ear length. The value of the indices which relate face breadth to head breadth (cephalo-facial) and the length of the ear to its breadth, are also unduly high. These bootleggers constitute anthropometrically an easily distinguishable offense group.

The residual small offense group containing persons convicted of arson and miscellaneous crimes is older than common, broader in chest and narrower in forehead. It has 7.7 per cent of significant deviations — more than enough to differentiate it from the total series, but, at that, nothing very striking.

All of the offense groups except other sex and assault are anthropometrically distinguished from random samples of the same size drawn from the total series. In the total of measurements we have a mean residuum of independently differentiated means consisting of 17.39 per cent, against an expectation in random samples of only 4 per cent. In indices (the relation of one measurement to another) the differences are not so marked. There remains independent of state sampling and age a total of 6.25 per cent of deviations, against an expectation of 4 per cent.

OLD AMERICAN CRIMINALS
MOSAIC OF EXCESS METRIC AND MORPHOLOGICAL FEATURES, INDEPENDENT OF AGE AND STATE SAMPLING
FIRST DEGREE MURDERERS

Deficiency of thick head hair
Foreheads narrow relative to face breadth
Deficiency of narrow nasal bridges
Compressed cheek-bones
Broad jaws
Jaws broad relative to face breadth
Large earlobes
Deficiency of submedium antihelices ①

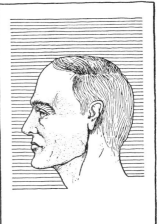

OLD AMERICAN CRIMINALS
MOSAIC OF EXCESS METRIC AND MORPHOLOGICAL FEATURES, INDEPENDENT OF AGE AND STATE SAMPLING
SECOND DEGREE MURDERERS

Low absolute head height
Low length-height index
Low breadth-height index
High nasal bridges
Facial wrinkles
Bilateral chins ①

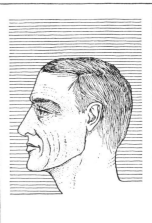

Thus, at present, we reach the conclusion that, so far as caliper measurements and derived indices are concerned, eight of ten offense groups of criminals are anthropometrically distinct each from the total series. In general, also, we may then assert that the average bodily form of the criminal varies with the type of offense he commits. This is our first positive criminal anthropological finding.

MORPHOLOGICAL DIFFERENTIATION OF OFFENSE GROUPS

In qualitatively observed morphological characters, the determination of offense group differences which are of ultimate criminological validity involves the necessity of correcting not only for state differences but also for differences which are due to age. Thus, if first degree murderers have higher proportions of gray and white hair than some other groups of offenders, the fact is of no criminological significance, because the excess of depigmented hair is due to the older age of the first degree murderer group, which is dependent upon their serving, for the most part, life sentences. Gray hair has no organic relationship to the nature of crime committed. Other groups of criminals, classified according to offense, differ in their mean ages according to the length of sentence usually pronounced for their particular type of offense, and for other reasons, most of which are irrelevant to the kind of crimes they have committed. For this reason the morphological differences which were found to exist between the various offense groups, and were proved to be independent of state sampling, were tested for their dependence upon age. It is unnecessary to enter into the details of the process. Each feature, such as color of hair, was tabulated for the entire series by age groups, arranged in five year classes. An inspection of these tables permits an appraisal of the extent to which the various characters change with advancing age. Then for each offense group a prediction of the expected character is made, which is, in

OLD AMERICAN CRIMINALS
MOSAIC OF EXCESS METRIC AND MORPHOLOGICAL FEATURES,
INDEPENDENT OF AGE AND STATE SAMPLING

ROBBERS

Low waved hair
High heads
Median eyefolds ①
Broad faces
Unwrinkled
Short ears
Lack of sparse beards
Relatively broad, short noses

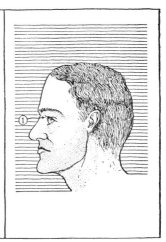

OLD AMERICAN CRIMINALS
MOSAIC OF EXCESS METRIC AND MORPHOLOGICAL FEATURES,
INDEPENDENT OF AGE AND STATE SAMPLING

BURGLARS AND THIEVES

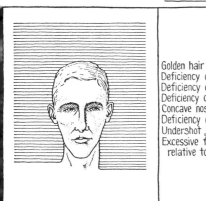

Golden hair
Deficiency of head length
Deficiency of head circumference
Deficiency of face breadth
Concave noses
Deficiency of jaw breadth
Undershot jaws
Excessive forehead breadth
relative to jaw breadth

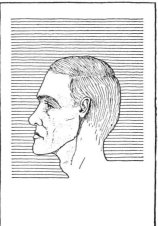

short, the proportion of that character based upon the number of individuals of the different ages found in that offense group and the mean proportions of the character found in the various age groups of the total series. When the difference between the proportion predicted for the offense group on the basis of age and the proportion actually observed in the offense group is compared with the difference between the offense group and the total series, it is possible to distinguish age-dependent differences from those which are independent of age, and to appraise the significance of the latter in terms of the sampling error.

We finally emerge with differences between the offense groups which are not due to accidents of sampling, are not due to state variations, and are independent of differences between the ages of the offense groups. Thus, in the case of first degree murder we find the members of that offense group deficient in persons with abundant head hair, deficient in individuals with narrow nasal bridges, presenting an excess of persons with pointed or median chins, and with compressed cheek bones. Large ear lobes are characteristic of the group, and a poor development of the antihelix of the ear is rare. The first degree murderers are also more square-shouldered than total criminals.

In the other offense groups, I shall state the residually independent features which differentiate them from the total series, in non-technical language, less precise, but at the same time less ponderous. Second degree murderers are notable for square (bilateral) chins, high nasal bridges, wrinkling of the face, markedly worn teeth, and lack of dental caries. The small assault group of criminals is independently characterized only by a tendency to deviate toward both extremes in the height of the root of the nose. Other differences shown by this group are complicated by age effects and it cannot be said that the group, as a whole,

OLD AMERICAN CRIMINALS
MOSAIC OF EXCESS METRIC AND MORPHOLOGICAL FEATURES,
INDEPENDENT OF AGE AND STATE SAMPLING

FORGERS AND FRAUDS

Thin head hair
Great head circumference
Great head length
No eyefolds
Long face
Nasal bridges of medium height
Deficiency of thin membranous
  lips ①

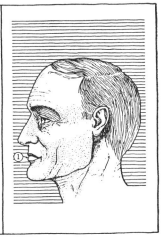

OLD AMERICAN CRIMINALS
MOSAIC OF EXCESS METRIC AND MORPHOLOGICAL FEATURES,
INDEPENDENT OF AGE AND STATE SAMPLING

VERSUS PUBLIC WELFARE

Excess of ear length
Low ear index
Free ear lobes ①
Excess of face breadth
Prominent cheek-bones
Excessive face breadth relative
  to head breadth
Excess of jaw breadth
Deficiency of thin integumental
  lips ②

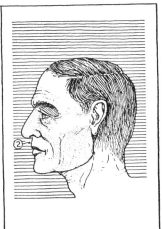

is certainly distinguishable from a random sample of the whole criminal series of the same size.

The surviving morphological distinctions of the robbery group are: lack of sparse beards and an excessive amount of low waved hair, diffused pigment in the iris of the eye, frequent median folds of the upper eyelids, lack of wrinkles, lack of edge-to-edge bite of the teeth, lack of pronounced protrusion of the ear.

The members of the burglary and larceny group have sparse body hair, an excess of golden shades of head hair, frequently concave noses and undershot jaws, rarity of edge-to-edge bite of the front teeth. Forgers and fraudulent criminals have thin head hair, but rarely thin beards; they tend to lack eye folds and to have nasal bridges of medium height; their lips are rarely thin and the teeth are not ordinarily characterized by pronounced wear. Rapists show an unusual prevalence of blue-gray eye color, deflected nasal septa, and facial asymmetries. Other sex offenders are notable for straight hair, thin lips, hollow cheeks, and facial asymmetry. Offenders against public welfare seem to be notable in the features which are disproportionately deficient: they are characterized by a lack of thin integumental lips, a lack of compressed malars (and an excess of prominent malars), deficiency of persons with narrow jaw angles and of persons with small ear lobes, and an excess of those whose ear lobes are free rather than detached.

The miscellaneous group of arson and all other offenses has but three morphological features which survive age and state correction. These are excess of ash-blond hair, and of eye folds across the inner corner of the eye (epicanthic), and an excess of slight amounts of facial protrusion (prognathism).

When only corrections for state sampling are applied, all of the offense groups are significantly differentiated from the total series in morphological features, with the exception of assault, and arson and all other offenses. These latter two groups are numerically very small. When age corrections are applied, rape and other sex offenses become morphologically indistinguishable from the total series, since the number of independently differentiated characters which survive the process of sifting is reduced in the case of these two subgroups of rather elderly men to a very few. There remain six of ten offense groups which are morphologically distinguishable from random samples of the entire series, after all allowances have been made for complicating and confusing factors.

These facts lead to the important conclusion that native White criminals of native parentage are not only distinguished from each other by offense groups in sociological characteristics, but also in anthropometric and morphological features. Thus, it is suggested that crime is not an exclusively sociological phenomenon, but is also biological.

CHAPTER III

OLD AMERICAN CRIMINALS: PHYSIQUE AND ALLEGED OCCUPATION, BODY BUILD AND BEHAVIOR, THE WILL-O'-THE-WISP OF CRIMINAL TYPE

THERE are many fascinating byways into which one may wander in the analysis of a huge mass of material pertaining to the physical and sociological characteristics of individuals. Almost none of these has been thoroughly explored, largely, I suppose, because of a widespread feeling that any attempt to relate anatomy to behavior is inadvisable, unedifying, or even indecent. One is permitted to regard the human body aesthetically or medically, as something beautiful or something pathological, but in the former case good taste requires the suppression of specific anatomical detail. In the latter one may only whisper in the confidential ear of the discreet physician.

In one of those peculiar organizations which are neither intellectual nor social, but, as it were, half-caste, featured by the preliminary reading of one paper and the eventual consumption of food, a subject was announced in advance which seemed to have corporeal implications. Whereupon one of the members wrote in to the secretary requesting that the author be asked not to mention "anything below the neck." I am sometimes afraid that our knowledge of man includes nothing below the neck and that this constitutes convincing evidence that we have nothing above the ears. Thus, we try to save our faces and get nowhere.

In each scientific field the specialist looks down his nose and fears the uncovering of his nakedness, and I fear that there is lacking even that sardonic humor of the Roman augurs, who, you recall, were said to be unable to refrain from laughing when they passed each other on the street. Now I am thoroughly tired of the *disiecta membra* of knowledge, the useless gobbets of information which science feeds to the public as sawdust to a jackass provided with green spectacles. Our scientific knowledge is like the processed foods of modern industry, sealed up in tin cans adorned with gaudy labels, but sterile and bereft of vitamins. What we really need is a variety and an abundance of raw facts served in a balanced ration, instead of synthetic and devitalized essences. Someone really must discover the essential relationships between organic matter and organic behavior before real progress can be made, except by the blind process of trial and error.

Now in the very elementary field of the relation of physique to occupation and economic status, almost nothing is known. Anyone who looks at me can state positively, on the basis of physical diagnosis, that I am neither Man Mountain Dean nor Miss America. Unfortunately not even science can go much farther than that, merely because science has never attempted to investigate such important though elementary matters. And that is why I say that Science is a stuffed shirt. It has never been able to "take the cash and let the credit go" merely because it simply does not know "tother from which."

So in this investigation which is concerned primarily with the relation of man's physique to man's antisocial behavior, I have been tempted to make a small foray into the subject of physique in relation to occupation, simply because I wanted to find out something about an obviously important unknown, whether or not it was any of my present business.

PHYSIQUE AND ALLEGED OCCUPATION

If criminals of similar ethnic and racial origin differ physically according to the types of offenses which they commit, it is reasonable to suppose that they may differ anthropologically and sociologically according to the types of occupations they claim. A serious deterrent to the investigation of putative occupational differences is one's skepticism as to the extent to which many convicted criminals have engaged in law-abiding pursuits. We know that they have committed crimes, but we are merely *informed* that they have practised law or carpentry. Some crimes of violence require considerable physical strength and so do also some occupations. Other occupations and offenses require no physical strength, as for example selling neckties and picking pockets. Both offense and occupation may require a fairly good education, as in the case of banking and the more elaborate types of fraud.

Our occupational categories, eleven in number, are not all so clear cut as is desirable, and some individuals have been put into the wrong classes, probably as a result of perplexity on the part of the clerical force which had to fit the criminals to the Procrustean bed of our code. For example, a bartender belongs under personal service, but does a saloon-keeper who tends his own bar? Our classification was adopted, not without some misgivings, from the scheme modified from the census by the State Department of Mental Diseases, under which our survey began.

Our extractive class is four-fifths farmers and one-sixth miners. The rest are fishers, foresters, nurserymen, lumberjacks, animal husbandmen, and a stray milkman or two. Our laborer class includes 81 per cent of unskilled day laborers, not otherwise specified, with 6 per cent of textile workers, 3 per cent of shoe workers, and about 10 per cent of persons claiming special occupations some of which might be otherwise classified. The factory category includes only persons who obviously work with machines. Transportation is a self-explanatory class, which includes no strays. Skilled trades is composed, for the most part, of the building trades, with 34 per cent of painters, 24 per cent of

carpenters, 15 per cent of electricians, 8 per cent of plumb-
ers, et cetera. Trade is largely monopolized by salesmen
and sales clerks, with some shopkeepers and odds and ends
of commercial workers, such as window-dressers, and insurance agents. Public service includes soldiers, policemen,
firemen, and persons holding public office or working
under some government auspice. When our survey was
carried on the federal government had not yet begun to ex-
haust the alphabet and our national resources with relief
projects.

The semi-professional class consists of 39 per cent of
printers, 29 per cent of musicians, and all sorts of persons
engaged in the various types of entertainment business.
Some of the square pegs in the round holes of this class are
embalmers, lithographers, and cartoonists.

The professional class was supposed to include only
teaching, law, medicine, and the clergy. Nevertheless, one
or two bank presidents have sneaked into this classification,
probably because some one of our coding clerks was unduly
susceptible to the prestige of capitalism. Personal service is
dominated by cooks, barbers, waiters, tailors, and bakers.
Thirty-five per cent of this class consist of cooks, presumably
bad cooks, and 22 per cent are barbers, a fact which hardly
occasions surprise. The clerical class of criminals is filled
almost exclusively with persons who deal with accounts, 63
per cent of bookkeepers and accountants, and with those who
handle other people's money with sticky hands, bankers,
cashiers, tellers, et cetera.

The closest mathematical relationship found in this survey is that between the occupations of criminals and their
educations. By far the best educated is the professional class,
with 74 per cent of college attendants and an additional
15 per cent who have been at professional schools. It is a
very small group consisting of but 27 men (0.66 per cent of
the series), only three of whom have had no better than high

school educations. Next comes the clerical class with 75 per cent of men who have gone at least as far as high school, then the semi-professional class with 54 per cent who have attained or surpassed this minimum, trade with 52 per cent, personal service with 32 per cent, and so on down to the extractives who include only 7.34 per cent of persons who have reached high school. Illiteracy rises from nothing at all in the professional and clerical classes to 14 per cent in the laborers and 19 per cent in the extractives. The educational rankings are: (1) professional, (2) clerical, (3) semi-professional, (4) trade, (5) personal service, (6) skilled trades, (7) factory, (8) transportation, (9) public service, (10) laborer, (11) extractive. The last two classes are not only the most ignorant, but the extractive is by far the largest numerically, and the laborer is third in rank.

The study of physical differentiation by occupational groups was confined to hair color, eye color, and 12 of the most important bodily measurements and indices. Eight of 11 occupational groups give clear indication of being anthropometrically distinct from the total series of which they form a part.

The extractives, who are most ignorant and rank highest in murder, are not distinctive in hair color, but have the largest excess of blue eyes, are significantly high in mean age, and have smaller head breadths and forehead breadths than the series at large. In the 12 metric features studied they show 3 statistically differentiated. They include an excess of tall men of medium weight.

The laborers, next to the bottom in education, rank among the darker haired group and have excessive proportions of dark brown eyes, as well as blue-gray eyes. They are younger, lighter in weight, shorter in stature, narrower in head breadth, smaller in head circumference, and more long-headed, or dolichocephalic, than the total criminal series. Short men of medium weight are in excess in this occupational class of criminals.

The factory group is undistinguished in pigmentation of hair and eyes. Although it ranks only seventh by the educational ratio it is low in illiterates and in the most poorly schooled and shows excesses in the higher grades up to college, in which, as a group, it is below the series level. It is notably deficient in mean age, and has broader heads and foreheads and a higher mean cephalic index than the total series. Evidently this group includes a large number of round-headed men. Tall-heavy and tall-slender body builds are excessively represented.

The transportation group ranks first in lightness of eyes and third in lightness of hair, but is not certainly distinguished in any measurement or index. It cannot be said to be anthropometrically differentiated from the total criminal series. The group of the skilled trades workers is without anthropological individuality. The class of persons engaged in trade — selling — is better educated than most, ranking fourth, and presents significant excesses of mean age and of head breadth. It is possibly high in weight and in head circumference. Anthropometrically, it is barely distinguishable from a random sample of the total series.

There are only 27 public servants in this criminal series, a number insufficient to show statistical differentiation unless its deviations are very great. This group ranks ninth in education and has the darkest hair color, being entirely devoid of the blond and red shades. However, in eye color it is sixth, the median class. The deviations of this group suggest that an adequate sample might prove to be older, heavier, narrower in head and forehead, and with shorter, broader faces and noses than the run of the mill of criminals. However, none of the differences can be relied upon wholly, because there are too few men in the subgroup.

The semi-professional group is rather small, with only 69 members. It is third in education, and especially strong in light brown eyes and light brown hair. This group is the most brachycephalic, or round-headed, and has an excess of forehead breadth. Of possible but not certain significance are excesses in head breadth and a deficiency in stature. It is the shortest of the occupational groups.

The professional class, though very small, is widely divergent from the physical mean of the total series. It is second in lightness of hair, but tenth in lightness of eyes. It is by far the oldest and heaviest group, being 11.65 years above mean age, and 19.60 pounds above average weight, and is distinguished certainly by excessive breadth of forehead and face, and probably by great head length, great head breadth, and a high nasal index. It is insignificantly below average height and somewhat rounder-headed than the total series. A disproportionately large number of short, heavy men are found in this group.

The personal service group has somewhat darker hair than the general series, and a deficiency of blue eyes. It is also shorter, probably lighter, and shows a relatively greater nose breadth, than is characteristic of the series at large.

The clerical occupational class includes only 117 persons, but is notable for several physical features in addition to its high educational ranking. Curiously enough, it is first in lightness of hair color and last in lightness of eye color. It is certainly deficient in stature and probably in weight, but the head breadth is excessive and the nose is narrower relative to its height than that of any other group.

The occupational differentiation of our criminals into physical types has not been exhaustively investigated. It seems not to be nearly so marked as is the differentiation by state groups, and is probably less pronounced than offense differentiation. Nevertheless, it is sufficient to indicate that most of these criminals probably actually have practised the occupations to which they lay claim. There is a rather

OLD AMERICAN CRIMINALS
MOSAIC OF METRIC AND MORPHOLOGICAL EXCESSES
OF THREE OCCUPATIONAL TYPES

PROFESSIONAL

PERSONAL SERVICE

CLERICAL

Second lightest hair
Oldest (excess 11.7 years)
Heaviest (excess 19.6 pounds)
Large head length
Large head breadth, round head
Excess forehead breadth
Excess face breadth
High nasal index

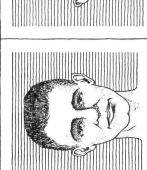

Dark hair
Deficiency blue eyes
Relatively great nose breadth
Small and light weight

Lightest hair
Darkest eyes
Excess head breadth
Relatively narrowest nose
Small and light weight

clearer suggestion of ethnic or racial influence in the occupational types than in the offense types. For example, tall, long-headed, lightly pigmented men seem to be at a maximum in the extractive class; shorter brunet long-heads in the laborer and personal service groups; round-headed and short men in the semi-professional group; and lightly pigmented round-heads in the professional and clerical classes; the former stout and broad-nosed; the latter, short, slender, and narrow-nosed.

It is almost certain that the same physical factors which tend to select a man for occupation are concerned in his criminalistic proclivities, but the interrelations of education, occupation, physique, and choice of crime are very involved. Occupation is .intimately related to nature of criminal opportunity, education to choice of occupation, and inherited or acquired physical and mental features seem to be potent throughout.

BODY BUILD AND BEHAVIOR

There is good reason for suspecting that body build is, in some way, associated with temperament and behavior. Shakespeare recognized that common belief when he put into Julius Caesar's mouth the well known remark about Cassius. Kretschmer, a German student of constitution, recognized three main varieties of body build — short-fat, medium, and tall-thin — which he christened with names derived from the Greek, and which he endowed with various psycho-pathological tendencies on the basis of clinical hunch, rather than by controlled scientific observation. A considerable amount of work has been done in Europe on the relation of body build to various diseases and some excellent beginnings have been made in this country. I think that there is no doubt that this subject will develop into one of the largest and most fruitful fields of research in medical science, if ever it is possible to overcome the inertia and

prejudices of a profession which is still steeped in the traditions of curative magic, and neither knows nor cares about
the biology of well human beings.

All sorts of elaborate volumetric and proportional indices have been contrived to express man's variation in body
build, many of them involving intricate and abstruse mathematical calculations. I have made a slight excursion into
this field in the present investigation of native White criminals of native parentage, utilizing a very simple method of
classification based upon the two main constituents of body
build, stature and weight. You will recall that the standard
deviation is a statistical constant which expresses roughly
the average extent to which individuals of a given series
deviate from the arithmetic mean of that series. I took 3910
criminals and divided them into three stature classes, using
as the limits of the medium class intervals equal to once the
value of the standard deviation above and below the mean
of the series. Such a division in an approximately normal
distribution results in a large middle class which might be
expected to include about 68 per cent of the series and two
extreme classes — short and tall — each of which might comprise about 16 per cent of the series. I then took each of
these three stature groups and calculated the mean and the
standard deviation of weight, and divided them similarly
into three weight subgroups. The final result was nine
groups of individuals classified according to their individual
combinations of body weight: short-slender, short-medium
weight, short-heavy; medium   height-slender, medium
height-medium weight, medium height-heavy; tall-slender,
tall-medium weight, tall-heavy. Actually, the nine body
build groups do not conform in respective numbers to
expectation in a normal distribution, partly because the
class intervals used in grouping measurements prevented
an accurate cutting of the series on the basis of standard
deviation.

The short-slender group consisted of only 64 men with an average stature of 158.01 centimeters (62.21 inches) and an average weight of 111.4 pounds. The short-medium weight group included 217 men who averaged 159.99 centimeters in stature (62.99 inches) and had a mean weight of 133.4 pounds. The short-heavy type numbered only 54 individuals with average stature of 159.96 centimeters (62.96 inches) and an average weight of 162.9 pounds. The medium height-slender type with 348 men had averages of 169.29 centimeters (66.65 inches) and 122.7 pounds. The medium height-medium weight type, including 1925 persons, had a mean height of 171.36 centimeters (67.46 inches) and a mean weight of 145.5 pounds. There were 729 men in the medium height-heavy class, who averaged 172.95 centimeters (68.09 inches) and 174 pounds. In the tall-slender class were only 114 men, who averaged 181.38 centimeters in stature (71.42 inches) and 141.7 pounds in weight. The tall-medium weight class consisted of 325 men with an average stature of 181.92 centimeters and an average weight of 163.9 pounds. Finally, the tall-heavy class of men numbered 134 and had a mean stature of 182.7 centimeters (71.93 inches) and an average weight of 196.9 pounds.

Thus, in each body build group the short men are very short, the tall men very tall, the thin men very thin, and the fat men very fat. We are now going to inquire briefly into sociological differences which may obtain between these nine groups of men of extremely diverse body builds. If we find that they are in any considerable degree distinct in their social and economic status, class by class, we shall then proceed to attempt to ascertain whether these sociologically differentiated body build types are of hereditary origin or have been selected by some concatenation of environmental forces.

Naturally, we are interested first of all in the offenses

committed by these nine types of criminals of different body builds.

Let us consider first the general trends of relationship between the nine body build types and specific offenses. In first degree murder the three short statured groups are, in general, lowest, the medium statured groups are intermediate, and the tall groups are highest. A similar regression may be noted in second degree murder. Within each trio of stature groups, the amount of murder, of either degree, seems to vary with weight. In the short groups both types of murder are most frequent in the short-slender class. In the medium statured groups murder seems to increase as one proceeds from slender through medium weight to heavy men, but this regression breaks down in the tall groups.

Assault is a small offense group, but it reaches its maximum percentage among short-heavy men and is not found at all in the short-slender and tall-slender men. However, we cannot be certain of the significance of these observations, because the samples are numerically too small.

Robbery is far less common among the short groups than among the medium and tall groups. It is especially connected also with men of slender build and reaches its maximum among the tall-slender men. Burglary and larceny are particularly associated with shortness and with slender or medium weight. These commonest of offenses tend to decrease as men grow taller and heavier in relation to their stature. Forgery and fraud, on the other hand, increase with weight in the short groups and are at a maximum in the tall groups.

Sex offenses, and rape in particular, decrease with stature and increase with weight. Thus the short-heavy men are the notable sex offenders and the tall-slender men seem completely uninterested in this type of activity. Bootlegging goes up with stature and weight.

In general, murder, robbery, forgery and fraud, and

versus public welfare offenses increase with stature, while assault, burglary and larceny, sex offenses, and arson decrease. Murder, forgery and fraud, and versus public welfare offenses generally increase with weight as do also sex offenses. Robbery and burglary and larceny diminish with increasing weight.

Records of previous convictions for criminal offenses decrease with increasing stature and also decrease generally with added weight. Thus, the minimum recidivism occurs in the tall-heavy group (29.06 per cent), and the maximum in the short-slender group (48.33 per cent).

In each trio of stature groups the percentage of single men declines from slender through medium to heavy builds. Also, as the groups grow taller, the tendency to be married seems to increase. Some of these marital relations are complicated by age, since the older men are usually both heavier and more married, but there is no consistent relationship of mean age of groups to marital status. Percentages of divorced and widowed men also seem to rise with increments of weight in each stature trio of groups, but there is no especial relation of divorce and widowerhood to stature.

The relationship of occupation to body build is rather complicated and not always clear. The extractive occupation increases steadily from short to tall classes. Unskilled laborers are especially common in the short-medium weight class. Professional occupations increase with weight. Perhaps an enumeration of the occupational characteristics of the body build types which seem distinct in these sociological categories would be most illuminating.

The short-slender type is very high in trade, semi-professional, and clerical occupations, and deficient in extractive and unskilled labor. The short-medium weight type is overloaded with unskilled laborers and has an excess of personal servants. The short-heavy type is high in transportation, professional, personal service, and clerical occupations. The medium height-heavy type is especially noted for its deficiency in personal service, and has small excesses of extractives, semi-professionals, and tradesmen.

The tall-slender men are especially active in extractive, factory, and transportation occupations. The tall men of medium weight are excessively represented in the extractive occupations. The tall-heavy type is especially strong in factory work and is notably deficient in extractive, unskilled labor, and personal service categories. The extreme occupational differentiations are found in the extremes of body build. Especially noticeable is the dearth of short-slender men in occupations involving heavy manual labor. There are twice as many statistical differentiations of occupation with body build as would be expected to occur by chance.

The body build groups are strongly differentiated in educational attainment, but there seems to be no consistent relation of education either to stature alone or to weight alone. The short-slender men are considerably the best educated, and the tall-heavy men come next. Short men of medium weight are the most unschooled. Illiterates are least common (6.25 per cent) in the short-slender type, and most frequent in the tall-slender type (12.28 per cent). The percentage of college men reaches its maximum of 8.21 per cent in the tall-heavy type, and falls to 1.67 per cent in the medium height-medium weight group.

Since many sociological differences between the body build groups are evident, it is desirable to examine more of the physical characteristics of the group for the purpose of finding out whether their combinations of stature and weight are associated with other anthropological characters. We shall, then, be in a better position to determine the nature of the groups and the reasons for their sociological differentiation.

A study of the age relationships shows that the tall-slender group is the lowest in mean age (29.15 years) and that the short-heavy group is oldest (mean age 36.70 years). Since increasing age tends to be associated with added weight and since the younger generations are increasing in stature, we might expect a regular regression of the body build groups in which age increases, weight increases, and stature decreases. However, no such exact correlation exists. Some of the slender groups are comparatively old and some of the medium weight groups are below mean age. Age enters into body build type as here classified, but it is by no means the single differentiating factor.

A few racial physical characteristics which are known to be of value as racial criteria may be tested in the body build groups in order to demonstrate whether these several groups are racially homogeneous or heterogeneous. The cephalic index (head breadth expressed as a percentage of head length) shows little difference in the nine groups. All kinds of head form occur in each group. There is a slight tendency for mean cephalic index to decrease with added stature. Shorter men are likely to be more round-headed, and taller men longer-headed. There is no apparent regression of cephalic index upon body weight.

The study of the facial index (height of the face expressed as a percentage of face breadth) shows that the heavier men are likely to have somewhat broader faces relative to face length. Also, the breadth of the nose relative to its length decreases as stature rises, but seems to depend even more obviously upon increased weight.

In general these indices show that the taller groups tend to have longer and narrower heads and noses; the shorter groups somewhat broader and shorter faces and rounder heads. There is, however, no metric indication that any one of these body build groups is racially unified, and that important racial differences in composition underlie the social differentiation of the body build types.

An investigation of hair color and eye color in the body

build types does nothing to clarify the situation. All shades of hair and eye pigmentation occur in each type. The medium height-slender group has, on the whole, the lightest hair, and the short-heavy group has the darkest hair. But this latter group has, in general, the lightest eyes, and the rankings in pigmentation of hair and of eyes do not agree. In fact, these body build types are almost undifferentiated in eye color. Hair color shows more variation, but it is not linked in intensity of pigmentation with eye color. Some of the lightest groups in hair color rank low in lightness of eye shades, and *vice versa.*

We may now summarize the physical and sociological characteristics of the body types. The short-slender type consists of 64 persons with an average stature of 158 centimeters and a mean weight of 111.4 pounds. Its mean age is 31.5 years. It contains rather more round heads than do the other groups and is predominantly medium in hair color, but contains more dark eyed persons than does the total series. In offenses this group ranks first in burglary and larceny, but last in robbery, forgery and fraud, and arson. It is second in second degree murder but low in rape and in liquor offenses. It has the most previous convictions and the second highest percentage of single men, although it ranks only fourth in mean age. Occupationally, it ranks first in clerical, semi-professional, and trade categories. It is high in personal service and contains fewest manual laborers and members of the extractive occupations. This group is, on the whole, the best educated, and contains fewest illiterates. It is overloaded with criminals from Massachusetts and Wisconsin.

The short-medium weight group consists of 217 men with a mean age of 29.9 years, an average stature of 159.99 centimeters, and an average weight of 133.4 pounds. It is in the middle of the types in pigmentation of hair, but has the darkest eye color. This group shares with the short-heavy type the honor of the lowest ranking in murder. It is also lowest in offenses against public welfare and below the median in robbery, forgery, and other sex offenses. It is first in arson and miscellaneous offenses and second in percentage of previous convictions. It is fourth in percentage of single men. This group heads the occupational ranks in unskilled labor and in personal service, and has the lowest percentage of factory workers. It is the most ignorant group of the nine, and is also unduly weighted by convicts from Massachusetts and Wisconsin.

The short-heavy group has only 54 men and is the oldest of the groups, with an average age of 36.7 years. This group consists of short, fat men, since they average 159.96 centimeters in height and 162.9 pounds in weight. Some of them weigh as much as 250 pounds. This group contains the second highest percentage of round heads and has the shortest and broadest faces, and relatively the broadest noses. It has, on the whole, the darkest hair of any type, but the lightest eyes. The short-heavy group is one of the most clear cut sociologically. It ranks first in rape, first in other sex offenses, and first in assault. It is last in murder, next to the last in percentages of previous convictions. It ranks first in divorcés and in widowers. It has the highest percentage of professional men and of transportation workers and is also high in clerical occupations. Its education is middling. These short, fat men appear to be lecherous, but not homicidal.

The medium height-slender men are 348 in number, 30 years in mean age, 169.29 centimeters in average height, and weigh on the average 122.7 pounds. They have the narrowest noses and narrowest faces of any of the body build types. The medium height-slender men have the lightest hair color, but are in the middle of the series in eye pigmentation. This medium height-slender group is not particularly distinguished in offenses. It ranks third in

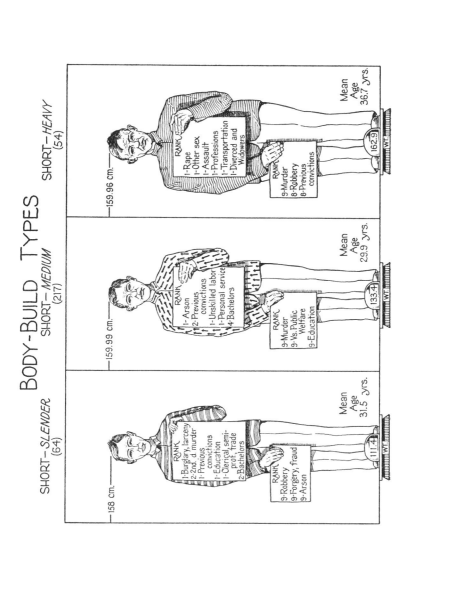

BODY-BUILD TYPES

SHORT – SLENDER
(64)

SHORT – MEDIUM
(217)

SHORT – HEAVY
(54)

SHORT – SLENDER (64)

— 158 cm. —

RANK
1-Burglary, larceny
2-2nd. d. murder
1-Previous
   convictions
1-Education
1-Clerical, semi-
   prof., trade
2-Bachelors

RANK
9-Robbery
9-Forgery, fraud
9-Arson

Mean
Age
31.5 yrs.

WT.
111.4

SHORT – MEDIUM (217)

— 159.99 cm. —

RANK
1-Arson
2-Previous
   convictions
1-Unskilled labor
1-Personal service
4-Bachelors

RANK
9-Murder
9-Vs. Public
   Welfare
9-Education

Mean
Age
29.9 yrs.

WT.
133.4

SHORT – HEAVY (54)

— 159.96 cm. —

RANK
1-Rape
1-Other sex
1-Assault
1-Professions
1-Transportation
1-Divorced and
   Widowers

RANK
9-Murder
8-Robbery
8-Previous
   convictions

Mean
Age
36.7 yrs.

WT.
162.9

robbery and in burglary and larceny, but is low in most other crimes. It has the highest percentage of single men and of skilled trades, and also ranks second in unskilled labor. It takes third place in educational attainment. This group is overweighted with Kentucky criminals.

The medium height-medium weight group is by far the largest with 1925 men. Its average age (29.25 years) is below the mean of the series. The means for stature and weight are respectively 171.36 centimeters and 145.5 pounds. Physically, it occupies a median position in the series, not only in height and weight, but in pigmentation and in indices of head and face. Offense differentiation in this group is not marked. It is second in arson and second in robbery. It is fourth in previous convictions and in the middle of the series in regard to marital status. This type is high in factory workers and unskilled laborers, and low in the professions which require more education. It is next to the bottom in educational attainment.

The medium height-heavy type includes 729 men, with a mean age of 33.7 years, an average stature of 172.95 centimeters, and a mean weight of 174 pounds. It leans slightly toward round heads, broad short faces, and broad noses. It is sixth in lightness of hair, but second in lightness of eye color. This type ranks first in offenses versus public welfare, which are usually violations of liquor laws. It is third in sex offenses and well up in murder. However, it is next to the bottom in burglary and larceny, and is seventh of the nine types in percentage of previous convictions. It is lowest but one in percentage of single men. Occupationally, this group is not outstanding. It is rather high in the extractive and semi-professional pursuits. It ranks sixth in education.

The tall-slender men are only 114 in number and are youngest in mean age (29.15 years). They average 181.38 centimeters in height and 141.7 pounds in weight. This

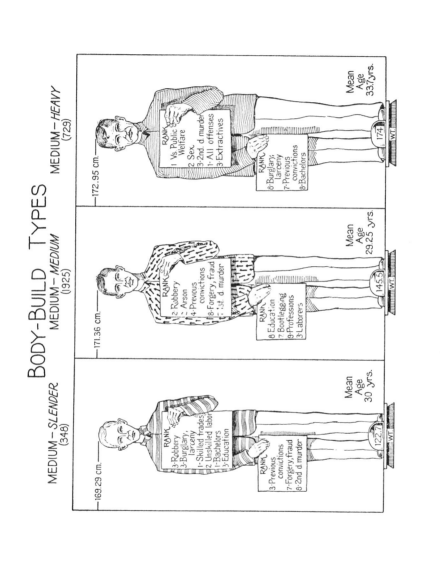

BODY-BUILD TYPES

MEDIUM – SLENDER
(348)

MEDIUM – MEDIUM
(1925)

MEDIUM – HEAVY
(729)

Panel 1 (Medium–Slender):
169.29 cm.

RANK
3-Robbery
3-Burglary;
  larceny
1-Skilled trades
2-Unskilled labor
1-Bachelors
3-Education

RANK
3-Previous
  convictions
7-Forgery, fraud
8-2nd. d. murder

WT. 122.7

Mean
Age
30 yrs.

Panel 2 (Medium–Medium):
171.36 cm.

RANK
2-Robbery
1-Arson
4-Previous
  convictions
8-Forgery, fraud
1-1st. d. murder

RANK
8-Education
7-Bootlegging
9-Professions
3-Laborers

WT. 145.5

Mean
Age
29.25 yrs.

Panel 3 (Medium–Heavy):
172.95 cm.

RANK
1-Vs Public
  Welfare
2-Sex
3-2nd. d. murder
1-All offenses
3-Extractives

RANK
8-Burglary;
  larceny
7-Previous
  convictions
8-Bachelors

WT. 174

Mean
Age
33.7 yrs.

type is rather long-headed and narrow-nosed, but is extremely variable in pigmentation of hair and eyes. These tall, thin men rank second in first degree murder, first in second degree murder, and first in combined murder. They rank first in robbery, but last in burglary and larceny, and in rape and other sex offenses. They are second in liquor offenses, third in forgery, but eighth in assault. In previous convictions they occupy the median rank. The tall-slender group is third in proportions of unmarried men and at the bottom in widowers and divorcés. Occupationally, it is very high in extractives and factory operatives, ranking second in each category. It has the highest proportion of illiterates, but also the second highest proportion of men who have had really good educations. It is probably compounded of ignorant mountaineers who murder and make moonshine whiskey, together with weedy urbanites who work in factories and stage holdups. Tennessee, Kentucky, and Texas furnish nearly all of the members of this group.

The tall-medium weight body build type contains 325 men, who average 29.9 years in age, 181.92 centimeters in height, and 163.9 pounds in weight. This group is second in lightness of hair, because it is preëminent in redheads and has a large proportion of blonds. It is fourth in lightness of eye color. These tall-medium weight men rank first in forgery and fraud, tie for second place in combined murders, and are otherwise undistinguished. The group is sixth in percentage of previous convictions and in proportions of unmarried men. It leads the list in extractive occupation and is badly educated, being in seventh place. This group has been recruited slightly in excess from Texas.

The tall-heavy type consists of 134 men who average 33.55 years of age. The stature, 182.70 centimeters, is very great, and so is also the average weight (196.9 pounds). This group has the lowest mean cephalic index — i.e. is most long-headed. It is second darkest in hair color. It leads in black

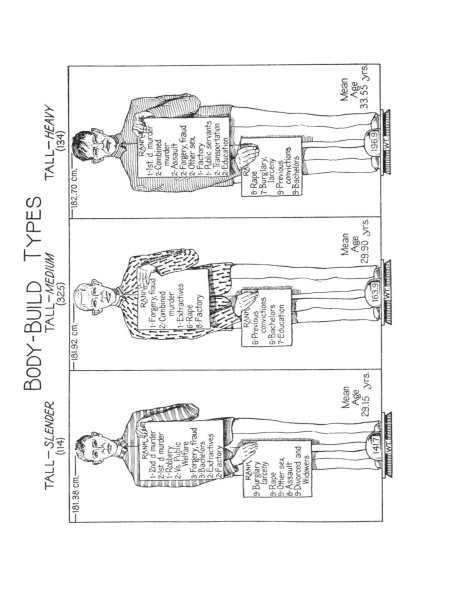

BODY-BUILD TYPES

TALL—SLENDER (114) TALL—MEDIUM (325) TALL—HEAVY (134)

181.38 cm. 181.92 cm. 182.70 cm.

TALL—SLENDER (114)

RANK
1-2d.d murder
2-1st.d murder
1-Robbery
2-Vs. Public Welfare
3-Forgery, fraud
3-Bachelors
2-Extractives
2-Factory

RANK
9-Burglary, larceny
9-Rape
9-Other sex
8-Assault
9-Divorced and Widowers

Mean Age 29.15 yrs.

WT. 147

TALL—MEDIUM (325)

RANK
1-Forgery, fraud
2-Combined murder
1-Extractives
6-Rape
8-Factory

RANK
6-Previous convictions
6-Bachelors
7-Education

Mean Age 29.90 yrs.

WT. 163.9

TALL—HEAVY (134)

RANK
1-1st.d. murder
2-Combined murder
2-Assault
2-Forgery, fraud
2-Other sex
1-Factory
1-Public servants
2-Transportation
2-Education

RANK
8-Rape
7-Burglary, larceny
9-Previous convictions
9-Bachelors

Mean Age 33.55 yrs.

WT. 196.9

hair and is very low in red and blond hair. Yet it is next to the darkest in eye pigmentation. The tall-heavy group ranks first in first degree murder and ties for second in general murder ranking. It is second in assault, second in forgery and fraud, second in other sex offenses, but seventh in burglary and larceny, and eighth in rape. The tall-heavy group has fewest previous convictions and the smallest proportion of unmarried men. It is highest in factory workers, in public servants, second in transportation, and low in most other occupations. This group has the highest proportion of men who have attended college (8.21 per cent), and is second in general educational ranking. Like the preceding type it is overloaded with Texans.

It is sufficiently evident from the facts stated above that our body build types are differentiated in offense, previous convictions, marital status, occupation, and education. The most important findings are the relationships of shortness and slenderness to burglary and larceny and to frequence of previous conviction, of tallness to murder, and the very curious predilection for sex crimes shown by the short, fat men. They almost justify the generalization that short, fat men rape; short, thin men steal; tall, thin men kill and rob; tall, heavy men murder and forge. But, of course, all body build types are likely to be associated with any particular kind of crime. A short, fat man might under sufficient provocation murder his wife in complete defiance of his body build proclivities.

Why do we have these associations between body build and crime? Racial differences between the several groups are not clearly demonstrable, although the taller and longer-headed men may have sprung from stocks in which Nordic and Atlanto-Mediterranean racial strains predominate; while the shorter and round-headed men of dark pigmentation may be Alpine, or something else. The racial strains in each group are, however, greatly mixed.

A considerable part of the sociological differentiation of the body build types may be due to the inequality of their individual derivations from the nine states represented in our criminal series. Thus, short and slender men are particularly common among the Massachusetts and Wisconsin criminals, while tall-heavy men are unduly represented in the Texas sample, and tall-slender men in Tennessee and Kentucky. In Wisconsin and in Massachusetts educational facilities are excellent, while the same cannot be said of Tennessee and Kentucky. Again, Massachusetts is a state with a large urban population, whereas most of the other states represented in our series are predominantly rural. It is all too clear that the several state environments, physical and cultural, are quite diverse. It may then occur to my readers that it would be possible to eliminate the complicating effects of state environment from this study of body build type by applying a correction for state sampling, such as was done in testing the physical differentiation of offense groups. I have not applied such corrections for state sampling, because I maintain that it is the organism which creates social environment and not the reverse. Only if each of the states possessed an exclusive physical environment and an exclusive physical type with its own particular and unvarying culture, could we conclude that environment is the common cause of body build and sociological status. Of course the physical environment of a state to some extent determines the occupations of the persons residing within that state, and may possibly, because of varying climate and food supply, exert some molding influence upon body types. But if short, fat men commit rape and come from Texas, I, for present purposes, am inclined to relate their criminal predilection to their bodily constitution and not to the sexuality of the Lone Star state. In other words, in this particular small investigation, I am interested in the sociological correlates of body build irrespective of the state of incarceration of the persons who possess a particular type of body build.

THE WILL-O'-THE-WISP OF CRIMINAL TYPE

So much nonsense has been talked about "criminal types" that it seemed necessary to make a foray into this field of subjective impressions, not in the usual manner of asseveration or denial, but by the use of multiple sortings of morphological features and by statistical analysis. People talk about "types" without having any clear conception as to what they mean when they use the word. A type is something which, literally, is struck out by a die or pattern, or cast from a mold. A physical type is recognized by the observer's visual impression of a combination of morphological features. The lay observer and, sometimes, the trained anthropologist recognize types, often without analyzing their component morphological variations. They depend merely upon impressions of likeness. Such visual recognition is the easiest and most valid method of type differentiation. Such identifications, however, have no scientific validity unless they are tabulated, analyzed, and confirmed by a statistical demonstration that persons classified within a type do, in reality, present similar combinations of morphological features and are actually distinct from other types.

To attempt to discover a type empirically by taking the morphological variations of separate features, singly tabulated, and by attempting to find their characteristic combinations in individuals is an almost impossible task. The reason for this is the appalling number of combinations which are mathematically possible when any considerable number of features and gradations of features are involved. If there are four gradations of each character and five characters involved, the possible combinations are equal to 4^5 or 1024. Thus, one would require at least 1024 individuals in order to secure all of the theoretically possible combinations.

Unless there is some sort of linkage in character gradations, by which certain combinations occur much more frequently than they would on a chance basis, there is virtually no mathematical possibility of dividing up small samples into a few morphological types of any degree of combination complexity.

Unless each offense group is characterized by the possession of a number of morphological features exclusively its own, and each found in an overwhelming majority of the individuals of that offense group, it is clear that there is almost no chance of establishing distinctive physical offense types, whereby the prognosis of a criminal's offense may be made from his physique. But every possible morphological variation occurs in each and every offense group, save those containing an insufficient number of individuals. Also, any morphological feature which in some specific variation characterizes the majority of any offense group is almost certain to occur also in a very large proportion of every other offense group. Contrariwise, any really distinctive feature is likely to occur in very few individuals of whatever group.

Differences between groups are generally established by deviations in the means of measurements or in the percentages of certain variations found in morphological features, these differences and variations being separately considered. We have distinguished our offense groups by tabulating the metric and morphological features in which each of them diverges significantly from a random sample of the entire series. Thus, we have a group of 414 robbers in which the following significant excesses have been found: (1) asymmetry — none, (2) ear protrusion — medium, (3) ear lobes — attached, (4) hair color — light brown, (5) eye folds — median, (6) hair form — low or deep waves, (7) beard quantity — large, (8) Darwin's point — pronounced, (9) iris — diffused in pigment. Now if each of these features is particularly characteristic of robbers, the more of them an individual possesses the more certainly he ought to be a robber. So we begin sorting robbers and all other criminals, keeping them separate, and if morphological combinations work, each successive sorting ought to increase the proportion of robbers to non-robbers, and we ought eventually to arrive at an exclusively robber combination. Accordingly, we start with the first character, asymmetry — none, which yields 10.28 per cent of robbers and 89.72 per cent of other criminals. Continuing these sortings, and throwing away the individuals who do not possess each successive robber variation, we arrive in the fourth sorting at two groups in which robbers comprise 19.65 per cent of the total and non-robbers 80.35 per cent. In the fifth sorting the percentage of robbers has risen to 88.89, and the sixth sorting gives us 100 per cent of robbers. However, this exclusive combination includes only one robber, out of 4212 criminals. Since we started with 414 robbers in total series, it is evident that by securing an exclusively robber morphological combination, we have emptied out the baby with the bath. In other words, a morphological type which is peculiar to robbers identifies but one of 414 of such offenders. Clearly, such a procedure has little practical utility.

One of the difficulties inherent in such a process of sorting for morphological type is that really distinctive characters are found in few persons. When we begin our sortings, we start with the most widely prevalent morphological feature, asymmetry — none (in which this offense group exceeds the total series), which is found in 77.33 per cent of robbers, but is also found in 73.16 per cent of non-robbers. When we get down to the ninth character, iris — diffused, we find it in only 11.74 per cent of robbers as against 8.60 per cent of non-robbers. Thus the largest percentage of robbers who could possibly have the nine robber characters in combination would be 11.74. Actually on the sixth sorting we had one robber and no non-robbers, and on the seventh sorting we still had the same one robber. On the eighth sorting we ran out of robbers also.

Of course, sorting in a specified order for each of nine characters really establishes a permutation rather than a combination. So in order to find all of the combinations of the nine excess morphological features which are notably present in robbers, our Hollerith operator went on with the sorting process of this group of robbers until every possible combination had been investigated. This process with an electrical sorter, running 450 cards a minute, consumed over six weeks. By any non-mechanical process it would have taken an incalculable length of time and probably the sanity of the person who attempted it.

What we actually found is of some theoretical interest. For instance, there were 6 robbers, or 1.45 per cent, who had none of the robber peculiarities at all. Only one individual had as many as seven of them. The commonest number was three, found in 31.64 per cent of the robber group. The next commonest number was two, with 27.05 per cent, and 20.29 per cent had four of the characters in combination. The actual number of combinations of the nine characters theoretically possible is 512, but we had only 414 robbers. In reality 127 different combinations were found, or 24.8 of those theoretically possible. Considering the fact that there were not enough robbers in our group to take care of 512 different combinations, the number actually observed is 31.91 per cent of those theoretically possible in the group of 414 men — namely 414 combinations.

We also tried out various fourfold combinations of morphological features which are especially common in robbers to see to what extent they were observable also in non-robbers. All that we were able to accomplish was the demonstration that certain of these combinations when found in an individual considerably reduce the odds against his being a robber. In fact, we were able to reduce those odds from 9 to 1 to about 4 to 1. Clearly, then, no one but an anthropological ignoramus and a mathematical ass would conceive it possible to utilize for purposes of practical criminal diagnosis any rigid multiple combination of morphological features supposed to constitute a criminal type.

It is perfectly possible, however, for a skillful and experienced anthropological observer to sort a large group of men into classes or types on the basis of mutual physical resemblances, as judged from visual impression. Such morphological types exhibit within themselves marked metrical and physical homogeneity, if they have been selected with sufficient skill and precision. They may be regarded as racial or subracial types, since they owe their distinguishing physical similarities to characters which are, presumably, inherited. The associations of such types with kinds of behavior, social or antisocial, are largely hypothetical, but that some behavioral tendencies are connected with bodily types, I, for one, do not doubt. In a later stage of this investigation I shall present the results of a study of the relation of offense to racial types selected on the basis of a conventional combination of physical characters, such as variations of head form, hair color, and eye color. But all types of offense are committed, to some extent, by every physical race which we can distinguish. Therefore, all that can be expected of the racial typing of criminals is that excesses of this or that kind of offense may be demonstrated for the several type subgroups.

Constitutional types, based upon body build, especially the relation of stature to weight, have been shown to be associated in a very interesting manner with the nature of criminal offense. These body build types are only in part racial. Family inheritance and individual variation enter into their makeup. They furnish some clue to antisocial proclivity,

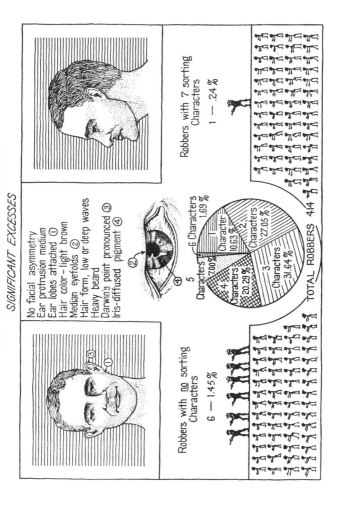

SORTING FOR INDIVIDUAL COMBINATIONS OF MORPHOLOGICAL EXCESSES IN OLD AMERICAN ROBBERS

SIGNIFICANT EXCESSES

No facial asymmetry
Ear protrusion medium
Ear lobes attached ①
Hair color – light brown
Median eyefolds ②
Hair form, low or deep waves
Heavy beard
Darwin's point pronounced ③
Iris-diffused pigment ④

Robbers with 7 sorting Characters
1 — .24 %

Robbers with no sorting Characters
6 — 1.45 %

5 6 Characters 1.69 %
Characters 1 Character
7.00% 10.63 %
2 Characters
4 Characters 12.
20.29 % Characters
27.05 %
3 Characters
31.64 %

TOTAL ROBBERS 414

but they also are not in themselves of definitive diagnostic value.

Pathological types, due to some definite dysfunction, often of the ductless glands, are easily distinguishable, but are confined to so few individuals that their use in criminal identification would be as limited, or nearly as limited, as our sorting combination of robber characteristics.

Criminals represent, on the basis of our findings, individuals from every racial group who are selected, for the most part, for constitutional inferiority. But they do not bear the brand of Cain, nor any specific physical stigmata whereby they can be identified at a glance. One can make a guess, by a careful inspection of an individual, whether he is more likely to be a professional criminal or a professor of criminology. Some of my unsolicited correspondents have assured me that I resemble the former more than the latter — a judgment which would suggest to me an overlapping of the physical characteristics of two widely diverse professions, did it not suggest much more forcibly that the writing of letters to unfortunate persons whose names have got into the press is the favorite pastime of the insane.

CHAPTER IV

OLD AMERICAN CRIMINALS AND CIVILIANS: DO THEY DIFFER?

ONE of the principal difficulties (or stupidities) of medical science is that it knows a great deal about people who are sick, but almost nothing at all about people who are well. It concerns itself almost exclusively with the pathological man, and is content to evolve the hypothetical normal man from its inner consciousness, like the notorious German investigator of the camel. Similarly, the criminologist is prone to carry on elaborate studies of the social, economic, and psychological status of the criminal and exhausts himself and his research funds in so doing, since he has neither the energy nor the resources to find out enough about noncriminals to provide a standard of comparison. He leaves the criminal out on the end of a felonious limb, suspended in a vacuum of postulated law-abiding citizens who are supposed to be sociologically "normal." Criminal anthropologists have committed this same scientific misdemeanor, in that they have studied the physical characteristics of delinquents, and have then concluded them to be "normal," pathological, degenerative, or atavistic, without knowing whether they are really different from the putatively law-abiding.

The present survey of criminals in the United States was designed to include comparable studies upon adequate samples of the civilian population. However, we soon discovered that the law-abiding population, if drawn from the lower social and economic levels, is singularly recalcitrant and suspicious when approached by an anthropometrist equipped with shining calipers and gleaming measuring rods. The man in the street fears a practitioner of a science named by the Greeks, even when bearing gifts. We set up an anthropometric booth at Revere Beach; we were unwelcome guests at the drill halls of the militia; we insinuated ourselves into the dispensaries of public hospitals; we interrupted firemen at their games of checkers and students in their more or less intellectual pursuits; but still we did not secure really satisfactory civilian samples with which to compare our criminals.

There is no such thing as a truly random sample of a human population; the concept is a statistical abstraction invented by mathematicians who toss coins, draw black or white marbles out of a bag, and then proceed to calculate probabilities and to write equations. None of these has even smelled the so-called "normal" man of the hypothetically "law-abiding" population — much less measured him. We did measure some thousands of men who were not in jail; in fact, we found in several instances that we had remeasured in our series of upright citizens individuals upon whom we had placed the calipers when in "durance vile." We were delighted to have the opportunity to measure a large series of respectable Jewish out-patients at the Beth Israel Hospital, but discovered after we had completed our criminal series that there were not enough Jews in jail to constitute an adequate sample with which to compare those at liberty.

In attempting to gather a civilian check sample of native Whites of native parentage, we were baffled by the fact that these Old Americans seem not to congregate in the cities, in which our check samples were necessarily gathered. Among the 3000 and more civilians whom we measured, only a few more than 300 were native Whites of native parentage. This seemed to us a barely adequate sample, and it was only after the field work was finished and analysis had been going on for several years that the dragon of incomparability raised its hideous head.

As I have pointed out previously, the entire field work of the survey was carried out when I labored under the erroneous belief that all native Whites of native parentage, because they were derived from only a few racial and ethnic strains, were sufficiently homogeneous physically, so that they could be lumped together in a single series. Consequently, our civilian check samples of Whites were gathered, from motives of economy, in two states only — Massachusetts and Tennessee. After I had discovered that the several states included in the survey had developed each its own differentiated and, in some respects, peculiar physical type, I found myself in the predicament of having civilian samples from two states only and no more money with which to fill the hiatus.

In this emergency I adopted the following expedient. The total criminal series of native Whites of native parentage derived from nine states was compared with the total civilian series of similar antecedents derived from Massachusetts and Tennessee. The significant differences were tabulated. Then the Massachusetts criminals in a separate series were similarly compared with the Massachusetts civilians, and their significant differences tabulated; likewise in the case of the two state series from Tennessee. My assumption was that significant differences of any measurement or observation which occurred not only in the total comparison but also in the two state comparisons, and in the same direction in all three pairs, were criminologically valid. What was sauce not only for the total series goose but also for the Tennessee gander and the Massachusetts buzzard was undoubtedly a valid condiment for all criminal birds. I have found no reason for changing that opinion.

In Tennessee the entire check sample of native White males of native parentage consisted of a group of 146 Nashville firemen, whom Observer A succeeded in measuring. This sample is far from ideal, because it is composed entirely of men belonging to one occupation for which the physical qualifications are rather stringent. The sociological status of these firemen is not diversified, but uniform. However, the principal objection to them is that they are inclined to be fat. Since our Massachusetts check sample was gathered in Boston from hospitals, drill halls, and beaches, it seemed to be sufficiently representative of what may be called the lower and lower middle economic classes. Now when the Tennessee firemen were thrown in with the militiamen, casual patients, bathers, et cetera, the general character of the combined check sample seemed fairly representative, apart from the fact that it was almost exclusively urban, whereas the majority of our criminals are of rural residence when not incarcerated.

When the total criminal series was compared in any sociological or anthropological feature with the total civilian check sample, the differences were validated or depreciated according to the agreement of the two separate state comparisons with the total result. This method works perfectly well and is conclusive when all three comparisons agree in direction and significance, or when all three agree in direction, even if the difference in one of the state comparisons does not attain full statistical reliability. However, when a significant difference is found in the total comparison which agrees in direction with that found in one of the state comparisons, but disagrees with the other, we find ourselves in a quandary. Which of the state comparisons between criminals and civilians is to be regarded as the more reliable? Originally I was strongly of the opinion that in such cases of state disagreement more weight should be given to the Massachusetts comparison, because the Massachusetts civilian check sample is occupationally diversified, whereas the Tennessee check sample consists only of the fat firemen. Ultimately, however, I was driven to change my opinion for two reasons. Firstly, certain probable racial differences manifested themselves between the Massachusetts criminals and civilians which ran contrary to the general series trend. Upon tabulation of the extractions of the Massachusetts series it became apparent that the criminals of Massachusetts, although Old American, include a large proportion of men of French Canadian descent, whereas this element is very feebly represented in the Massachusetts civil sample, and, in general, very scarce throughout the entire criminal series, except in the samples from Massachusetts and from Wisconsin. Again, a large proportion of the Massachusetts civil sample was measured by a third anthropologist, Observer C, who seemed to have introduced into some of the data his own personal equation, different from that of Observer A who studied all of the Massachusetts criminals.

On the other hand, a study of the extractions of the Tennessee criminals and their civilian check samples showed them to be ethnically comparable, and both series were measured and observed by one anthropologist. Thus, in spite of the corpulence of the Nashville firemen, they seem to furnish a better basis for the determination of differences between criminals and civilians physically than does the otherwise more satisfactory Massachusetts civil sample.

SOCIOLOGICAL DIFFERENTIATION

In marital state it is abundantly evident that our criminal series is differently constituted from the civilian check sample. The criminals include far more single men, divorced men, and widowers, with a corresponding dearth of the wedded. However, since the criminals are on the average 3.8 years younger than the civilians, it is evident that some of the marriage deficiency of the felons is attributable to this circumstance. Our criminal series includes over 10 per cent fewer of men in the age group 25–29 years, which, I take it, is one of the most dangerous ages for men as regards marriage susceptibility. It is a curious fact that the excesses of single men and the deficiencies of married men are overwhelming and significant in the Tennessee and total series comparison but are statistically insignificant and absolutely small in Massachusetts. The Tennessee criminals have a much higher marriage rate than the Massachusetts criminals but the Tennessee firemen enormously exceed the Massachusetts civilians in their addiction to matrimony. I do not think, however, that there can be any serious doubt of the general deficiency of criminal marriage rates as compared with those of civilians.

All of our comparisons indicate a pronounced excess of divorced men among criminals as compared with civilians, for the simple reason that not a single one of our law-abiding citizens admitted that he was divorced or separated. Of course we have only 307 civilians, but it seems to me that, since not all of them were Catholics, some of them must have been liars. We had to ascertain marital status from personal interrogation, and not, as in the case of the criminals, from records.

The excess of widowers in the criminal series found, to some extent, in all three comparisons, is puzzling. Since our criminals are somewhat below the average age of the civilians they should include fewer widowers. Some of the disparity may be due to the probability that a certain number of criminals have been widowed by their own homicidal activities. We have recorded in our civilian check sample but one widower out of 307 men, but I cannot think that this paucity is due to civilian mendacity, because certainly no one need be ashamed to confess himself a widower, unless he has killed his wife, and there is no reason for suspecting our civilians of such irregularities.

It is easy enough to explain why there are fewer married men among criminals than among civilians, because one cannot acquire a wife while he is in jail, and a considerable proportion of our criminals seem to lead a life of penal servitude, interrupted only by short periods of freedom,

MARITAL STATE

4160 Old American
Criminals
303 Old American
Civilians

48.6 42.0   44.8 57.7   4.23 0   2.4 .33
SINGLE MARRIED DIVORCED WIDOWER

during which they scarcely have time to publish the banns. Again, the fellow who is liable to protracted absences from the matrimonial bed and board while an enforced guest of the state probably does not appeal to the majority of young women as an ideal husband and head of a family. Finally, there is no particular reason for supposing that men who break the laws designed to protect property and persons are likely to toe the mark in the matter of matrimonial statutes. It is conceivable that a blushing bride might encounter considerable difficulty in dragging into the office of the justice of the peace a prospective bridegroom with a long police record. I for one should be happy if I thought that the matrimonial state of the criminal to be that of heaven, where we are told that they "are neither married nor given in marriage." One cannot, however, banish the lurking suspicion that many of these criminals propagate their undesirable kind outside of the holy state of matrimony.

There are some very marked occupational differences between criminals and civilians, but a good many of these are wholly, or partially, attributable to the fact that our civilian sample is exclusively urban, or almost so, whereas the bulk of our Old American criminals are of rural origin. However, an excess of unskilled laborers, amounting to nearly 15 per cent in the criminals, and an excess of personal servants, amounting to more than 5 per cent, are confirmed in all three comparisons and are undoubtedly valid. On the other hand, our huge excess of criminal extractives (30.64 per cent) must not be taken to signify that agriculturalists are excessively criminalistic, but only that Old Americans are, perhaps, most numerous among the farming population. Our occupational comparisons are well nigh ruined by the fact that nearly 48 per cent of our check sample are Nashville firemen — a circumstance which piles up numbers in the public service category to the detriment of all other classes of occupation. Yet, an excess of factory workers among the criminals as compared with the civilians may possess some measure of validity. In general there can be little doubt that the occupational status of criminals is, on the whole, markedly inferior to that of ethnically comparable civilians. Yet I should be the last to claim that this has been demonstrated in the present comparison, because of the obviously specialized character of our civilian check sample, as compared with the great criminal series. Then, too, it is difficult to avoid the pessimistic conclusion that the real occupation of many of these criminals is crime and nothing else. This in spite of the fact that our special studies of criminal occupation have led us to attribute a moderate credibility to criminal claims of law-abiding occupations.

I see no reason for regarding with suspicion our findings that Old American criminals are very inferior in educational attainment to comparable civilians. Actually, however, there is no unanimity of significant deficiency of criminal education in any single one of our numerous educational categories, manifested in the total series comparison, in Tennessee and in Massachusetts. While Massachusetts criminals are abysmally inferior to Massachusetts civilians in the higher categories of educational attainment, and the same is true in the total series comparison of all criminals with all civilians, the Tennessee state comparison is peculiar. The Nashville firemen are men of very modest education, and the Tennessee criminals exceed them not only in illiterates and those who can read and write only, but also, significantly, in the proportions of men who have reached the first two years of high school, and, insignificantly, in the proportion who have attended college. I suppose that it is perfectly natural that some criminals, but no firemen, should have enjoyed the advantages of university education. It is quite possible that higher education is more useful to a criminal than to a fireman. At any rate, Massachusetts criminals are better educated than Nashville, Tennessee, firemen — a fact which does not reflect discredit upon firemen, but upon the general status of education in Tennessee.

Of course our general sociological data indicate that criminals are vastly below civilians in sociological status, but that is nothing new. It is capable of proof and doubtless has been proved by the analysis of many bodies of statistics which are much larger and more valid than ours. We deal with this rather unsatisfactory sociological comparison of our civil check sample with our criminals only because it is an essential preliminary to the consideration of their physical differences. It would be a perfectly simple matter to introduce here a comparison between the physical and sociological status of the criminals and our very large sample of law-abiding citizens whom we studied at the Century of Progress Exposition, but it would be manifestly unfair to the criminals. For our exposition visitors represent a class selected for economic and social superiority — economic because each of them presumably possessed at least the fifty cents which was the price of admission to the fair, and social because our anthropometric laboratory was unfortunately situated in the Hall of the Social Sciences, a building mainly patronized by school teachers, students, and others interested in education, aside from those of the general public who had become lost in the maze of exposition buildings. Of course these exposition visitors are vastly more superior to criminals in physique and in education and occupation than are the humble citizens included in our civilian check sample gathered specifically for comparison with criminals. We really want to compare the man in the street with the man who has been taken off the street and put in jail, not the man in the prison yard with the man in the Harvard Yard. Although some who have been in the latter are at present in the former, only 3.3 per cent of our Old American criminals can be credited to higher education.

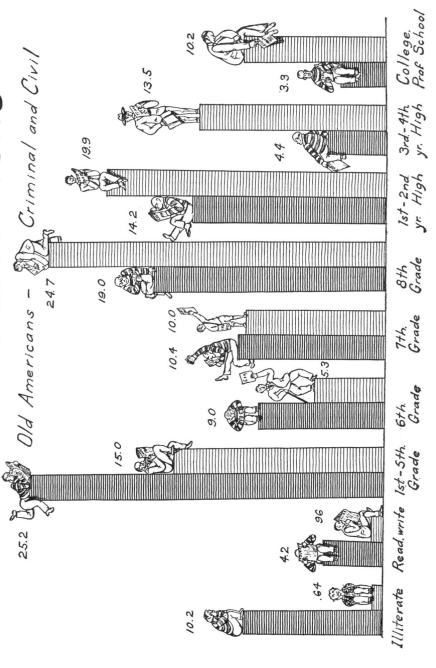

COMPARATIVE EDUCATIONS

Old Americans — Criminal and Civil

	Illiterate	Read.write	1st-5th Grade	6th Grade	7th Grade	8th Grade	1st-2nd yr. High	3rd-4th yr. High	College. Prof School
Criminal	10.2	.64	15.0	9.0	10.4	24.7	14.2	13.5	10.2
Civil		.96	4.2	5.3	10.0	19.0	19.9	4.4	3.3

PHYSICAL DIFFERENTIATION

METRIC AND INDICIAL DIFFERENCES

Since the civilian check sample which I am comparing
physically with our Old American criminals consists of *hoi
polli* rather than *haute élite*, I do not feel in the least
apologetic about the incompatibilities which have resulted
from the limited state distribution and the restricted occupational status of the check sample. As I have said, I have
tried to circumvent the difficulty by accepting as ultimately
valid only those differences which are substantiated in Massachusetts, in Tennessee, and in the total comparison — all
three unanimous in their testimony. Now in the first and
most positive category of unanimous and truly significant
differences are 7 measurements, or 21.1 per cent of those
taken. Criminals are deficient in age to the extent of 3.80
years, in weight to the amount of 11.7 pounds, and also in
chest breadth, head circumference, upper face height, nose
height, and ear length. Of almost certain validity also are
5 criminal deviations in which all three comparisons agree
in direction, and the total comparison difference and that of
one of the two state comparisons attain statistical significance. For example, the comparison of total criminals with
total civilians shows that the criminals are inferior in stature
or body height to the extent of 1.02 cm., a difference which
amounts to 4.25 times its probable error. Massachusetts
agrees in direction and significance of criminal statural
inferiority, but Tennessee shows a criminal diminution of
stature which is not certainly of statistical significance.
Similarly, in shoulder breadth and chest depth all three
comparisons agree, but in one state the criminal inferiority
is insignificant. In this same category fall the nasal index, in
which criminals show an elevation indicating a relatively
shorter nose, and the zygo-frontal index, in which the crimi-

nals show a greater forehead breadth relative to the total breadth of the face across the cheek bones.[1] Differences of this class, amounting to virtually certain validity, occur in 5 metric features or 15.15 of the total. Finally, there is a third category in which the total comparison difference between criminals and civilians is significant, and both of the state comparisons agree in direction but fail to attain statistical validity. The one measurement in this category is total face height in which criminals are inferior to civilians in the total comparison by 1.5 mm., which is 5.56 times the probable error. There are other classes of difference in which the probability of ultimate criminological importance is strong, but we may neglect these in this cursory summary.

Altogether we have 39.39 per cent of differences in metric features between civilians and criminals which seem to be of general validity. Of course this amount is vastly in excess of the deviations which might be expected to occur by chance, and it is far more than could be attributed to the restricted character of our civilian check sample as regards state provenience and occupational diversification. However, before a final acceptance of these metric differences between criminals and civilians which are attested in both state comparisons and in the total series, we must consider the effect of the age disparity of 3.8 years which obtains between the great group of the criminals and the small check series of civilians. The most simple, direct, and satisfactory method of handling this problem of age disparity is to select from the large criminal series subgroups of adequate size which are exactly comparable in age composition with the civilian

[1] I entertain some doubt as to the significance (logical rather than statistical) of this particular difference. It may mean that the excessive breadth of the criminal forehead relative to face and jaws is a result of mere retardation in facial breadth development. It is possible, though unlikely, that the difference is spurious, arising from a variation between observers in the measurement of this minimum frontal diameter.

check sample and to determine whether the differences in measurements found in the total series persist in these subgroups of the same age as the civilians. This process involves the restudy of two subgroups of criminals — those in the age group 35–39 years, consisting of 409 men, and those between the ages of 35 years and 69 years, including some 1223 individuals. This enables us to compare within the criminals a subgroup of ages centering about the mean ages of the civilian check sample, and a larger subgroup of all of the older age grades in which criminals are deficient, each with the total criminal series and with the total civilian check sample. In this way we can ascertain whether a group of criminals of the same age as the majority of civilians presents the same difference from the latter as is exhibited by the entire criminal series, and, further, whether the older criminals *in toto* persist in their metric differentiation from the civilians, when the excess of young criminals has been removed from the series. After this tedious and laborious process has been carried out, it emerges that only one of the 13 metric features in which differences between criminals and civilians were validated on the basis of sampling error and state agreement is possibly affected by disparity of age composition. This is head breadth. While we cannot be sure that the difference between criminals and civilians is due to an age factor, yet the counsel of caution bids us to discard head breadth as a differentiated feature. Hence, for the moment, we are left with 12 metric differences between criminals and civilians: criminal deficiency in age, weight, stature, shoulder breadth, chest depth, chest breadth, total face height and nose height, criminal excesses of the nasal index (indicating shorter noses with respect to their breadth) and of the zygo-frontal index (meaning that the criminal forehead is broader relative to face breadth than that of the civilian), a deficiency in the facial index of criminals (who thus have relatively shorter, broader faces), and finally in criminals a slight elevation of sitting height expressed as a percentage of stature.

MORPHOLOGICAL DIFFERENCES

However, before we can discuss the meaning of these metric differences between criminals and civilians, we must tackle the vastly more difficult task of appraising the number, significance, and validity of the morphological differences — those numerous graded observations of the soft parts of the body which depend upon the morphological judgment of the field observer. This business is much more troublesome than the testing of metric differences, because qualitative features — attributes — are far more subject to the personal equation of the observer than are caliper measurements; they are much more difficult to handle statistically, and apparently they are more seriously affected by age changes. For example, the shape of one's cranium as expressed by the cephalic index is little altered by senile changes, but the amount and color of hair on that cranium is likely to change radically with advancing years.

I have no intention of dragging this circle of readers through the entire length of the Slough of morphological Despond across which I have struggled and splashed, to emerge eventually with a head that is muddy but unbowed, because I fear that the hardy survivors of such a crossing would be not only muddied but also muddled. So I propose to hop across directly to the more or less firm ground on the other side of the morass and to present the results which have been cleansed of adhering impurities. They may still smell a bit, but they have been thoroughly scrubbed.

Tattooing, a practise of stupid and ignorant persons, is commoner among criminals than among civilians, but in this group of criminals it occurs infrequently, in about one of seven prisoners. Lombroso and his school attributed great significance to the extent to which criminals adorned themselves in this primitive fashion and to the character of the designs, which, indelibly printed in their hides, facilitated their identification by the police. It seems a pity to delete from scientific criminology the entertaining consideration of this practise with all of its wealth of lurid detail, but, to tell the truth, our findings indicate that tattooing in this country has little, if any, criminological significance.

Probably criminals have less beard and body hair and more head hair than civilians, apart from differences which may be due to age, but the data on these points are somewhat conflicting and unsatisfactory. It is quite certain, however, that criminals include a larger percentage of straight-haired men as compared with wavy-haired, curly-haired, and frizzly-haired individuals in the general population of the same ethnic origin, but some of the excess of criminal straight hair may be due to prison hair crops, since a wave in the hair is hardly perceptible when the latter is clipped close to the head.

Criminals have much higher proportions of red-brown hair than civilians, and the latter have excesses of gray and white hair, but the difference is probably attributable in large measure to the fact that the criminals of our series are, on the average, considerably younger than the civilians of the check sample. I suspect that red-brown hair is particularly susceptible to graying, and, if that is the case, the excess of this shade in criminals may also be affected by the age disparity between the two groups.

Criminals (always as compared with our check sample of civilians) are deficient in the very dark and very light shades of eye color (browns and blues) and include an unduly large proportion of men with mixed eyes. In the Old American criminals individuals with homogeneous irides (the pigmented part of the eye consisting of a flat color without apparent patterning) are comparatively rare. The prevailing arrangement of the iris in a mixed eye is a rayed pattern of brown or yellow-brown pigment extending outward from the pupil of the eye toward the periphery, which shows a lighter background of blue, gray, brown, or green. This predominant rayed pattern of mixed eyes, of course, is common enough in criminals, but they also show considerable excesses of the far less usual iridical patterns, especially those in which the brown pigment is arranged in a concentric zone around the pupil, and the speckled type, in which brown spots and blotches are irregularly scattered over the lighter background.

The entire pigmentation of the body — hair, skin, and eyes — seems to me to present, in general, little of criminological importance, except in so far as pigment types assist us to separate various racial elements in a mixed population. That matter of the racial differentiation of criminals is not our present concern. We are here comparing a racially mixed group of criminals with a group of civilians, also racially mixed, and from essentially the same ingredients. All sorts of pigmentation combinations occur in each group, and perhaps the only comparatively safe generalization which we are permitted is to the effect that, in these pigmentally heterogeneous Old Americans, there is evidence that the criminals present fewer of the extreme and pure type combinations of color of hair, skin, and eyes, than do our civilians.

Quite apart from complicating influences, criminals seem to have more eye folds of the upper eyelid than do our civilians, especially the fold across the inner corner of the eye which is often called the Mongoloid fold, but is likely to happen in the best of our supposedly non-Mongoloid families. This fold is found in cretins, and in so-called Mongolian idiots — individuals suffering from defective functioning of the ductless glands — but the possession of this fold, a tiny skin flap across the inner angle of the eye slit, makes its owner neither an idiot nor a criminal, and, in fact, not even a member of the Mongoloid division of mankind.

Our materials substantiate the findings of the Lombrosian School that criminals display more low and sloping foreheads than do civilians, but the personal equations of observers cast some little doubt upon the complete validity of this result. A low and sloping forehead is not ordinarily considered a noble physiognomic attribute. Most persons who have low, sloping foreheads are likely to consider themselves as, at any rate, medium in brow development, and to judge others accordingly. In fact, I am about the only person I know who is willing to admit that he has a pronouncedly sloping forehead, and as soon as my hair recedes a little farther, I shall deny that I have ever had a low forehead. Nevertheless, the balance of the evidence does indicate that low and sloping foreheads are more prevalent in criminals than in civilians and this is perfectly consonant with the fact that criminals have the smaller brain cases.

In addition to its diminished length and relatively slightly greater breadth, the nose of the criminal tends to be higher in the root and in the bridge, and more frequently undulating or concavo-convex than in our sample of civilians. The septum of the nose (the partition between the nostrils) is prevailingly inclined upward and is more frequently skewed to one side or other than in the civilian noses. The tip of the criminal nose is likely to run to extremes of thickness and thinness. On the whole, the pudgy, blobby types of noses not generally admired by sculptors, but found in satyrs, Socrates, and in some anthropologists, seem unduly common in Massachusetts criminals and in the total series, although the Tennessee criminals do not show this nasal bulbousness when compared with Nashville firemen.

Our series of Old American criminals shows a larger proportion of thin-lipped individuals than the comparable non-criminal group. Now, in general, thin lips are not a

OLD AMERICAN CRIMINALS AND CIVILIANS
CRUDE METRIC AND MORPHOLOGICAL DIFFERENCES

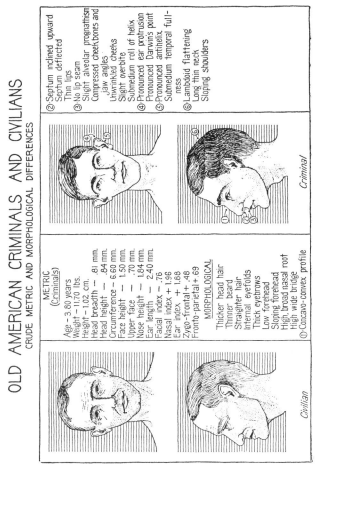

METRIC
(Criminals)

Age – 3. 80 years
Weight – 11.70 lbs.
Height – 1.02. cm.
Head breadth –   .81 mm.
Head height   –   .84 mm.
Circumference – 6.60 mm.
Face height   – 1.50 mm.
Upper face   –   .70 mm.
Nose height   – 1.84 mm.
Ear length   –   .76
Facial index   –   .76
Nasal index + 1.96
Zygo-frontal+ .48
Fronto-parietal+.69

MORPHOLOGICAL

Thicker head hair
Thinner beard
Straighter hair
Internal eyefolds
Thick eyebrows
Low forehead
Sloping forehead
High, broad nasal root
High wide bridge
①·Concavo-convex profile
②·Septum inclined upward
   Septum deflected
   Thin lips
③·No lip seam
   Slight alveolar prognathism
   Compressed cheekbones and
      jaw angles
   Unwrinkled cheeks
   Slight overbite
   Submedium roll of helix
④·Pronounced ear protrusion
   Pronounced Darwin's point
⑤·Pronounced antihelix
   Submedium temporal full-
      ness
⑥·Lambdoid flattening
   Long thin neck
   Sloping shoulders

Civilian

Criminal

sign of avarice, meanness, or determination, but of advanced age and loss of teeth. However, our criminals are younger than our civilians, and have lost fewer teeth than their law-abiding elders. Consequently, these thin criminal lips go contrary to the expected age difference. Actually, when the difference in mean ages is taken into consideration, criminals do not differ significantly from civilians in the degree to which their teeth are worn and in the number of teeth they have lost, but they do display a higher percentage of marked overbites — that condition in which the lower jaw is recessed, and the upper front teeth bite over, or in front of, the lower incisors. This dental deformity is very common in present generation children, and in economically well situated families involves the unfortunate youngsters in years of orthodontic treatment with its concomitant wire bands, braces, and wedges, and their parents in financial difficulties.

The hinder angles of the jaws in our criminals are oftener compressed and less often prominent than among our comparable civilians. Compressed jaw angles often accompany poor facial development.

The ear of the criminal was particularly stressed by the Lombrosians as manifesting malformations and evidence of degeneracy. The Bertillon system of individual criminal identification, still used in many European countries, taught police officers to memorize the details of the morphological variations of the external ear, which are numerous and intricate. Since the external ear in man and most of the primates is in an evolutionary degressive stage, abnormalities of conformation are frequent, and perhaps especially so in persons of inferior heredity. It is a curious fact that, unless one is trained to look at ears, they are ordinarily overlooked and completely escape attention. Perhaps that is all for the best in view of the ugly, degenerative features which they often show in otherwise apparently normally developed individuals. I, myself, when I go to the moving pictures, or when I ride upon street cars, am to such an extent fascinated by the aural turpitude (I use the word in a purely evolutionary context) which I observe, that I forget all about the plucked eyebrows, the hair-line moustaches, and other artificial physiognomic modifications, and concentrate solely upon the auricular evidence of human degeneration which is naïvely displayed in all of its naked ugliness. It is probable that my anthropological fieldworkers on the criminal survey may have been less sensitive to ear variations than I am. At any rate, the occurrence of out-and-out abnormalities of the external ear in our criminal series is very rare. Our data do not confirm the Lombrosian contention that criminals manifest a higher percentage of atavistic and degenerative features of the ear than civilians, except in the following details: The rim of the ear, or the helix, is more frequently unrolled, or almost so, in criminals than in civilians. Further, the cartilaginous nodule on the hinder border of the ear rim, which marks the site of the former free tip of the ears in mammals, is apparently oftener well developed in criminals than in civilians. Again, the ear of the criminal is somewhat more primitive in proportions, or perhaps less degenerate, in that it is shorter absolutely and broader relatively than in comparable civilians. Thus, while it may be stated that the criminal ear does differ from the civilian ear on the basis of the records of our comparisons, we certainly have found nothing to substantiate the theory that extreme aural malformations are criminal stigmata.

Finally, this series of native born American criminals of native parentage is distinguished from the civilian check sample by the inclusion among the delinquents of many more individuals with long, thin necks and with sloping shoulders, features associated with the prevailingly weedy build of the criminals.

Thus, the physical contrast between the criminal and his

civilian mate emphasizes the smaller size of the felon, his inferior weight and poorer body build, his smaller head, straighter hair, absolutely shorter and relatively broader face, with prominent but short and often snubbed nose, his narrow jaws and his rather small, and relatively broad, ears. I cannot reiterate too often and too emphatically the statement that the differences here presented do not distinguish every native born criminal of native parentage from any law-abiding person of similar stock. They are average or composite differences and cannot be relied upon for purposes of individual diagnosis. There is no single metric feature or morphological variation which is, in any sense, peculiar to criminals. Differences between criminals and non-criminals are in the relative frequency of the occurrence of certain variations in groups.

Now if, in this comparison of criminals with a civilian check series, we divide the criminals up into their ten offense groups and compare each of these groups with the total civilian check sample, we encounter a rather remarkable phenomenon. The general trend of criminal physical difference from civilians is practically the same, whatever offense group is compared with the civilian series. In other words, our criminals tend to present a more or less uniform array of physical differences from civilians, irrespective of the nature of the offense of which the prisoners have been convicted. This does not mean, of course, that there are no offense group variations in the nature of criminal-civilian difference, because there are a great many, which need not be listed here. It means rather that the majority of the differences which seem to have been validated as between the total series of criminals and civilians, after careful allowance has been made for state differences, age difference, and for the errors due to observational equation, are found to manifest themselves again as the outstanding differentiae between specific offense groups and the general sample of civilians.

The burglars and thieves are physically farthest removed from the civilian check sample and the assault criminals least so. Of course the number and significance of deviations are somewhat affected by the size of the various criminal groups, since very large groups, such as burglary and larceny, yield more numerous and more reliable differences than small groups, such as assault, which are subject to a large sampling error.

This unanimity of criminal physical differences from civilians of comparable ethnic composition is capable of two alternative explanations. The first is that our civilian check sample does not, in fact, so deviate from the criminal population, but that the differences are due to the faulty techniques of anthropometry and the vacillating morphological judgments and personal equations of the fieldworkers who collected the data. I have investigated this matter scrupulously, and (in the proper sense of the word) meticulously, and I have not attempted to gloss over my doubts and suspicions as to accuracy when they have arisen. I have, moreover, steadfastly refused to accept as valid differences which seem to me to have been occasioned by any such extrinsic methodological causes. However gratifying it may be to an investigator to secure startling positive findings, he can find no real or honest satisfaction in the presentation of results which he suspects to be in any sense spurious or, to speak vulgarly, "phony." To me the most convincing argument in favor of the validity of this physical difference between criminals and civilians is the fact that these morphological and metric deviations are of about the same magnitude and in the same direction as are their respective sociological differences, which are based upon the accumulation of objective facts. These sociological facts may be, and presumably are, in some cases, erroneously reported or recorded, but they are not subject to the personal equations of the fieldworker.

This leads me to the second alternative explanation of the unanimity of offense group differences of criminals from civilians in physical features. This is, in short, that the real basis of the whole body of sociological, metric, and morphological deviations of criminals from civilians is the organic inferiority of the former. Now physical, anatomical inferiority in persons who are not obviously diseased can manifest itself only, presumably, in a limited number of metric and morphological characters, and we do not pretend at the present stage of knowledge to assert precisely what these characters are, and what particular variations of them indubitably indicate the defective organism. We may assume, however, that these physical marks of inferiority are fewer and perhaps more restricted in their range than are the varieties of abnormal and antisocial behavior which the inferior organism can manifest. In other words, general organic deterioration is likely to result in diverse antisocial attitudes and in a multiplicity of different types of criminal offense. This I believe to be the most satisfactory explanation of the phenomenon which we are discussing — that criminal behavior is capable of considerable diversification in the manner and kind of the overt act, but that, whatever the crime may be, it ordinarily arises from a deteriorated organism which, so far as we now know, manifests its inferiority in comparatively few and uniform ways.

You may say that this is tantamount to a declaration that the primary cause of crime is biological inferiority — and that is exactly what I mean. To the human being who is organically sound — physically and mentally fit — the savior of society (a rôle to which I assuredly do not aspire) might say, "Thou art Peter, and upon this rock will I build my social order." Certainly the penitentiaries of our society are built upon the shifting sands and quaking bogs of inferior human organisms.

CHAPTER V

NEW AMERICAN CRIMINALS – IMMIGRANTS' PROGRESS FIRST GENERATION AND FOREIGN BORN NATIONALITY AND CRIME

THE process of transforming alien immigrants and their offspring into residents and citizens of the United States is usually called "Americanization." All too frequently Americanization might be described as criminalization. I remember in my youth attending one of the Chautauqua lectures which used to be shouted up and down the rural United States in churches, high schools, and colleges by verbalists with lungs of brass, and tongues which were at least silverplated. This lecture dealt with the "Melting Pot," and its climax was reached when, after vivid descriptions of the oppression suffered by the immigrants in their homelands, and heart-rending accounts of their struggles upward from penury in the land of the free, the orator portrayed a Fourth of July parade of New York school children: Danes, Germans, Italians, Czechs, Poles, Croats, Slovenes, Letts, Lithuanians, Greeks, Bulgars, Jews, Russians, Armenians, Turks, and Chinese — "and everyone of them waving the American flag and singing 'My country, 'tis of thee, sweet land of liberty'!" This peroration elicited from the audience cheers, hand-clapping, nose-blowing, and eye-swabbing, because those were the halcyon days of the new century in which we had not realized how many of these little New Americans were going to wave automatics instead of American flags, and hold up the corner grocery store rather than uphold the Constitution. Now I have no genealogical reason for disparaging New Americans, since I am not a Son of the Revolution, but of an English immigrant who came to this country devoid of noble pedigree, and even, I suspect, of aspirates. Nevertheless, I must admit that we New Americans have, as a class, availed ourselves too fully of the opportunities for gainful offenses against society in a country where there is insufficient popular discrimination between liberty and license.

The material for this portion of our criminal survey consists of some 1553 native Whites of foreign parentage and 1097 foreign born Whites, all inmates of the prisons and reformatories of our nine states in the years 1927–28. Now, after more than a decade, some have undoubtedly died, some are still, or again, in jail, and the remainder are at large, engaged in I know not what legal or illegal activities.

These criminals, diversified by nativity and by country of origin, present a problem which is more complicated anthropologically, as well as criminologically, than do the Old Americans. Not only are they racially heterogeneous, but, in the case of the native born of foreign parentage, they have undergone physical modifications away from their ancestral types, as a result of their transplantation in a new geographical and social environment. Many years ago Professor Franz Boas, the veteran anthropologist of Columbia University, demonstrated marked bodily changes which have taken place in the offspring born in the United States of immigrant parents. It is a part of our task to examine the extent to which these changes, generally in the direction of increased stature and body bulk, manifest themselves in first generation Americans who have been convicted of antisocial acts. If these first generation criminals do show superiority of physique over their kindred delinquents born in their mother countries, it may be suggested that their antisocial careers are not, at any rate, due to depression of their physical environment, involving such factors as light, air, nutrition, and living conditions, beyond the depth to which their

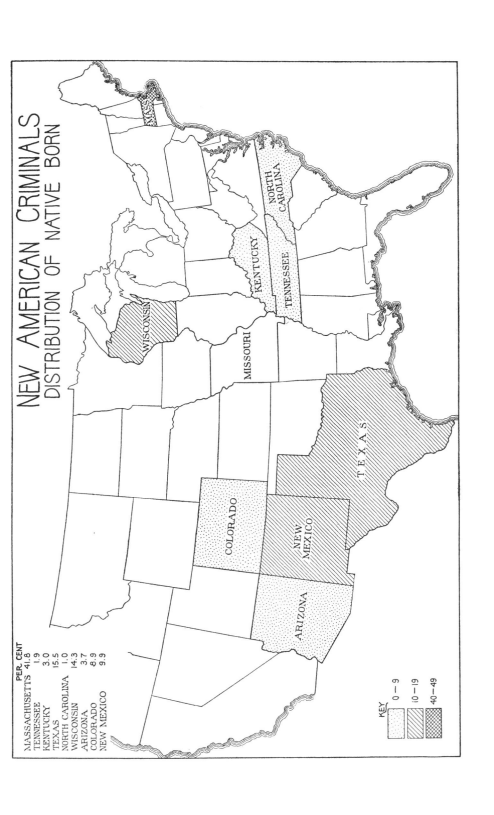

NEW AMERICAN CRIMINALS
DISTRIBUTION OF NATIVE BORN

	PER CENT
MASSACHUSETTS	41.8
TENNESSEE	1.9
KENTUCKY	3.0
TEXAS	15.5
NORTH CAROLINA	1.0
WISCONSIN	14.3
ARIZONA	3.7
COLORADO	8.9
NEW MEXICO	9.9

KEY

0 — 9

10 —19

40 —49

European ancestors were accustomed. Under such findings we should be inclined to seek for the cause of first generation American criminality in certain untoward sociological conditions which they may encounter, or in organic variations which may be of hereditary origin, and which do not manifest themselves in evidences of malnutrition and undergrowth; or, finally, in mental and temperamental deviations from the norm which are not obviously related to physique.

An opportunity is afforded here for studying the differing criminal propensities of several nationalities, of appraising the variations of the foreign born and the native born of the same nationality; finally, also, of discarding criteria of birth, parentage, and nationality, and regrouping all of our criminals according to physical criteria of race, to see whether such groupings associate themselves with type of crime.

DISTRIBUTION

In addition to sizable national groups, there are in our prison series of native Whites of foreign parentage and foreign born Whites, so many odds, ends, rags, tatters, and bobtails of alien origin that they must either be combined into groups large enough for study or thrown away entirely. If we combine them, we do violence to the principle of nationalistic self-determination, but not necessarily to any anthropological criteria, since European nationalities are, in any event, mixtures of several racial ingredients which have obstreperously disregarded national boundaries. If we discard all of these minority nationals, we have wasted a good deal of time and money in collecting our data and have neglected the study of a criminal element which is, in the aggregate, of fair size. In this unpleasant situation, we seize the dilemma boldly by its two horns, twist one off and blow a loud blast on the other, summoning the nations of Europe to a new alignment, which is, at worst, an anthropological advance upon the Treaty of Versailles.

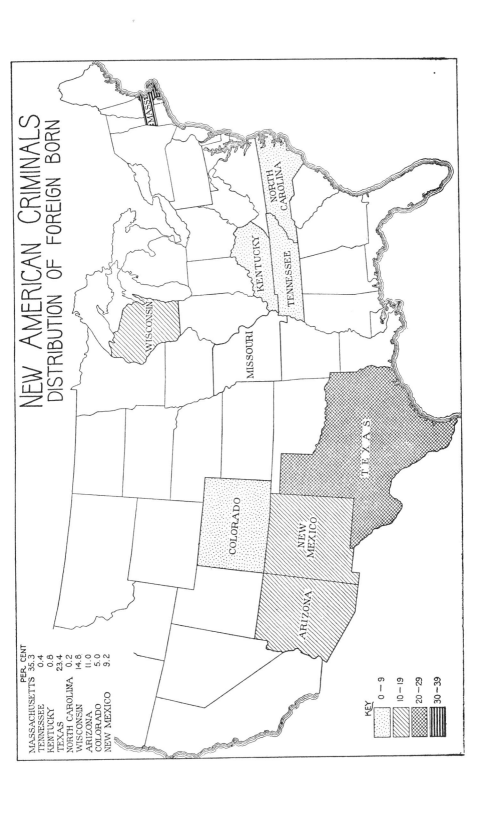

NEW AMERICAN CRIMINALS
DISTRIBUTION OF FOREIGN BORN

	PER CENT
MASSACHUSETTS	35.3
TENNESSEE	0.4
KENTUCKY	0.8
TEXAS	23.4
NORTH CAROLINA	0.2
WISCONSIN	14.8
ARIZONA	11.0
COLORADO	5.0
NEW MEXICO	9.2

KEY

0 – 9
10 – 19
20 – 29
30 – 39

Purely national groupings can be made only in the case of the Irish and the Italians, who alone have been sufficiently accommodating to furnish large and adequate samples of their natives and their natives' sons to our prison series. We have thrown into a combined British group, English, Welsh, Scotch, and British Canadian, because they represent only slightly different racial combinations which have become inextricably intertwined by marriage. All of the Scandinavians have been lumped together, and at that, constitute a wretchedly small group. Deliberately a few Dutch and Swiss have been allotted to a large group of Germans, and the slightly adulterated whole has been dubbed "Teutonic." We have also merged the identities of sundry French and Belgians with a large French Canadian group. Again, our Spanish-Portuguese series is 90 per cent Mexican, but includes also a smattering of Portuguese, and a few individuals of South American descent. This group has, at least, some common heritage of Mediterranean race blood, and is physically not too heterogeneous. Nothing could be done about the criminals stemming from the old Austro-Hungarian empire with its welter of peoples, except to leave them in one group — Croats, Slovenes, Czechs, and Austrians doubtless cheek by jowl — with Poles thrown in to boot, and possibly some of those pestiferous Sudetens. Finally, the dregs of the melting pot have been poured into one receptacle which has been called the Eastern and Near Eastern group. This broth includes Russians, Lithuanians, Greeks, Jews, Syrians, and an occasional Turk.

These ethnically mixed brews are not so noisome as they sound, because, on the whole, the racial elements within each group are much the same, although blended in different proportions in the nationalities of which they are composed.

We have also cut a Gordian knot by assigning the progeny of American marriages with foreigners or with the natives of foreign parentage to the foreign parentage grouping, and children of mixed foreign parentage have been allotted arbitrarily to the group of the father, since we stand firmly for the patriarchal family. One cannot deal anthropologically with any group which is merely designated as of "mixed parentage." Such statistical and marital mélanges may be left to the United States census for tabulation.

The parentage groups thus established in our New American criminals come in pairs, the American born of a certain group descent, and the foreign born of that descent. The marriages from which each individual is sprung have been analyzed, so that the degree of purity and proportion of adulteration can be calculated approximately in each group. The dubious element in each computation arises from the mixed marriages in which an American mate figures. The term "American" may cover a multitude of strains.

The native born group of British parentage has between 83 and 98 per cent of British blood (including Irish). The foreign born British criminals are 91 to 96 per cent British. The Irish Americans are at least 85 per cent Irish, and the Irish proper have at the minimum 89 per cent of Irish blood. The Scandinavian groups contain each less than 10 per cent of alien blood. There are about 17 per cent of Danes in each group. Swedes comprise 47 per cent of the American born, and 61 per cent of the foreign born. The rest are Norwegians or Icelanders. The German-Americans are at least 79 per cent German, and the foreign born 71 per cent. In the French Canadian groups the proportion of persons of more recent European French descent rises from 6 in the American born to 18 in the foreign born, while the pure Belgian figures are in the native born 2 per cent and in the foreign born 11 per cent. The Spanish-Portuguese groups are 91 per cent Mexican in the American born, and 95 per cent in the foreign born. The other members of the group are mostly Portuguese. Both Italian groups are virtually pure Italian.

The Polish-Austrian groups are, in both parentage divisions, two-thirds Polish. The other elements are roughly classified as Austrian, Hungarian, German, et cetera. Finally, the Near Eastern or Southeastern groups are fairly constant in the leading element, which is 36 per cent pure Russian in the native born, 38 per cent in the foreign born. Other elements vary, except the Jews which have about 11 per cent in each group. The American group includes 32 per cent of Lithuanians, but the foreign group only 6 per cent. Greeks, Syrians, and Turks are commoner in the foreign born series.

The shift in ethnic origins of criminals from Central and Eastern Europe to Northwestern Europe in the first generation Americans is interesting. The national shift amounts to about 39 per cent. The fact that native born criminals of foreign parentages are more largely British, Irish, Scandinavian, Teutonic, and French than the foreign born criminals is probably due in fact to the longer residence of these stocks in the country, which gives them more time to breed criminalistic offspring. Again, recent immigration has militated against the Eastern and Southeastern immigrants. Finally, it is possible that Portuguese, Italians, Poles, et cetera, raise more law-abiding children than do Western Europeans, or, at any rate, more elusive varieties of first generation delinquents. Massachusetts contributes more than half of the totals in each pair of groups of British, Irish, French, Italian, and Near Eastern criminals, native or foreign. Wisconsin furnishes more than half of the Teutonic and Scandinavian groups. Texas leads in Mexicans, with 36.9 per cent of the total native born and 47.3 per cent of the foreign born. Tennessee, North Carolina, and Kentucky contribute very few to these series of criminals of recent foreign origin, presumably because their fields of criminal

NEW AMERICAN CRIMINALS

Significant Offense Differences – Native Born and Foreign

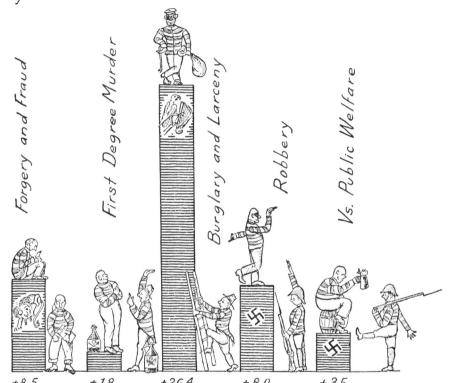

Forgery and Fraud — First Degree Murder — Burglary and Larceny — Robbery — Vs. Public Welfare

+8.5 Brit-Am. Brit. +18 Irish-Am. Ir. +26.4 Irish-Am. Ir. +8.0 Teut-Am. Teut. +3.5 Teut-Am. Teut.

activity are so thoroughly cultivated by the Old Americans and the Negroes, and are not very rich, at that.

The native born of foreign parentage tend to be domiciled in the reformatories to a greater extent than the foreign born, who more commonly inhabit the prisons. The native groups are younger and hence are attending the reformatory schools of crime, while the Old American graduates reune in the penitentiaries.

SOCIOLOGY

OFFENSE

The social statistics of our two series of New American criminals tabulate not only the gross numbers and percental occurrences of various categories of crime for each ethnic group, but also the offense differences between the American born of any ethnic origin and the foreign born of the same antecedents. In general, the total native Whites of foreign parentage tend to differ from the total foreign born Whites in that the American born are less addicted to crimes against the person and show marked increases in offenses against property, especially robbery, burglary and larceny, and forgery. "God's country" offers endless opportunities for the criminally acquisitive.

Differences between native and foreign born are considered fully significant and valid only when they exceed three times their probable errors. British-Americans commit 8.5 per cent more of forgery and fraud than do native Britons — the latter having, no doubt, failed to realize fully the confiding nature of a New World clientele. Irish-Americans increase slightly but not significantly in first degree murder, as compared with native Irish, and display a huge excess of burglary and larceny (26 per cent), an activity which yields probably meager returns in the homeland. German-Americans indulge significantly more in robbery and possibly in offenses against public welfare than do their foreign born

OFFENSE DIFFERENCES

Native and Foreign Born

French

Spanish

prison mates. The French-Americans desist from rape to the extent of 14.6 per cent and go in for bootlegging, a more lucrative pursuit, in an added proportion which is not certainly significant. American born Mexicans commit less of both kinds of murder, but more of burglary, larceny, and arson than do those born across the border. The Italians run counter to the general tendency of American born groups, since the Italian-Americans show, as compared with native Italians, a 30 per cent increase of first degree murder, a 16 per cent decrease of second degree murder, and a large excess of assault (12.6). The Italian-Americans also commit less rape and other sex offenses. The Polish-Austrian group of American nativity desists partially from both kinds of murder and rape, but shows an immense increase over the foreign born amount of burglary and larceny (34 per cent). The Southeastern or Near Eastern group diminishes activity in second degree murder, probably in assault and rape, and concerns itself vigorously with burglary, larceny, and robbery. There are in the aggregate 23 per cent of significant differences in offense between the native born and foreign born series.

The rankings of the nine pairs of ethnic groups in the various offenses, based upon the percentage of each convicted of specific crimes, bring out national propensities and some interesting shifts in position between the pairs of identical descent. Unpleasantly conspicuous are the Italian groups. The Italian-Americans rank first in first degree murder, first in second degree murder, first in assault, but last in robbery, last in burglary and larceny, in forgery and fraud, and sex offenses other than rape, and eighth, or last but one, in rape. They seem to have profited in full by American opportunities for individual self-expression. The foreign born Italians rank first only in second degree murder and are quite respectable in first degree murder, being in fifth place, and ultra-respectable in occupying the eighth

OFFENSE DIFFERENCES

Italians and Italian-Americans

+29.8

First Degree Murder

Assault

Second Degree Murder

Other Sex

+12.6

Rape

WPA

Foreign

Born

Level

−5.3

−9.1
Italian-American

−15.6
Ital.-Am.

OFFENSE DIFFERENCES
Polish - Austrians

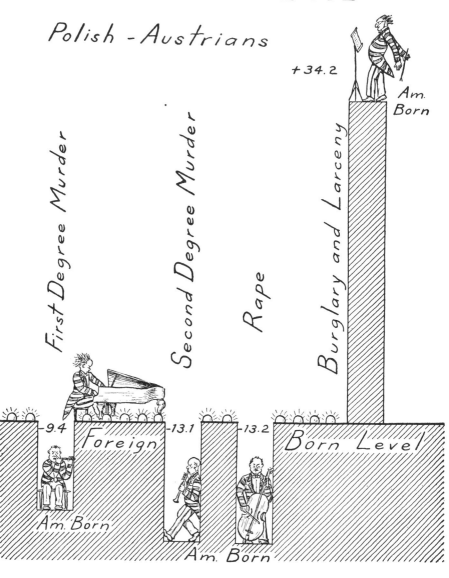

+34.2

Am. Born

First Degree Murder

Second Degree Murder

Rape

Burglary and Larceny

-9.4 Foreign

-13.1

-13.2 Born Level

Am. Born

Am. Born

OFFENSE DIFFERENCES

Near Easterners — +27.6 Native and

+17.3 Foreign Born

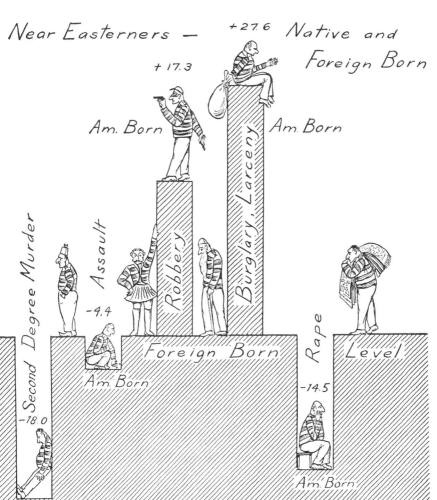

Am. Born   Am. Born

Second Degree Murder

Assault

Robbery

Burglary, Larceny

Rape

Level

Foreign Born

Am. Born

-4.4

-14.5

-18.0

Am. Born

Am. Born

Am. Born

place in assault. They are higher in sex crimes than the Italian-Americans, but like them are last in burglary and larceny, in forgery and fraud.

The British groups attain but two first places — burglary and larceny in the foreign born series and arson in the native series. The British-Americans drop to seventh place in the former offense, and rise from fifth to second place in forgery and fraud. The American born are a little higher in general ranking in offenses against persons, and both British groups are in second place in offenses against property.

The foreign born Irish rate two firsts — in robbery and in versus public welfare. The Irish-Americans do not capture a single first, but are second in robbery and last in arson. However, our transplanted sons of Erin are much higher in offenses against the person than are those born in the mother country. They move up in general ranking to second place, whereas the foreign born are in eighth place. On the other hand, the foreign born Irish rank first in offenses against property, while in their series the Irish-Americans are honorably in seventh place.

The Scandinavians of foreign birth rank first in sex offenses other than rape, and also first in forgery and fraud. The American Scandinavians achieve first place in rape, but sink to second in other sex offenses and have to be content with third place in forgery and fraud. In murder the American born are lower than the foreign born.

The Teutonic groups are very high in first degree murder. The foreign born rank first and the native born second in their respective series, but they are low in second degree murder and in assault. Again they forge to the front in fraudulent offense, the native born being in first place and the foreign born in second place. Both of these groups achieve second place in rape in their respective series, and are conspicuously high in other sex offenses. We now begin to understand why Wisconsin is so perniciously active in sex

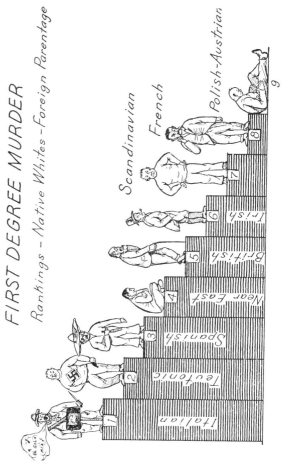

FIRST DEGREE MURDER

Rankings – Native Whites – Foreign Parentage

Italian 1
Teutonic 2
Spanish 3
Near East 4
British 5
Irish 6
7
8
9

Scandinavian
French
Polish-Austrian

crimes. The native Teutonic group holds first place in offenses against property, while the foreign born drops to fifth. Both are third in rank in their series in offenses against persons. The French group of American birth rises one place in each general ranking, as contrasted with the foreign born — from sixth to fifth place in personal offenses and from fourth to third in property. The only first place taken by the French is the primacy in sex offenses other than rape attained by the American born.

The Spanish, Portuguese, and Mexican groups shine forth in versus public welfare, mostly bootlegging, but also illegal possession of firearms. The natives are first in their series and the foreign born second. Both are third in first degree murder, well to the fore in second degree murder, and in burglary and larceny, but way down in robbery, in forgery, and in sex offenses other than rape. The native group achieves higher ranking than the foreign group in both personal and property offense.

The Polish-Austrian groups display the most interesting shifts in ranking. In assault they lead, with the foreigners in first place and the natives in second. However, these native born hold last place in both categories of murder, as against second and fifth in the two degrees held by their foreign born cousins. The Americans of these stocks have relinquished the primacy in rape held by the foreign born but have achieved first place in burglary and larceny. Both groups do well in robbery. The Polish-Austrians of American birth display a strong trend away from the personal offenses in which the foreign born rank first.

Finally, the mixed Near Eastern and Eastern European group can boast of but two first places: arson and all other offenses in the foreigners, and robbery in the natives. This group displays the most notable shift in the native born to much lower rankings in both personal offenses and property crimes.

FORGERY and FRAUD

Rankings of Native Whites
of Foreign Parentage

Teutonic

British

Scandinavian

French

Polish-Austrian

Italian   Spanish   Irish   Near Eastern

Taking ethnic pairs together, the highest general batting average is maintained by the Teutonic groups in their mean rankings in both large categories of offense. However, the British are a close second. Our Northwestern Europeans and Germans produce descendants in this country who appear to excel in all around criminal activity. They try to do "their bit" antisocially without undue fastidiousness in choice of offense.

Of course these results are not necessarily valid for all criminals of these ethnic origins in the United States, but only for our sample. Some of the groups are quite small, and, in any event, these rankings must not be taken too seriously. To me it is a striking fact that our purest group from the point of view of nationality is the Italians and that they are also the most consistent in the types of their criminal activity. They refuse to be seduced by American wealth and remain true to their national tradition of violence to the person. Their resolute adherence to homicide reminds us of the Old American Kentuckians. Perhaps they alone have become truly Americanized. On the other hand, some of the more acquisitive persons from farther east in Europe tend to stop wasting their time in unprofitable bloodshed and try to make a little money out of crime. This change would seem to be more in accord with the ideals of American industrialized civilization.

PREVIOUS CONVICTIONS

Of the native born of foreign parentage 55 per cent have records of previous convictions, as against 30 per cent of the foreign born. The American born are much younger, but have lived in the United States from birth and have had a much longer period in which to become Americanized and to practise crime. Again, the foreigners by birth have probably emigrated without their criminal records, perhaps tactfully suppressed by the emigration officials speeding their departure from their natal shores. Nevertheless, it is fairly

1 Polish-Austrian

2 Spanish

3 French

4 Near Eastern

5 Irish

6 Scandinavian

7 British

BURGLARY
AND
LARCENY

Rankings
of
Native Whites
of
Foreign Parentage

Italian

8 British

Teutonic

9

certain that recidivism is much more common in the sons of immigrants than in the immigrants themselves.

It is difficult to compare the previous convictions of New Americans with those of the Old Americans, because the latter are principally domiciled in states which seem somewhat casual in the keeping of their prison records. The Old American criminals in Massachusetts have a record of 71 per cent of previous convictions, a fact which seems to indicate considerable individual persistence in wrong-doing.

Every single parentage pair shows an increase of recidivism in the American born over the foreign born. These increases are insignificant only in the British, Scandinavian, and Teutonic groups. The most notable increases in native born recidivists occur in the Irish, Near Eastern, Italian, and Polish-Austrian pairs. The Spanish-Mexican group ranks lowest in recidivists, irrespective of nativity. The group of American birth which leads in percentage of recidivism is that which includes Russians, Greeks, Lithuanians, Syrians, Jews, et cetera, with 77 per cent. The Teutons head the foreign born with 52 per cent of repeaters. The greatest percental increase in recidivism is that of the Irish-Americans with 39 per cent gain. However, our foreign born Irish group of criminals is unreliably small, as is also the Scandinavian group.

MARITAL STATE

There are about 62 per cent of unmarried men in the American born criminals of foreign parentage, and about 10 per cent less in the foreign born. However, these differences are apparently due in large part to age, since the native born groups average from 3.3 to 15.6 years younger than their corresponding foreign born groups.

OCCUPATION

The Old American criminals differ occupationally from those of foreign birth or recent foreign descent in the larger percentage of persons among the older settlers who are living in rural areas and engaged in extractive occupations. The New American criminals show excesses of unskilled laborers.

When the native born of foreign parentage are compared with the foreign born criminals of the same descent, it is evident that some of the former have improved their occupational status by entering vocations which require more education and, probably, a better command of the English language.

Some of the older immigrant groups, such as the British and Irish, show comparatively little change in occupational status between the two series. In fact, the native born seem not to have risen above the foreign born to any significant extent. The Mexicans also remain much the same. The Italians of both groups are essentially urban dwellers, but the native born rise considerably in the occupational scale, notably in the shift from unskilled labor to skilled trades and clerical work. Polish-Austrians of American birth seem to have abandoned the extractive pursuits and unskilled labor and have risen to first ranking in skilled trades. The Eastern and Near Eastern American born tend to leave the ranks of the extractives and manual laborers and get into factory work and other semi-skilled or skilled pursuits. However, both native and foreign born groups hold first ranking in trade. Occupational shifts between the groups are most marked in the more recent immigrant nationalities, and, apparently, in those which have to learn English. The occupational data are quite in accordance with expectation.

EDUCATION

The contemplation of the remarkable improvement of educational status which the American born of foreign parentage show when compared with their foreign born relatives would be most heartening, if we did not stop to recall the fact that these newer Americans, with their superior schooling, are none the less convicted felons. If anyone can derive any satisfaction from the knowledge that we are raising more and better educated criminals, his optimism exceeds mine.

Illiteracy drops in the American born of foreign parentage to 8 per cent, whereas in the foreign born criminals it is 24 per cent. With the exceptions of Irish, Teutonic, and French, the criminals of native birth in general show decreases of the proportions which have reached only the first five grades, or have had no education at all, and increases in most of the grades thereafter up to professional school and college. On these highest educational levels there is no significant difference between the foreign born and the native born. The biggest gains in the native born occur in the Polish-Austrians, the Italians, and the Eastern and Southeastern Europeans.

For ranking the educational attainments of the two groups of foreign birth or descent, we use again the ratio which divides the number who have reached the last two years of high school, or some higher institution of learning, by the percentage of those who are illiterate plus those who can read or write but have never attended school. On this basis the Eastern and Near Eastern group of Russians, Greeks, Syrians, Lithuanians, et cetera, takes first place in education among the native born of foreign parentage with 7.97 times as many well educated as uneducated. The British come second with a ratio of 6.03, the Irish third with 3.43, the Scandinavians fourth with 2.00, the Polish-Austrians fifth with 1.67, the Teutons sixth with 1.33, seventh the Italians with 1.00, eighth the French with .68, and ninth the Mexicans and Portuguese with .03.

Among the foreign Whites the Irish lead in learning, but their educational ratio cannot be calculated because they (incredibly) have no illiterates, and none who can read and write but have not attended school. However, there are, unfortunately, only 27 Irish born criminals in this series, an altogether inadequate sample and one which can hardly be hoped to be representative. This dearth of Irish born criminals is remarkable, for we have 273 Irish-Americans in our series, and there are certainly plenty of the Irish foreign born in Massachusetts. The second rank in the foreign group is held by the British with 2.40. Thereafter follow in order: French, Scandinavians, Teutons, Eastern- and Near Easterners, Italians, Polish-Austrians, and finally Mexicans and Portuguese. The last two groups have educational ratios of .026 and .022 respectively. Their scholastic achievement, like that of Old American Kentucky criminals, is microscopic.

The three groups of native born which lose rank as contrasted with the foreign born educational standings are the Irish, Teutonic, and French. We may discount the Irish drop because of the small and inadequate sample of the foreign born. The American French Canadians are down in eighth place in educational ranking, while their foreign born cousins are in third place. Several groups hold the same rank in both series: British second, Scandinavians fourth, and Italians seventh. The Mexicans born in this country, like the foreign born, are in last place, and their infinitesimal educational ratios remain virtually the same. The big educational advancements are found in the Eastern-Near Eastern group which rises from sixth place in the foreign born to first in the native born, and the Austrian-Polish group which jumps from eighth place to fifth place. However, they are still criminals and the net effect of educating potential criminals as here exhibited is to divert them from crimes of violence to crimes of pecuniary profit. Recall that the jump from sixth place in the foreign born to first place in education in the native born corresponds in the Eastern Europeans to an advance from fourth place in robbery to first place, and that the Polish-Austrians moving from eighth place to fifth place in education also move from seventh place to first place in burglary and larceny, and sink from second place to ninth in first degree murder, from first to fourth in rape. Those ethnic groups which do not improve their educational ranking in the native born tend to go on murdering, raping, and committing other crimes of personal violence, while those who have been swift to acquire book learning try also to acquire property swiftly and illegally.

As a matter of fact, our 4180 Old American criminals have an educational ratio of .54, which places them below every native White group of foreign parentage except the Mexicans, and below the foreign born Irish, British, French, and Scandinavians. This inferiority of educational status of the Old American criminals is, however, conditioned by the fact that most of them come from the southern states. More than one-half of our first generation American criminals have enjoyed the educational opportunities afforded in Massachusetts.

I suppose that one might feebly hope to eradicate murder, assault, and sex crimes by cramming more and more education down the throats of the criminalistic. There would result probably a concomitant and disproportionately great increase of robbery, burglary, larceny, and fraudulent crimes. Possibly no one would then get killed except by cataclysms of nature, in automobile accidents, and in war; or possibly the highly educated murderers and rapists would, by dint of their learning, escape conviction, and more than ever of us would be killed and raped. Certainly we should have a hard time in protecting our property. When I was a college youngster, I spent two summers in the Wisconsin penitentiary, purely voluntarily, as a paid civilian employee. One of my occasional odd jobs was to follow round and keep watch upon the chief convict electrician, who was the only one in the institution who knew enough to fix the electric clock system. He was said to be a graduate of the engineering school of the University of Wisconsin, also my Alma Mater, and was known to have broken or "crushed out" of the prisons of several other states. So they set a Badger to watch a Badger, each utilizing his higher education according to his ability and opportunity.

SUMMARY OF SOCIOLOGICAL DIFFERENTIATION

Now if we summarize the degree to which our native born groups of foreign parentage are statistically differentiated in sociological characters from the foreign born of similar descent, we find that every group except the British and Scandinavian is so differentiated. The aggregate of differentiated sociological subcategories in the New Americans as contrasted with the foreign born is overwhelming.

The British change between the paired groups consists of a single significant increase in the amount of forgery and fraud committed by the British-Americans. It should be noted, however, that we have no record of their achievements in the field of international diplomacy.

The Irish shifts are contradictory and somewhat unreliable, probably because of the small size and peculiar character of the Irish born criminals. The huge excess of burglars and thieves in the Irish-Americans is probably valid, as is also their increase of recidivism. But our Irish of American birth also show an increase of unskilled laborers, which is very queer in view of the fact that they ought to have better educations than their foreign born cousins. As a matter of fact, more than twice as many proportionally of the native Irish have good educations (last two years of high school and college), as have the foreign born, but, as previously stated, the small group of the foreign born incredibly includes no illiterates at all. Thus, it is possible that the anomalous changes in the Irish pair are due to the enigmatic and wretchedly small group of the foreign born.

Scandinavians of American birth differ significantly from the foreigners only in having better educations. Teutons born in this country show proportionately more convictions for robbery. They also have more factory workers and clerks and are better educated.

The French Canadians of American birth tend to have many more previous convictions; Mexicans and Portuguese show only the conventional shifts of the native born: more crimes against property (burglary and larceny, arson), less against persons, more recidivism, and a very slight improvement in education.

Italian-Americans in general seem to go in for murder more than do the native Italians, although the former emphasize first degree homicide and the latter second degree. The American born also commit more assault, but seem to be less engaged in illegal sex activity. There are among the Italian-Americans proportionately many more recidivists, skilled tradesmen, and clerical workers, and many fewer unskilled laborers. The Italians born in the United States are much better educated, but nevertheless go on murdering. This recalls the sapient words of that greatest of Italians, Quintus Horatius Flaccus: "Caelum non animum mutant qui trans mare currunt." [1] The Polish-Austrian group shows the conventional sociological shift away from personal crimes, illiteracy, and lowly occupations, toward crimes against property, recidivism, good jobs, and better educations. The Near Eastern and Eastern European group shows similar changes in crimes, recidivism, and education, but no significant occupational difference.

PHYSICAL DIFFERENTIATION

METRIC AND INDICIAL

The determination of the degree to which each native ethnic group differs from its related foreign born group in sociological characters is a preliminary to the real task of the physical anthropologist, which is to distinguish such physi-

---

[1] "They change their sky, not their soul, who run across the sea."

cal differences as obtain between the pairs, and to relate them to the sociological phenomena. The finding of physical differentiae is much more precise and soul satisfying, but only, I fear, to the hardened specialist. To work through the comparison of pairs in 33 measurements and indices necessitates the analysis of some 115 complicated statistical tables, each of which is built up from the means, standard deviations, coefficients of variation, differences, and probable errors of constants of nine groups. From this monumental mathematical travail there issues, however, something more than a mere statistical mouse — a sizable litter of clear cut results which can be summarized briefly and without terminological verbiage.

Just as the British-Americans are not significantly distinguished from the foreign born British in their sociological characters, so they are also indistinguishable from them in anthropometric features. Like Harvard men, they are indifferent, or, at any rate, undifferentiated. The Irish-Americans are younger than the foreign born and have narrower noses, but otherwise display no marked differences, perhaps because the foreign born group is so small that we must allow a large leeway for inaccuracy of its measured characters. The American-Scandinavians are younger, taller, and greater in head height and in the head height indices than their foreign born mates, but really they, too, are barely distinguishable from the latter on the basis of conservative statistical estimates.

However, the American born Teutonic group differs from the foreign born group in 6 of 23 measurements and in 7 of 16 indices. The Americans are younger, taller, narrower in head and face, shorter in nose and ear, more dolicocephalic (long-headed); have higher heads relative to head breadth, narrower faces relative to their head breadth, relatively longer and narrower faces, broader foreheads relative to face breadth, and to the breadth of their jaws.

The American born French are younger and taller than the foreign born, and that is all. Generally speaking, they are not anthropometrically distinct.

The Mexican, Portuguese, Spanish group, born in the United States, again is notably different from its foreign born counterpart. It is younger, taller, heavier, shallower of chest, longer-headed, longer in the upper face, and shorter in the nose. It shows a relatively narrower head, relatively narrower shoulders, narrower and longer face, and greater jaw breadth relative to facial breadth.

The Italian-Americans are even more strongly differentiated from the foreign born Italians. The first generation Americans are younger, lighter, narrower in the shoulders and inferior in chest measurements, wider of head, narrower in face, nose, and jaws, and have probably higher heads and shorter ears. Sitting height relative to stature is diminished; heads are rounder, faces narrower relative to head breadth and forehead breadth, foreheads narrower in relation to head breadth, and jaws narrower in comparison with forehead and face breadth. Some of these differences are due to age disparity and possibly some of them may be caused by diversities of the Italian strains represented in the two series. However, most of them are probably ascribable to the change in environment from Italy to this country.

The Polish-Austrians born in this country are remarkably different from the foreign group. They are inferior in age, weight, shoulder breadth, chest diameters, head breadth, head circumference, forehead and face breadth, nose breadth, jaw breadth, upper face height, and ear length. Many of the index values have changed. The American born are relatively narrower of shoulder, and narrower of face relative to head breadth; their jaws are narrower in relation to breadth of forehead and face; they have probably lower nasal and higher ear indices. Here, again, the change may be due in part to age and in part to the fact that the recent immigrants possibly represent somewhat different racial elements than do the American born children of the earlier arrivals from the Austro-Hungarian empire.

Finally, the Eastern, Southeastern, and Near Eastern group of the American born also shows a significant number of metric differences from the immigrant group. These are virtually the same as have been recited *ad nauseam* in the preceding groups. The natives are younger, taller, narrower in shoulder, and smaller in chest diameters, narrower in face, shorter in ears; with diminished relative shoulder breadth, relative sitting height, cephalo-facial index; and with higher zygo-frontal index, and the additional possibility of shorter and broader ears.

From a statistical point of view only the British-Americans are undifferentiated from their foreign cousins, but the Irish, Scandinavian, and French groups are only slightly, if at all, distinguished from their old country relatives. The other five pairs of groups deviate widely, each from its mate.

A clear idea of the trend of changes can be gained by noting the number of times the same probably significant alterations occur in the nine different ethnic pairs. Thus all 9 native born groups are younger than the foreign born. Five of the 9 are taller; 7 of 9 have shallower chests; 5 groups have narrower faces; 6 have narrower noses; 5 have shorter ears; 7 have relatively narrower shoulders; 5 have relatively diminished sitting heights; 5 have faces narrower in comparison with head breadths; 6 relatively longer and narrower faces; and 5 have broader foreheads proportionate to face breadth.

The study of the statistical relation between age and the various measurements and indices, obtained by a device known as the coefficient of correlation, suggests that the length and breadth of ear are the only measurements seriously affected by the constant age disparity of the paired groups. When one begins to grow middle-aged and senile,

one's ears get bigger, and especially longer. This late bloom-
ing may be due to the fact that as one gets harder of hearing
the ears reach out farther and farther to catch more and more
of the elusive sound waves. I am afraid, however, that the big
ears of old age are nothing more than the manifestations of
senile exuberance in the decay of vestigial organs.

MORPHOLOGICAL DIFFERENTIATION

I shall now attempt to summarize the differentiation of
nine pairs of native born and foreign born of similar ethnic
extraction in some 148 subcategories of morphological variation. From a purely anthropological point of view some of
the most interesting of the data concern the ranking in different features of the nine pairs of ethnic groups. Each of
these features involves the analysis of several complicated
tables and a discussion of the meaning of the group variations. Even a very brief epitome of the results of these
individual analyses of numerous characters would protract
this course of lectures through the winter, a consummation
devoutly to be avoided. I propose to give but a single example, as tightly compressed as possible, of the results obtained by intensive study of the distribution of one character
in the nine pairs of groups. Let us take hair color, which is
classified into numerous shades, varies with the age of the
individual, and is one of the most interesting criteria of
racial distinction in Whites, though sometimes a fickle and
changeable thing in women.

First of all we have really black hair, in which the Spanish,
Mexican, Portuguese groups rank first in both series, with
27 per cent in the native born and 33 per cent in the foreign
born. In the foreign group the Near Easterners rank second
in this shade, but the Italian group nearly ties them. In the
native born series Italians and French divide second place.
In both Spanish and Italian groups of American birth the
percentage of black hair diminishes markedly. A similar

phenomenon is noticeable in the case of the Eastern European-Near Eastern group. However, the French maintain about the same proportions of black hair in both series (14.3 per cent in the foreign born and 15.4 per cent in the native born). The groups of partially Nordic origin are very low in this shade of hair and the Scandinavians have none of it at all.

Dark brown hair is very common in all groups of both series (29–47 per cent), but the American born Teutons lose heavily in this shade when compared with the foreign born. Reddish-brown hair is commonest among the foreign born French (36 per cent) and the American born Italians (41 per cent). The Teutonic and Italian groups of American birth gain markedly in this shade of hair over the proportions found in their respective foreign cousin groups.

The leaders in light brown hair in the foreign born are Irish, Scandinavian, British, and Polish-Austrian, in the order named. In the American born criminals the Scandinavians rank first, with the Teutons second and the British third. Teutonic-Americans, Scandinavian-, Italian-, and French-Americans gain in this shade of hair color, while the Irish-Americans lose. Light brown hair in both series is rarest among the Spanish, Mexican, Portuguese groups.

Ash-blond and golden hair are much commoner in the American born of most groups than in the foreign born, because the American born are younger and blond hair usually darkens with advancing age unless chemically preserved. In both of these shades the Scandinavians lead the foreign born, but in the native born the Eastern group captures first place in golden hair, probably because it has received a large increment of Lithuanians, an ethnic stock with frequent blond hair which is poorly represented in the foreign born Eastern-Near Eastern group. The American born Polish-Austrians gain strongly in the ash-blond and golden shades, while the Irish-Americans and the native Near Easterners manifest increases over their foreign mates in golden hair as contrasted with ash-blond.

There is little change between the two series in the amount of red hair, and the Irish lead in both (6 per cent in the native born and 8 per cent in the foreign born).

Gray and white hair are much commoner in the foreign groups than in the American born, doubtless because of the higher mean ages of the former, although possibly these gray hairs might be attributed to the disappointment and frustration of the ambitious criminalistic immigrant. Significant decreases in these depigmented varieties of hair occur in the American born Teutonic, Mexican, Italian, and Polish-Austrian groups. On the other hand, in the British and Eastern-Near Eastern groups gray hair increases insignificantly in the American born, in spite of their lower mean age. This single example will give you an idea of the weighing of factors which demand consideration in the case of each morphological character examined for the nine pairs of ethnic groups. Are the differences due to age changes between the American born and foreign groups? Are they rather to be referred to shifts in the ethnic composition of the American groups or to the change in environment of the first generation born in the United States? Or is it possible that the variations may be due to the sampling process or to the shifting personal equations of observers? Since few males dye their hair, we can at least be sure that the changes in color are biochemical rather than pharmaceutical.

Since our principal interest here is criminological rather than anthropological, no further time will be spent in this summary upon the ethnic and parentage variation of single morphological details. However, the principal physical differentiae between the native and foreign born pairs of the same ethnic groups must be enumerated.

The only groups of the native born which are not clearly different from their foreign born cousins are the British and

French. We can expect between 6 and 7 significant deviations out of 148 subcategories to occur by chance alone in
random samples drawn from the same population, although
the conditions of independent random sampling are not precisely fulfilled in these subcategories of observation. The
American born British show 8 such deviations and the
French-Americans 7. Every other group is overwhelmingly
differentiated from its foreign born mate. The maximum
differentiation occurs in the Italian-Americans with 49 significant deviations.

We may recall that the British-Americans were undistinguished from the foreign born British in sociological and
anthropometric features, and we need not delay to enumerate the few significant morphological differences which the
American born show.

We may also dispose summarily of the French-Americans,
who have fuller lips, and include fewer individuals with
more pronounced temporal fullness than the foreign born,
but are otherwise not clearly distinguishable from them, and
might be considered merely a younger sample of the same
physical population, with equally bad teeth and characters.

The Irish-Americans have 10 significant morphological
differences from the foreign born, but the foreign group is
so small that one distrusts results even when safeguarded by
statistical devices. One native Irish difference from the foreign born is certainly due to age — decreased amount of
slight or medium wrinkling. The American born Irish also
have more zoned patterns of the iris of the eye, thicker nasal
tips, more nasal septa deflected to the left, thinner membranous lips, less alveolar protrusion or prognathism, less
pronounced jaw angles, more pronounced wrinkling of the
cheeks in spite of their younger age, fewer Darwin's points
on the ears (remnant of the free tip of the mammalian ear).

The 7 differentiated features of the Scandinavian-Ameri-
cans include two which have to do with diminished wrin-

kling and consequently may be attributed to the lower age of the native born. Others are fewer deflected nasal septa, more men with moderate lip seams, and with ears having attached lobes. Several of these differentiae of the American born Scandinavians are not entirely independent of age change, and, in general, they are scarcely sufficient to differentiate the groups.

The Teutonic groups again show 10 significant differences between the native and foreign born. Those obviously affected by age difference are, in the native born, less gray hair, more men without wrinkles, fewer who have lost many teeth. The American group also has more red-brown and light brown hair, more straight nasal profiles, thicker membranous lips, more Darwin's points on the ears, and fewer ears with pronounced antihelices.

The Mexicans and Portuguese born in the United States differ from the foreign born in 28 morphological subcategories — nearly 20 per cent. Differences due to age disparity are diminution in gray and white hair, in wrinkles, in wear and loss of teeth. Others probably not seriously affected by age are thinner head hair in the native born, in spite of their lower mean age (3.4 years), more pale white skin, more light brown eyes and fewer dark brown, more rayed iris patterns, less depression of the nasal root and more high nasal bridges, more nasal septa inclined downward, fewer deflected septa, thicker integumental lips, less protrusion of the jaws (facial and alveolar prognathism), less flaring cheek bones, better rolled ear rims (helices) and fewer Darwin's points, fewer long thin necks. These differences of the American born Mexicans are largely away from Indian types of features and in the direction of the White variations. We have no proof of a greater admixture of White blood, although it is conceivable that the Mexicans long resident in the United States carry less Indian blood than the recent immigrants.

The Italian-Americans are differentiated from the foreign

born in 33 per cent of all characters. A considerable number of these are, however, due to age disparity. These are such features as thicker head hair, thinner body hair, less gray and white hair, fewer external eye folds, fewer wrinkles, lower foreheads (since foreheads look higher in persons going bald), and others having to do with wear of teeth, loss of teeth, decay of teeth, and type of bite. The younger Italian-Americans naturally have not suffered so much dental impairment as the older foreigners. Characters not obviously affected by age, in which the native Italians differ from the foreign born, include: more red-white skin, more deeply waved hair, less black hair and more red-brown hair, fewer rayed irides and more zoned and speckled irides, fewer thin eyebrows, nasal roots less deeply depressed, more roots of medium breadth and septa directed upward, fewer septal deflections, thinner integumental lips and fewer thin membranous lips, more compressed jaw angles, fewer small ear lobes, less facial asymmetry or lopsidedness, fewer short thick necks, fewer shoulders of pronouncedly sloping form and more of the medium variety.

The Polish-Austrian group of American born criminals averages 15.6 years younger than the foreign born — the greatest age disparity between any of the pairs. Consequently, 10 of the 24 differentiae between the two groups are due to age changes — largely matters of change in the hair, teeth, and skin. Other differentiated characters not obviously due to the age factor, but not always entirely independent of it, are (among the first generation Americans): more ash-blond and golden hair, more gray-brown eyes, fewer rayed irides and fewer thick eyebrows, fewer low foreheads, less marked depressions at the root of the nose, higher nasal bridges, fewer straight noses, fewer deflections of the nasal septum, fuller membranous lips, smaller ear lobes, a deficiency of short, thick necks.

The Eastern and Near Eastern group of first generation

Americans also differs notably from the foreign born in its inferior age. The discrepancy is 13.5 years. As a result, 18 of 28 differences depend largely upon age. These are the usual hair, teeth, skin manifestations, with also fewer of the curved nasal profiles which are usually developments of maturity rather than of adolescence and early years of adult life. The more or less independently differentiated features are: less black hair and more golden hair, fewer green-brown eyes and more blue eyes, fewer rayed irides and more zoned irides, more foreheads of medium height, fewer pronounced depressions of the nasal root, less pronounced development of the lips seams, fewer slight protrusions of the ear, and less facial asymmetry.

A critical appraisal of the 148 morphological subcategories in which the native born may differ from the foreign born of similar ethnic descent shows that 20 subcategories, or 14.2 per cent, are clearly dependent upon age variation and that 27 more, or 18.2 per cent, may be indirectly affected by age change. Therefore, a total of a little more than 32 per cent of potential differences between the pairs is of no significance in our present attempt to find out whether American born criminals of a certain stock are anthropologically different from foreign born criminals of the same stock, apart from variations due to disparity of age. If, then, we discard the virtual third of observational differences between the groups which are statistically significant but conditioned by age disparity, we still find that five of nine pairs of criminal groups are independently differentiated. The exceptions are the British, Scandinavian, the Teutonic, and the French. In the British, Scandinavian, and French groups the American born may be said to be barely distinguishable from the foreign born, and in the Teutonic groups the differences seem mostly due to age.

There are also certain trends of difference between first generation Americans and foreign born of the same antecedents which carry through most of the pairs. Those which are ascribable to age we need not enumerate. There are, however, some 10 other metric features in which the American born tend to diverge in a constant direction from their foreign born relatives and 16 morphological features. I have already described these metric trends of the New Americans.

The morphological differences from parental stock prison mates commonly displayed by those criminals of similar descent but born in the United States are: fewer irides of the eyes with rayed pattern, fewer sloping foreheads, less depression of the nasal root, narrower and higher nasal roots and higher nasal bridges, thinner integumental lips (parts of mouth covered by moustache or goatee), much less prognathism or protrusion of the jaws (both total facial protrusion and alveolar protrusion which involves only the forward thrust of the tooth bearing portions), cheek bones and hinder jaw angles less prominent, normal bites or tooth occlusions commoner, and marked overbites involving "buck teeth" rarer, Darwin's point on the ear (a primitive feature) less common, less lopsidedness or asymmetry of the face, less pronounced slope of the shoulders.

In general, then, the New American criminals tend to differ from their foreign born cousins in having a more elongated and slender body build, with which also go a narrow, lantern-jawed face, higher head, less sloping forehead, a higher and more pinched nose, thinner integumental lips, fewer dental malocclusions, less warping and skewing of the face and nose. All of these differences confirm the impression of the transformation of a squat build and a broad face and head to a linear weedy build, in which horizontal dimensions have been compressed and vertical dimensions stretched. They are paralleled, to a great extent, by the changes which Bowles observed in the Harvard sons of Harvard fathers, both groups of Old American ancestry.

It is difficult to account for these sweeping changes manifested in the last two generations of persons born in the United States from rather diverse ethnic and racial stocks. It is hardly possible to attribute them facilely to radical change of environment undergone by immigrant stocks, since shifts of bodily proportions in a similar direction have been observed in various countries of Europe, among the Japanese, and in the Old Americans. It is possible, of course, to assume that these modern bodily trends are due to improved hygiene, to superior nutrition, and to the preservation by medical skill of the many who used to die in infancy in the old crude days. However, it seems doubtful that the infancies of many of these young criminals were presided over by pediatricians with their incomparable knowledge of the vitaminic virtues of cod liver oil and spinach.

First of all it should be understood clearly that the increase in the tall and skinny does not signify a general improvement of physical status, but rather the contrary. Bigger men are not necessarily better than smaller men, just as big mistakes are not better than small mistakes. Vertical growth at the expense of lateral expansion is nothing over which to enthuse. In terms of the ductless glands it may mean nothing more than that a sluggish thyroid has been dominated by a perniciously active pituitary. My own impression is that inferior organisms are likely to come in long, thin packages, and that the net result of modern medicine and hygiene has been to preserve more and more of what, in human material, is less and less fit to keep.

The New American criminals then differ from the foreign born kindred criminals as conspicuously in physical characters as in their sociological traits. On the whole, it could be said that these new American criminals have been favored more in environment and have achieved better educations and occupations. But they have not improved physically and are definitely more antisocial, as measured by frequency

NEW AMERICAN CRIMINALS

GENERALIZED CRANIOMETRIC AND MORPHOLOGICAL DIFFERENCES BETWEEN NATIVE BORN CRIMINALS OF FOREIGN PARENTAGE AND FOREIGN BORN OF SAME STOCKS.

(PURELY SCHEMATIC AND SOMEWHAT EXAGGERATED)

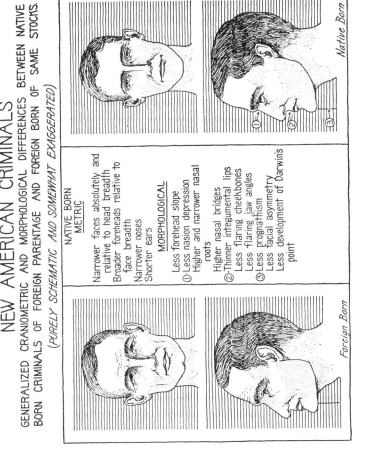

NATIVE BORN

METRIC

Narrower faces absolutely and relative to head breadth
Broader foreheads relative to face breadth
Narrower noses
Shorter ears

MORPHOLOGICAL

Less forehead slope
① Less nasion depression
Higher and narrower nasal roots
Higher nasal bridges
② Thinner integumental lips
Less flaring cheekbones
Less flaring jaw angles
③ Less prognathism
Less facial asymmetry
Less development of Darwins point

Native Born

Foreign Born

of prior criminal convictions, than are the persons born in other countries who come here and commit crimes.

As soon as we turn to the task of ascertaining whether burglars and thieves within a given ethnic group are different physically and sociologically from, for example, murderers, we encounter an almost insuperable difficulty. For the 18 ethnic and parentage groups are too small to be split up into 10 offense subgroups each. Such division would result in wretched little handfuls unworthy of statistical treatment, because they would be too small to be representative or reliable. At the time when we were grappling with this difficulty it was decided to combine the burglary and larceny group with the forgery and fraud group, thus creating a composite class of property criminals which could be compared in each ethnic group with the total criminals of that group. The procedure was not so irrational as it perhaps sounds, since a great deal of larceny is fraudulent crime, and no little of fraudulent crime is, in its essence, larceny. Larceny is only theft in full dress legal terminology. Even by this process of pooling, it was possible to secure samples adequate for treatment in but 6 of the 9 groups of American born criminals of foreign parentage. The Scandinavians, Polish-Austrians, and Eastern Europeans had to be neglected.

All groups of the first generation property offenders except one show appreciable increases over their total series in previous convictions. This exception is the Mexican group. Only in case of the Irish, Teutonic, and Italian groups, however, are the increases of recidivists certainly valid from a statistical viewpoint. There is also a general trend toward a larger number of single men among the property offenders than in their total series, but this excess is certainly significant only in the Mexicans. Occupationally, the property offenders of the first generation are not markedly different from their total series. We should expect fewer extractives (especially farmers) in the property group, and five of the six groups do show deficiencies, but they are dependable only in case of the Mexicans.[2] The Teutonic group shows a decrease in unskilled laborers and the Italian group a deficiency in clerical occupations. But there are only three certain cases of occupational differentiation in a total of 66 subcategories.

The property criminals ought to be better educated than their total groups, according to our findings in the Old American criminals. This expectation is realized in that most of the groups of property criminals show deficiencies of illiterates, of those who have learned to read and write without going to school, and of persons who have reached only the first six grades, but excesses in the higher educational ranks. The French manifest this educational superiority most clearly; the Mexicans do not show it at all; and the Irish tend to vary in an opposite direction, since their property criminals are deficient in men who have reached the last two years of high school. Presumably, Irish-American criminals are precocious.

On the whole, the property criminals of the first generation Americans of six different ethnic groups are not very different sociologically from their total groups. This lack of differentiation may be due to a confusion created by our combining forgery and fraud offenders with thieves and burglars. Again, it may be the result of the small size of samples. Lastly, it is possible that in these first generation offenders sociological differentiation in correlation with type of offense has not proceeded so far as in the Old Americans.

[2] This term "extractives" is a census occupational classification which I deprecate because in criminology it causes confusion. An extractive is a man who extracts his living from the soil, as a farmer, or from the bowels of the earth, as a miner. It does not mean a person who extracts your wallet from your pocket, or your savings from your bank by fraud. Extractive criminals are much more likely to extract an eye for an eye or a tooth for a tooth.

I am inclined to feel that the probabilities favor this last explanation.

When we proceed to examine the anthropometric measurements and indices of the property offenders in comparison with their respective totals, the results are perfectly clear cut. In the Teutonic and Mexican groups the property offenders are significantly younger than their total series, and in general all groups of the property offenders, except the Italians, tend to show slight size inferiority to the totals of their ethnic series. But nowhere do these deviations reach the margin of dependability. Consequently, it may be stated that the property offenders may well be regarded as random samples of their total series and they are not, in fact, shown to differ in measurements and indices from their total groups. This lack of differentiation is quite contrary to what we have found in the Old American criminals. In morphological features these six property offense subgroups of first generation Americans differ from their total series in occasional characters. Irish property offenders may, for example, differ from their total series in having fewer individuals with slight shoulder slope, while French offenders against property may include more individuals with compressed jaw angles than are found in the total first generation French criminals. However, these variations attain statistical significance only sporadically, probably because of the insufficient size of the samples studied. The same difficulty creates a probably false impression that the significant morphological differentiae between the various ethnic groups of property offenders are haphazard and irrelevant.

The attempt to test offense differentiation in physical and sociological characters was also made in two other cases. The Irish-Americans furnish a sufficiently large group of robbers to warrant a comparison of that subgroup with the total series. However, these robbers proved not to differ from their total series in measurements and indices more than any random sample of the series would be expected to differ. Hence, no effort was made to pursue this profitless task further through the mazes of numerous morphological variations. The other test was made by constituting a violence against persons group in Mexican-Americans. This test revealed nothing except that the violence criminals were older and had longer and narrower noses. They are probably older because they have longer sentences, and they have longer noses because they are older, or contrariwise, as Tweedledee would say.

In the case of the foreign born groups of criminals another effort was made to study offense differentiation, whenever the size of the groups permitted separation of an offense group large enough to be compared with the total criminals. Such comparisons were possible only in three instances. In the Mexicans a property offense group was made by combining forgery and fraud with burglary and larceny, as in the case of the native born of foreign parentage. Also in the Mexicans a violence against persons group was distinguished by combining both degrees of murder with assault, and a sex group by taking rape together with all other sex offenses. In the case of Italians it was possible to segregate only a personal violence group.

The property group of foreign born Mexicans is distinguished from total foreign born Mexican criminals in 9 of 26 sociological subcategories. These acquisitive criminals have more previous convictions, are less often married, are more rarely engaged in the extractive occupations and oftener in personal service, and apparently go in more for certain semi-skilled pursuits, such as factory work, transportation, and trades. They are also much better educated than the total foreign born Mexican criminals. They differ sociologically from their total groups in much the same way as property offenders among the Old Americans diverge from their total series. However, the physical differences are not so marked. The Mexican property offenders are much younger than the total group and have narrower shoulders and shallower chests. They seem somewhat smaller and more slender than Mexican born criminals in general. In morphological features they are distinct from their total series. Particularly, they have less body hair and not so many thick eyebrows; they have fewer convex noses and more straight noses, fewer wrinkles, less worn teeth, more edge-to-edge bites of the incisor teeth, and smaller ear lobes. All of these features thus far mentioned are, to some extent, explicable in the light of the younger mean age of the property offenders. But, in addition, these thieves, burglars, forgers, and confidence men have fewer light brown eyes, fewer rayed irides, more of light brown skin color, fewer median eye folds, more nasal septa inclined downward, less thickness of the integumental lips, and more prominent jaw angles than have the total Mexican criminals. These features are not dependent upon age difference.

The Mexican criminals convicted of offenses of violence against the person show the same excesses of married men, the same increases of persons in the extractive occupations, with corresponding deficiencies in urban occupations, and the same general inferiority of education as characterize the murderers among the Old American criminals. In measurements and indices they differ not at all from the total Mexican criminals, except that they have longer faces and are older. A considerable number of differences in morphological features are obviously connected with the older mean age of the violence criminals. Those not so conditioned are excess of rayed eyes and thicker integumental lips. It can then be concluded that Mexican violence criminals are sociologically differentiated from total Mexican born criminals, but that physically they exhibit virtually no differences which are not ascribable to their superior age.

The Mexican sex offenders are really not strongly distinguished sociologically from the whole group of foreign born Mexican criminals. They include more persons who can read and write but have not attended school, more persons in semi-professional occupations, and some other possible, but not certain, sociological differentiae. Metrically, they differ from their total series only in having shorter faces. There are, in addition, a considerable number of morphological characters in which these sex offenders differ from the whole group of Mexican born convicts. A few of these are affected by a slight age superiority (1.3 years) of the sex group. Those which are not influenced by age are excesses of dark brown skin color, of blue-gray eyes, of low nasal roots and low nasal bridges and of concave noses; more thin nose tips, excess of downward directed nasal septa, more extreme variations in thickness of integumental lips, more pronounced lip seams, less wear of the teeth. Some of these features suggest that the Mexican sex offenders retain a rather more primitive physiognomy than the group as a whole. If the samples were larger, it is probable that the differentiae would be multiplied and rendered more distinct.

Since the Italian violence criminals were found not to differ from total foreign born Italian criminals, as far as metric features are concerned, except in being older, the matter was left without further investigation of their potential sociological and morphological differences. So many of the Italians are offenders against persons that they impart their physical characters to the entire group of Italian delinquents. The typical Italian criminal is a murderer, someone who assaults another, or someone who is prone to rape.

The apparently negative findings of these initial efforts to test offense group differentiation in the native born of foreign parentage and the foreign born are probably due to two principal reasons: the inadequate size of the samples, and the extremely stringent statistical method of differentiating offense subgroup differences which has been utilized up to this point in our survey. The small size of samples renders differences statistically insignificant, unless they are of comparatively large magnitude. The statistical method of comparing a subgroup with the total series of which it forms a part loads the dice strongly against differentiation when the subgroup comprises nearly half of the total series or more than half. It may be desirable to apply to this problem some less exacting test of offense group differentiation, such as the comparison of the subgroups with the remainder of the series. At any rate, all that has been demonstrated up to now is that, in the present small samples and with the methods used in our larger series, statistical differentiation of offense subgroups is not satisfactorily established. The trends of differences between offense subgroups and totals are sufficiently defined as to suggest that there may in fact be considerable differentiation.

Consequently, I do not believe that first generation Americans and foreign born criminals are in reality undifferentiated anthropologically when classified according to their several offenses. Nevertheless, there are certain factors in their general environmental situation which would tend to prevent or to impede such offense group differentiation.

The first generations of the American born of alien extraction have been subjected to certain impacts of the new physical environment which seem to have produced in them, generally irrespective of ethnic origin, more or less uniform trends of bodily changes; or, alternatively, they have all been affected simultaneously by certain evolutionary forces which have brought about the shift toward taller stature, more slender body build, and other anthropological changes, which are so noticeable in the last two generations of the American population and are discernible elsewhere. These bodily changes, whatever their cause, seem to have confused and overcome the differentiation into the physical types which are closely related to sociological characteristics in the Old Americans. Even clearer are the uniformities of sociological change which have acted upon these children of immigrants. The acquisition of a new language, education in the American public schools, introduction into the social and economic life of the country, have conspired to break down the family traditions brought over from the countries of parental origin and have tended to disrupt families and to cause conflict between parents and children. Thus, the currents of anthropological and sociological change have, in the case of these children of immigrants, set so strongly in the same directions as to sweep with them the New Americans of delinquent tendencies, almost irrespective of race and nationality.

However, it is quite remarkable that several of these first generation groups have resisted to a great degree both types of change. Thus, the first generation of British descent has hardly varied from the foreign born in physical and sociological features. It is conservative in an anthropological sense. This condition is easily understandable when it is recalled that many of these British-Americans are of Canadian descent and that their parental stocks have already been acclimatized in the New World. Further, they have continued to use their linguistic heritage with which are bound up many psychological and sociological concomitants, so that they have been the more readily assimilated into American life, and have avoided many of the conflicts into which the children of the alien-speaking immigrants are forced. To a lesser extent, the same factors have influenced the Americanization of the children of French Canadians, although these have indeed shifted their linguistic adherence and have probably undergone more violent sociological changes.

In the case of the children born in this country of Mexican parentage there seems to have been the minimum modification of social status as compared with the foreign born domiciled in this country. Apparently both groups adhere to types of rural life which may not be profoundly different from those pursued in their home country. Antisocial offenses are prevailingly of the same type in foreign born and native born, with a swing toward acquisitive crimes less marked than in many other ethnic pairs. Offenses against property naturally increase most rapidly in the immigrant children who are settled in the more prosperous industrialized areas where there are more things to steal and more persons worth robbing.

However, the most remarkable of all the phenomena considered in this treatment of New American criminality is the unswerving loyalty of the Italian-Americans to their national homicidal propensity, in spite of sociological and anthropological change. To the anthropologist there is something beautiful in this steadfast Italian adherence to their traditional criminal *mores*, all, as it were, shouting "Viva Lombroso! Lombroso was right!"

CHAPTER VI

NEW AMERICAN CRIMINALS AND CIVILIANS: SOCIAL AND PHYSICAL DIVERGENCE

ENVIRONMENT is the universal alibi of human failure. It is the excuse of those who have shown themselves to be social liabilities, and the extenuating circumstance for those who appraise human conduct sympathetically rather than intelligently. Environment is impersonal and has to serve as the mute scapegoat for all of our sins, because it is inarticulate and presumably unresentful of false accusations. Men go into a desert and die there of hunger and thirst, and the desert is to blame. Men create a desert by removing the covering of vegetation which holds the soil, and curse the resulting dust storms. They cut down the forests and drown indignantly in the ensuing floods. Then, belatedly, other men, scarcely more wise, formulate vast and expensive plans for moving the dusty denuders of the soil into new regions where they can begin over again, and organize "flood control." Why is there no beneficent control of man himself? Why is human control undertaken only by rapacious dictators for purposes which are usually evil? I think it is because man dares not look himself in the face.

Man makes his own environment and if he makes a mess of it, it is his own fault. The pig is unjustly reputed to be a dirty animal, because dirty men keep him in a dirty sty. But men who live in dirty houses are dirty men. If this be treason, make the most of it.

Long residence in the same geographical area, with inbreeding and adaptation, tends to differentiate the Old Americans into physical and social types, of varying qualities. Each type then finds its own environment; inferior types sink; superior types rise. When environmental equilibrium has been attained, there is set up a benevolent or malignant interaction between environment and the organism. The superior type is improved by a good environment; the bad environment still further deteriorates the inferior. The organism holds the balance of power only if it is a good organism.

The marked physical and sociological differentiation of Old American criminals, and of the criminals from law-abiding Old Americans, is largely attributable to the process of selection, organic and social. Inferior types are selected for social inadequacy and for crime. When we pretend that it is environmental hard luck which is the ultimate cause of human failure, we are simply ministering to our own inferiority complexes.

We ought to expect less social and physical difference between immigrant delinquents and immigrant law-abiding citizens than in the case of the long settled and extremely differentiated Old Americans. For immigrants have at least displayed the initiative which brings them to a new country. Further, all of them have to undergo the shock of a change of physical and social environment. Their environmental alibis are sounder than those of Old Americans who have gradually bogged down into crime.

SOCIOLOGICAL DIFFERENTIATION

If crime is mainly or exclusively a sociological phenomenon, it ought to manifest itself most commonly and most pronouncedly in a sociological environment which encourages criminalistic tendencies. Poverty conceivably prompts its sufferers to secure by theft or other illegal means the necessities and luxuries which they lack. Lowly occupational status means low wages and a low standard of living. It fosters discontent. Depressed living conditions foment family discord, breed strife and hatred, and are likely to lead to crimes of violence, both within and without the family.

Most immigrants come to the United States with the hope of bettering their economic status, and perhaps with some additional aspiration toward a greater measure of political and religious liberty. They have been foiled in their efforts to obtain a comfortable livelihood in their home countries, have become dissatisfied, or have involved themselves in trouble of one sort or another which makes it expedient for them to emigrate. Many of them arrive in the United States with a past record of failure and frustration. Probably all, or nearly all, have had roseate dreams of golden opportunities in the United States. The shock of disillusionment is sudden and brutal. They find themselves in a country which seems to provide no place for the alien except in the ranks of menial and badly paid labor. They may suffer the dreadful disadvantage of being able neither to speak nor to understand the language of the country; its customs and methods of life are utterly strange to them. They are laughed at and despised as inferiors. It is very easy to understand the difficulties of this period of adjustment and to comprehend how strong are the incentives to criminal behavior for those who are unable to secure the advantages of American life which they had confidently anticipated. Only a very stupid person would ascribe the greater part of the antisocial behavior of the newly arrived immigrant to sheer innate wickedness. On the other hand, it is undeniable that hundreds of thousands do overcome the difficulties of the situation and succeed in spite of adversity, gradually bettering their scale of living and becoming assimilated into the ranks of the substantial law-abiding population. Many persist in honesty in spite of continued poverty and disillusionment.

However rapacious our industrialists may be, however stupid and dishonest our politicians, however cheap and tawdry our American civilization, we can and do offer, to the most humble and ungifted immigrant, opportunities for a decent and safe existence which are afforded by few European homelands. It is high time for us to recognize that the moral and cultural superiority asserted for themselves by supercilious Europeans, and admitted by sycophantic American expatriates, is nothing but a sham. The crude "100 per cent" American who scatters his money in European capitals and returns thankfully to "God's country" is nearly 100 per cent right.

It is not so easy to explain the increased criminalistic tendencies of the children of immigrants, even when one invokes the well known factors of family disruption, the development of antagonism between parents and children, the disregard of the offspring for the ethnic traditions and sanctions of the old country, the linguistic barrier which is likely to arise when the parents have an imperfect knowledge of English and the children refuse to learn the native tongue of the parents. All of these familial and intergeneration difficulties no doubt contribute to the potential delinquency of the New Americans, but they seem to me to be quite insufficient to explain it entirely. It seems probable that, on the whole, the criminals of native birth but foreign parentage have sprung from the less successful of the immigrant parents, whose inhibitions and traditions may have kept them law-abiding, but who have been able neither to provide for their children such upbringing as will minimize temptation toward antisocial behavior, nor to prevent them from succumbing to such temptation. In other words, it is wholly conceivable that the immigrants who are inferior in ability and unsuccessful in the process of assimilation produce the majority of the criminalistic first generation Americans.

If these considerations are sound, we should expect civilian immigrants to show a minimum sociological and physical differentiation from their criminal mates, since in these groups the strain of adjustment to the life of a new country is greatest and, under equal environmental adversity, small factors may determine the antisocial fate of the individual — factors which are not entirely obvious either sociologically or anthropologically. However, in the first native generation blood ought to tell, and the offspring of inferior immigrants, destined for delinquency, should exhibit their lack of capacity in a wider divergence in sociological traits from the children of the immigrants who have successfully adjusted themselves, and who, perhaps, have been given a more favorable environment and at the same time have inherited more qualities which are likely to bring them social and economic success.

We have attempted, in securing samples of the civilian population with which to compare our criminals, to derive them, in general, from the same social and economic levels of the population from which we know the criminals, in large part, to have sprung. If we were to compare with our first generation Irish-American criminals the Irish-Americans who are attending the colleges of Massachusetts, we should in so doing adopt a procedure which would magnify the physical and social differentiation of the two groups, since the college students would be selected from the most capable of the Irish-American population, the criminals from the least capable and not *vice versa* as some cynics would assert. It is desirable to equalize environmental factors, so far as possible, in order that we may compare two groups in which similar occupational and social status might seem to afford about equal incentives toward criminality. It is for this reason that we have drawn our civilian samples from the out-patients of our great city hospitals, from the ranks of militiamen which include a majority of persons of humble status, and even from the casual patrons of the public bath houses at Revere Beach, which is not especially exclusive, but, as far as I know, not particularly infested with criminals.

We have but 5 ethnic pairs of first generation Americans in whom both criminal and civilian samples are sufficiently large to warrant inter-group comparison. These are British, Irish, French, Italian, and Eastern, Near Eastern. Every one of these pairs except the French shows marked sociological differentiation, and the lack of differentiation between these groups seems to be due to the small size of the civilian sample (21 men) rather than to an absence of crude differences.

Marital Status

Significant differences in marital status are confined to the divorced and separated categories of marital classification. In both of these British and Irish criminals exceed their comparable civilian samples. It is easy to understand the excess of divorced criminals, since a criminal is not commonly a satisfactory husband and father, and, in any event, the almost total absence of divorces reported among our civilians is quite incredible. On the basis of our findings among Old American criminals we should expect these New American criminals to include far larger proportions of single men than do the law-abiding of the same ethnic antecedents. This is not the case, and it seems indicated that criminal behavior is not so strong an obstacle to matrimony among the New Americans as in the older stock. Alternatively, it is possible that marriage among the New Americans does not inhibit the expression of criminal propensities so markedly as in the population of longer residence in the United States. I do not suggest, however, that the wives of first generation Americans are less able to control their husbands than the Daughters of the Revolution the Sons of Cincinnatus.

Occupation

The British and Irish criminals have significantly more in the extractive occupations than their civilian check samples. Italian criminals show a huge excess of unskilled laborers, and all groups, except the Near Eastern, show statistically insignificant deficiencies of factory workers. The Irish-American criminals are more heavily represented in the skilled trades than are the civilians. There are significantly fewer Irish-American, French-American, and Italian-American criminals in public service than civilians, and this is as should be. Personal service is overweighted with British and Italian criminals in comparison with the civilian distribution. In clerical work British and Irish criminals also fall below the civilians.

Lowly occupations which are heavily patronized by criminals of the first generation are manual labor and personal service. On the whole, the criminals seem occupationally inferior to their civilian check samples.

Education

The educational inferiority of the first generation American criminals to the paired civilian groups is very pronounced. Generally speaking, the criminals show excesses in the illiterate class and up to the first year of high school, and deficiencies, when compared with the civilians, in the succeeding higher categories.

Summary

It is hardly necessary to detail by ethnic groups the sociological differences which distinguish the native born criminals of foreign parentage from comparable civilian series. The British-American criminals exhibit all-around sociological inferiority, but the Irish-Americans, although generally of lower occupational status, have more criminals in the skilled trades than do the civilians, but fewer in public service. Significant educational deficiencies of the Irish criminals are restricted to the last two years of high school and to college and professional school. The French criminals fall significantly below the civilians only in public service, and their educational deficiencies do not attain statistical significance, probably because of the small size of the civilian sample.

Italian-American criminals seem to have been drawn largely from the most ignorant and those occupationally lowest placed (unskilled laborers, personal servants, transport workers). Eastern and Near Eastern criminals show sociological differentiation of a reliable character from civilians only in their educational abasement. However, they have strong tendencies, also, toward the lowlier occupations.

Altogether, there is marked and general sociological inferiority on the part of the delinquent New Americans — strongest in educational qualifications, although educational opportunity in this country is perhaps most nearly equal for all.

FOREIGN BORN

When we turn to the comparison of foreign born criminals by ethnic groups with corresponding civilian check samples, we note that their sociological differentiation takes a somewhat different form. All of the criminal groups, except the French, display a significant number of reliable deviations from their civilian mates. The French-American criminals differ significantly in but one of 25 sociological categories and are otherwise indistinguishable from the civilians.

Marital State

Marital differences vary in the several pairs. British and Near Eastern delinquents include more unmarried men than their check samples. Near Eastern criminals have more

divorced men, and the British have an excess of widowers.
French show a significant deficiency of widowers, and Irish
criminals do not deviate significantly from their check series.

Occupation

Occupational differences in the several groups are not
especially enlightening. There are fewer unskilled laborers
and more skilled tradesmen among the Irish delinquents,
contrary to expectation, but more unskilled laborers and
fewer in personal service among the Near Easterners, which
is in accordance with what might be expected. The foreign
born Italian criminals, as contrasted with their civil check
sample, show a dearth of factory workers and a probably
valid excess of unskilled laborers.

Education

In education the Irish criminals are definitely superior to
the Irish of the civilian check sample. The British criminals, too, are better represented in the highest educational
brackets, but they include a possibly significant excess of
illiterates. French criminals have about the same educations
as French civilians, whereas Near Eastern criminals are, in
general, inferior in education to their check samples. Nevertheless, more Near Eastern criminals than civilians have
reached the last two years of high school. One is left with
the impression that amount of education is rather unimportant as a criterion of distinction between foreign born
criminals and civilians. On the whole, of course, the
criminals are less well educated, but the situation is full of
contradictions.

Generally speaking, sociological differentiation is more
marked in the first generation than in the foreign born
groups. Inequalities of educational opportunity and of
linguistic handicapping in the foreign born immigrants
tend, doubtless, to confuse the sociological differentiation of

the various pairs and make them seem contradictory and inconsistent. Their children and the children of law-abiding immigrants start life on more nearly equal terms in the matter of opportunity, and consequently exhibit much more consistent sociological differences, and really greater ones, from their more socially disposed check samples.

The conviction grows that it is not inequality of opportunity, but inferior capacity for grasping environmental opportunity, which stigmatizes the antisocial New Americans.

PHYSICAL DIFFERENTIATION

NATIVE BORN

After all of the data have been collected by field anthropometrists, the troubles of the person who is to analyze them multiply and increase like the offspring of the mentally deficient. Thus, after several years of labor on the Old American criminals, with all of its grief occasioned by troublesome variations due to state sampling and the personal equations of Observers A and B, we encountered a new and nasty difficulty in dealing with the comparison of the series of native born Whites of foreign parentage and those of the foreign born. For, to secure additional check samples of civilians with which to compare these New Americans, it was necessary to utilize the services of a third observer, whom I designate as C, although I should rate him A minus, at worst. This anthropometrist, also a trained and careful worker, developed his own personal equation in morphological judgment, so that a prolonged process of sifting and appraisal was necessary before it became apparent that only a restricted number of his observed features could be compared legitimately with those of Observer A, who was responsible for most of the New American criminal series. These personal equations, however, were apparently operative only in morphological observations, not in measurements.

We were able to test the differences in anthropometric features between civilians and criminals in the case of five pairs of the native born of foreign parentage, namely: British, Irish, French, Italian, and Near Eastern. Each criminal group was found to differ significantly from its civilian mate. In 20 bodily measurements the statistically valid differentiae varied from 10 per cent in the French to 50 per cent in the Irish, and in 13 indices the significantly differentiated ranged from 23 per cent in French and Italians to 61.5 per cent in the Near Easterners.

The British-American criminals are older than their civilian check sample by 3.65 years and are vastly inferior in stature, sitting height, and nose height. They have wider foreheads, noses, jaws, and ears. They have heads higher relative to length, broader noses relative to nasal height, relatively broader ears, wider foreheads relative to face breadth and relative to head breadth, and faces shorter in relation to their breadth. Thus, they are very different from the civilians.

The Irish-American criminals also contrast markedly with their civilian check sample. They are five years younger than the civilians, have smaller chest diameters, shorter upper faces, noses, and ears. As in the case of the British, the Irish criminals exceed the civilians of the same antecedents in head height, forehead breadth, nose breadth, and jaw breadth. Consequently, they also differ from the civilians in the indices derived from this last named group of breadth measurements. The criminals have higher length-height and breadth-height indices of the head, noses broader relative to their height, and foreheads broader relative to face and head breadth. The upper facial proportions of the criminals are shorter and broader. The criminal ears are also relatively shorter and broader.

The value of our French comparison is seriously impaired by a very small number in the civilian check sample (only 21). This fact probably accounts for the comparative scarcity of significant differences, because small samples have large probable errors and differences are regarded as reliable only when they exceed three times their probable errors. Nevertheless, the French criminals born in this country are distinguishable anthropometrically from their civilian brothers. They have, certainly, shallower chests and broader foreheads, and are probably significantly younger (4.35 years), narrower in chest, shorter in nose and in ear. Valid indicial excesses are in the ear proportions and the relation of forehead breadth to face breadth and head breadth. There is, also, a probability that the criminals have shorter and broader noses.

We are similarly hampered in our Italian comparison, since the Italian-American civilians of the check sample number only 29. The criminals are certainly inferior in weight, height, chest breadth, sitting height, and ear length, and probably in head circumference, upper face height, and nose height. It is probable also that the criminals have the broader foreheads. In indices the criminals are superior in shoulder breadth relative to stature and in relative breadth of the ear. They have shorter, broader upper faces, and probably shorter and broader noses.

Differentiation of indices is at a maximum in the case of Eastern and Near Eastern criminals and civilians, both, of course, born in this country of foreign parentage. Again chest breadth and also shoulder breadth are inferior in the criminals; noses and ears are shorter. On the other hand, criminal foreheads, jaws, and possibly noses, are broader than those of the civilians. The criminals exhibit greater sitting heights relative to stature, more brachycephalic or rounder heads, higher heads relative to head length, relatively broader and shorter noses and ears, and foreheads broader relative to head breadth and jaw breadth.

FOREIGN BORN

The foreign born criminals differ even more radically from their civilian check samples. The British criminals are considerably younger (8.75 years), and are notably inferior in chest diameters, nose height, and ear length. They have higher heads, broader foreheads, noses, and ears. They have greater relative sitting heights, higher cephalic indices, length-height indices, as well as breadth-height, nasal, and ear indices.

We are baffled again in the Irish born criminals by the small size of the group (only 27 individuals). Nevertheless, there are great differences between the criminals and their civilian mates. Criminals are much younger (10.4 years), inferior in weight, stature, shoulder breadth, chest diameters, head length, head circumference, and face height. They exceed the civilians in forehead breadth, nose breadth, and ear breadth. The criminals have higher relative sitting heights, nasal and ear indices, and exceed the civilians also in breadth of forehead compared to face breadth and maximum head breadth.

The comparison of foreign born French criminals with the civilians is completely unsatisfactory because there are only 18 civilians in the check sample. The criminals are more than 13 years younger and are shorter, inferior in chest diameters, in jaw breadth, and probably in weight. They have higher heads and broader noses than the civilians. In the criminals significant elevations of relative sitting height and the nasal and ear indices are to be noted, while they fall below the civilians in the breadth of jaws relative to forehead breadth. In spite of inadequate numbers of civilians, the differences between the two groups are numerous and significant.

Italian criminals are not significantly younger than civilians. Both samples are adequate in size. The criminals have narrower chests, shorter noses, and probably narrower shoulders and shorter ears. They have higher heads, broader foreheads, noses, and ears. Relative deficiencies of shoulder breadth, and shorter, broader upper faces and ears are distinguishing indices of the criminals. They also have heads which are higher relative to their breadth, and foreheads wider in relation to head and face breadth.

Finally, the Eastern and Near Eastern criminals are markedly different from their civilian check sample. The latter averages 5.6 years older. Criminals have shorter noses and ears, but greater sitting heights, head heights, and breadths of forehead, nose, and ear. Nine differences in indices distinguish them from civilians. These concern the relatively greater skull heights and forehead breadths in comparison with other parts of the face and head, and the shorter, broader noses and ears. The upper face of the criminal is also shorter and broader, and face breadth bears a higher relation to maximum head breadth.

The general trends of metric and indicial differences between the native born criminal and the foreign born criminal, each compared with a civilian check sample of similar ethnic origin, are found by taking the ten pairs of groups together. When all ten criminal groups vary in the same direction from their civilian mates, there is reason for believing that a real metric difference separates criminals from civilians.

Every one of the 10 criminal groups has a greater breadth of forehead than the corresponding civilian check sample; all criminals have narrower chests, broader noses, shorter noses, shorter ears, broader ears, and higher heads. Not all of the differences are statistically significant, but most of them are. From these differences arise certain similarly unanimous trends in index deviation. The criminals have higher nasal and ear indices, higher indices of forehead breadth to face breadth, greater head height relative to head length and head breadth. A number of other metric features deviate so strongly in a uniform direction in the criminals as to be almost universal. Thus the chest depth is less in 9 of 10 criminal groups than in civilians, as is also weight and shoulder breadth. The upper facial index 9 times out of 10 is lower (i.e. the criminal face is shorter and broader). The following measurements and indices total 8 of 10 deviations in one direction on the part of the criminals: inferior stature, head circumference, total height of face, and total facial index. The sitting height of criminals expressed as a proportion of stature is higher in 8 of 10 groups. Eight of 10 groups of criminals are younger than their civilian check sample; 7 are inferior in sitting height, 7 in relative shoulder breadth; 6 have broader bigonial diameters or jaw breadths; 7 criminal groups are more brachycephalic (i.e. have broader heads relative to head length).

It is safe to conclude on the basis of these data that native born criminals of foreign parentage and foreign born criminals both deviate from their comparable civilian groups in the following ways. The criminals are usually shorter than civilians and tend to be lighter — these differences established by trend rather than by significance of difference. Of the following we may be even more certain: criminals have shallower and narrower chests, higher sitting height relative to stature, breadths of forehead absolutely greater, and greater relative to head breadth and face breadth, faces proportionately shorter and broader, noses shorter and broader, absolutely and relatively broader jaws, shorter and broader ears.

There are some of these differences which may conceivably depend upon great age disparity, since 6 of the 10 groups of criminals are significantly younger than their civilian check sample. We might expect younger criminals to have slightly shorter noses and ears than their elders, and possibly to weigh somewhat less and to have smaller chest diameters. Now the native born criminals of British parentage constitute the only delinquent group which is significantly older than its check sample. They exceed the civilian mean age by 3.65 years. They do not differ significantly from the civilians in weight and in chest diameters, although they are definitely shorter than civilians. But the criminals nevertheless have shorter and broader noses, and probably shorter, but certainly broader, ears. Again, the Italian foreign born criminals are insignificantly older than their civilian check sample (.35 years). Yet they display inferiorities of weight, chest diameters, nose height, and ear length. In other words, they differ from the civilians exactly as do the criminal groups which are younger than their check samples, instead of older. I doubt, then, that age plays any very great part in these trends of metric difference.

Here there is a disturbing possibility of a factor which may invalidate some of these striking differences. Personal equation rears again its horrid head. Nearly all of the criminals of these particular series were measured and observed by Observer A and the civilians by Observer C. Perhaps they developed slightly different techniques which have made the differences in their series when the various groups are compared. I can deal with this possibility only in an indirect way. Observer C was to a considerable extent trained in his techniques by Observer A and both worked together in the study of the Massachusetts militia civilian sample. I think it very improbable that Observer C subsequently diverged greatly in his methods of measurements from Observer A. Only a few of the bodily measurements present great difficulties which are likely to lead to differences in the results between the two observers. Frankly, I rather suspect that the excess of forehead breadth of criminals may be due in part to a tendency of Observer A to take this measurement in such a way as to get rather too high caliper readings. But I do not think that any considerable part of the deviations between criminals and civilians is really due to observational equation. Most of the differences are correlated (e.g. an initial height inferiority in criminals is accompanied by shorter broader faces, broader noses, broader heads, broader foreheads). The general run of differences between the criminals and the civilians is much like that which obtains between native born criminals of foreign parentage and the foreign born of the same stocks. That is to say, the criminals resemble the foreign born in that they are shorter and more "squashed down," if I may use that inelegant expression. Again, these New Americans differ from their civilian check samples in much the same ways that Old American criminals differ from their check samples, most of which were measured by Observer A himself.

I am the last person who would desire to deceive himself by accepting as of criminological importance variations which are merely due to chance or to the idiosyncrasies of individual anthropometrists. In the Old American series I was able to hunt down the personal equations of Observers A and B in measurements and observations, by detailed comparison and sifting of those of their series which ought to be nearly identical and by many, many observations as to the consistency of deviations of one observer from the other in specified measurements. The only measurements which seemed to exhibit marked personal equations were ear measurements and head height. In the latter case the observers used entirely different instruments and techniques — a fact of which we were fully aware. So it seems to me that most of these differences between criminals and civilians have been exaggerated only slightly, if at all, by personal equations.

MORPHOLOGICAL DIFFERENCES

We did find that Observers A and B had some serious divergences in standards of morphological observation. In the case of native born British and Irish it was possible to restrict the criminal civilian comparisons to check samples measured principally by A himself, who had also done the work on the criminals. In the rest of the groups the morphological comparisons were limited to the 16 main categories of features in which detailed examination showed that A and C had the same standards of judgment.

The first generation British criminals differ from their civilian mates in 36 of 155 morphological subcategories or nearly 23 per cent. The criminals have thicker head hair and body hair, straighter hair, more frequent zoned pattern of irides, more external eye folds, higher and more sloping foreheads, thicker eyebrows, higher and broader nasal bridges, fewer concave noses, and fewer nasal septal deflections. The criminals also have thinner membranous lips, more protrusion of the jaws, more pointed chins and more prominent cheek bones, fuller cheeks, greater loss of teeth, less roll of the rims of the ear, more pronounced ear protrusion, more facial asymmetry, and more flattening of the crown of the head.

The Irish first generation criminals show 17 per cent of morphological differentiae from civilians. The criminals have more head hair, more irides with a zoned pattern and fewer of the speckled variety, more median and external folds of the upper eyelids, higher foreheads, broader and higher nasal roots and bridges, thicker nasal tips, thinner integumental lips and less marked lip seams, more facial protrusion or prognathism. The criminals have poorer teeth and fewer of them, more outstanding ears with larger lobes and commoner development of Darwin's point, and more extreme variations of shoulder slope.

We may now throw in the French, Italian, and Eastern-Near Eastern pairs for an added summary of some 16 morphological traits relatively unaffected by personal equation, and epitomize the general trend of differences. All of the criminal groups have thicker head hair than their civilian check samples. They all show less gray hair than the check samples, probably because they are usually younger. Mixed eye colors are more frequent among the criminals than among the civilians, and clear whites (sclerae) less common. Foreheads are higher among the criminals and depressions of the nasal root more pronounced. Moderate degrees of facial prognathism or protrusion are also more to the fore in delinquents. Pointed chins and prominent cheek bones are in excess in all criminal groups. The criminal ear appears generally to have a more primitive and less deeply rolled rim or helix, with a stronger development of Darwin's point. These are all of the general morphological features in which trustworthy comparisons can be made between Observer A's criminal series and Observer B's civilian check samples. Other data on numerous morphological features have been discarded, because we want to find out criminological differentiation rather than differences due to the subjective judgments of Observers A and B, respectively. It is heart-rending to throw away great masses of carefully collected and elaborately analyzed data, which have meant the expenditure of much time and money, but it really does not pay to eat spoiled and tainted food in order to save it.

The same limitation of comparison to 16 morphological features had to be imposed upon the foreign born groups of criminals and civilians. In this condensed account of the results of a large survey, it is hardly worth while to "niggle" about with a description of this or that individual difference between one or another criminal group and its check sample. We are more interested in general trends of difference. So we find that both criminal series, native born and foreign born, tend to diverge in similar directions from their own ethnic check samples of civilians in the following morphological observations — not always to diverge significantly, but at any rate uniformly. The criminals have thicker head hair, and more extremes of straight and curly hair, more black hair and more reddish-brown hair, more red hair, and less gray and white hair. The pure dark and light shades of eye color are rarer in the criminals, in whom mixed colors prevail. The whites of the criminal eyes are oftener splotched and speckled with pigment flecks of yellow. Forehead heights appear to vary more in criminals, and the nasion depressions (at the root of the nose) are commonly deeper. In deflections of the nasal septum the criminals and civilians do not differ. However, the primitive or degenerate facial protrusion known as prognathism is more characteristic of the criminals than of the civilians. Square chins are not so frequent among the delinquents as among the law-abiding populations of similar derivation, and pointed chins, conversely, are commoner. The criminals tend to have more prominent malars or cheek bones. The criminal ear seems less highly evolved, in that the helices are more frequently unrolled, or slightly rolled, and Darwin's point is oftener observed. Facial asymmetry is commoner among the criminals.

Now I think we are in a position to state that criminals, native born of foreign parentage and foreign born, are as clearly and consistently different from their comparable check samples in physical anthropological features as in sociological features. This is a very remarkable fact when it is considered that the classification of samples of the population into criminal and non-criminal series is sociological and not anthropological.

You may argue, if you like, that environment makes the criminal physique in addition to the criminal behavior. But all of the physical differentiae which so nearly uniformly distinguish the delinquent from the law-abiding, whether first generation American or foreign born, are not easily referable to environment. The shorter stature, inferior weight, and lesser chest diameters of the criminals may conceivably be due to poorer nutrition during growth. Smaller size does indeed suggest biological inferiority, but only within groups which are ethnically, racially, and to some extent environmentally comparable. I seriously doubt that our civilian militiamen and out-patients of dispensaries have been born with silver spoons in their mouths in contrast to the criminals of similar origin. I think that both alike were born with nothing at all in their mouths except the usual equipment of tongue and toothless gums. It is not in the slightest degree probable that the inferior growth and underweight of the prisoners is due to their prison environment, since it is notorious that criminals on the whole are better housed and fed inside of prison than when at large. Within each stock criminals are derived disproportionately from individuals who are either stunted hereditarily or through unfavorable environmental conditions during growth, or more probably by both adverse factors operating together.

It cannot be stated that such metric features as superior breadth of forehead, greater head height, broader jaws and noses, and relatively shorter, broader faces — all of which seem to characterize New American criminals in contrast to similar ethnic groups of civilians — are in any way indicative of evolutionary or general physical inferiority. The more prominent malars, shorter and broader noses, excess of facial prognathism and of ears with unrolled helices and Darwin's point are, it is true, primitive characters. I do not wish to overemphasize them, because, in spite of all precautions, some effect of personal equation may still be left to enhance these differences. I have found no evidence of any weight to support the Lombrosian supposition that the criminal is in general a sort of primitive man at odds with civilized society. The indications are merely that criminals are somewhat deficient in organic adaptability and that a certain number of the gross and outstanding differences point toward poorer physique.

The most interesting suggestion of the direction and quality of difference in the criminal as contrasted with the non-criminal is the closer adherence of the former to what seems to be the alien, conservative bodily type of the foreign born immigrant, as contrasted with the new American type which seems to be evolving in the Old American stocks and in the children of immigrants alike. Usually the criminal, be he Old American, native American of foreign parents, or foreign born, tends to stay closer to the vertically compressed and, in head and face, laterally extended body build of the European than do comparable civilians. The shorter, broader faces with the higher nasal index and the more prominent malars and jaw angles, with the shorter stature usually shown by criminals, contribute to this impression. Are the criminals then selected from the less plastic, more conservative physical types, and can this organic rigidity and lack of adaptability be related to their social maladjustment?

There is an alternative possibility. If the foreign born who immigrate to the United States owe their squatness to ancestral or individual stunting and undernourishment, it is possible that the criminal approximation to them may be due to the fact that those who eventually become delinquents have not suffered release from adverse environmental and nutritional conditions in this country to the extent that is true of their longer and more linear civilian counterparts. All of this boils down to the statement that it is impossible to settle the eternal question of the relative influences of heredity and environment by logic or by dialectic.

It seems pertinent to point out here that in comparing criminals with civilians all of the dice are loaded in favor of sociological differentiation and against physical differentiation. The reasons for sociological differentiation are inherent in the basis of selection; the odds against physical differences are concealed. The supposedly law-abiding population is both the source and the receptacle of the criminal element which passes into jail and out again. Any large sample of the so-called civilian population is likely to include some proportion of ex-convicts, unapprehended criminals, and potential criminals. Actually we picked up in our civilian check samples a few individuals who had previously been measured in houses of correction, reformatories, or penitentiaries. On the other hand, it seems extremely improbable that many of the really respectable law-abiding individuals of the population are to be found among the ranks of convicted felons. But anyone who has had the opportunity to inspect the records of arrests which result in probation, of cases put on file, and of acquittals and paroles and pardons, can hardly fail to be convinced that the portion of the criminal element actually serving sentences in penal institutions at any one time must be comparatively small. How much greater would be the physical differentiations between those in jail and those outside, if all who ought to be in jail were actually there?

CHAPTER VII

RACE AND CRIME IN WHITE AMERICANS

WHEN I was a boy, it used to be considered funny for a bucolic wit to remark, "It's a great day for the race!" Some innocent was expected to ask, "What race?" Whereupon you replied, "The human race." This feeble jest of the gay nineties exemplifies not only a misconception of humor, but also of anthropology. The human animal does not constitute a race but one or more species each made up of several physical "races."

Up to this point our survey of the relation of physique to crime in the United States has been restricted to the study of various groups of so-called "Whites," classified on the basis of nativity and of national descent. Such groups are ethnic rather than racial. A race is a great division of mankind, the members of which are characterized by similar or identical combinations of physical features which they owe to their common heredity. Race is, in short, a matter of group heredity. Individuals are identified as members of the same race when they look alike, because they have inherited their bodily features from the same group of ancestors. Consequently, the physical tests of race must be principally of hereditary origin and not merely features which vary radically from individual to individual in accordance with their differing environments. We know of no physical feature in the animal organism which is wholly impermeable to the influence of environment, but some bodily characters are less modifiable than others and are traceable, in the main, to inheritance from one's immediate ancestors. The larger the number of hereditary features which are included in the combination which is common to two or more individuals, the closer is the probable relationship between the individuals. Two persons of the same sex who are so nearly identical in all of their bodily characteristics that they create in the observer the illusion of seeing double, are not merely members of the same race — they are identical twins and exemplify the closest possible blood relationship. When we wish to divide mankind up into large racial groups we restrict the number of hereditary features in the testing combinations to a few broad characters of known hereditary origin and diagnostic worth. More than one feature must always be used in race selection. Thus, black skin is not enough to distinguish a Negro, because Australians and Dravidians also have black skins, but are in many other features quite distinct from Negroes and only remotely related to them. If, however, we select a person who not only has black skin, but also woolly hair, flat broad nose, and puffy everted lips, we have an indubitable Negro and have succeeded in putting together a combination of inherited physical variations which has racial diagnostic value. Actually, however, we conceive of race as a somewhat finer classification than that which divides mankind into four great principal divisions: Negroid, Mongoloid, White, and Australoid.

Our present task is to distinguish several races within the great "White" division of mankind for the immediate purposes of criminal anthropology. The term "White" is rather a misnomer, since the skin color in this division ranges from a dead "fish-belly" white through various shades of pink and ruddy, sallow or yellowish white, down to such a brunet or swarthy shade as might more fittingly be described under the term "light brown." Within this great human division, sometimes "white" only by courtesy, we can afford to disregard skin color which runs through many shades and is very difficult to measure and to classify, and depend for pigmental characters rather upon combinations of eye color and hair color, which are a good deal more obvious. For we know that blond hair and blue eyes are acquired by inheritance. It is perfectly true that you can bleach your hair, and we have to look out for that in women, but you cannot alter your eye color, although it may change with age. The various shades of eye color and hair color, in combination, generally correspond with lighter or heavier amounts of skin pigment and constitute fairly dependable criteria for subdividing into races the major White division of mankind.

Another racial criterion of value is head form. Some people have long and narrow heads (dolichocephals), some have short and broad heads (brachycephals), and some have head breadths which are medium in relation to head length (mesocephals). We cannot assert that a long and narrow head is biologically preferable to a short broad head, or *vice versa*, except, purely theoretically, in the land of the Nazis, or that a specified type of environment produces one shape of head rather than another. We do know that head form is in a general way inherited, and that in the great divisions of mankind, with the exception of the Whites, there is a certain tendency toward a common type of head form. Negroes, for example, are, in the majority of cases, long-headed. Mongoloids are prevailingly round-headed, and Australoids are invariably long-headed. Among the so-called Whites there is a great diversity of head form, which thus furnishes a convenient means of subdividing them into races if correlated with other hereditary features.

The breadth of the nose, expressed as a proportion of its length, is called the nasal index. It is also, within limits, and in combinations, a useful criterion of race. Long, narrow noses, are called leptorrhine. A long, narrow nose is likely to be high in the bridge and may be straight or convex in profile, rarely hollow-backed or concave. On the other hand, a short, broad nose may be straight in profile, but is much oftener concave than convex. The nasal index is a short cut to nose form, which, as a matter of experience, varies widely in the White races and mainly by reason of heredity.

So then, when we select among our White criminals sub-groups with similar combinations of head shape, hair color, eye color, and nose form, we find that we have nine races, or at any rate nine different physical combinations with many similar individuals in each. We postulate that these persons within any single race group are, in general, of the same heredity, or at least have more ancestors in common than individually they would have with the members of other racial groups.

The cephalic index (head breadth expressed as a per-centage of head length) was divided for our purpose into two categories: a more or less long-headed moiety with in-dices under 80, and a rounder-headed half with indices of 80 and above. Hair and eye color were divided first into pronouncedly light and dark combinations, then the various medium shades of hair color associated with the several varieties of mixed eye color, and, finally, the disharmonic combinations in which hair is light and eyes dark, or *vice versa*.

A bipartite division of stature (under 170 cm. and 170 cm. or over) was used to aid in the discrimination of sec-ondary racial types in the case of certain individuals of mixed pigmentation. Similarly, the nasal index was divided at 63, to be used as a subsidiary criterion for distinguishing between certain types otherwise identical in the few criteria employed for sorting.

Now the anthropological critic may assert that the nine different groups distinguished by the use of these combina-tions of criteria are not races at all. However, they do con-sist of individuals who, within each separate group, have been selected upon the basis of the possession of like physi-cal characters in combinations which are generally considered of racial significance by all students of European races. The principal difference between this selection and other attempts at race classification of White groups is that our method involves the sorting of a very large sample according to the actual possession by individuals of combinations of the same features which other students have talked about as combinations but have studied only, for the most part, as isolated characters.

There are 5689 individuals in this sorting, including native White criminals of native parentage, native Whites of foreign parentage, and foreign born Whites. They are divided into nine groups as follows: the Pure Mediterranean, including all persons with cephalic indices under 80, dark eyes, and black, dark brown, and red-brown hair; the Keltic, also long-headed (cephalic index under 80), blue eyes combined with black hair, dark brown hair, red hair, and red-brown hair; the Nordic Mediterranean blend, long-headed with dark hair and mixed eyes, red-brown hair and mixed eyes, light brown hair and dark eyes, red hair and mixed eyes in persons with statures under 170 cm. (evidently a long-headed race with mixed pigmentation); the Predominantly Nordic, long-headed, ash-blond or golden hair with mixed eyes, light brown hair with mixed eyes, light brown hair with blue eyes, red hair and mixed eyes with statures over 170 (a long-headed group of near blonds); Pure Nordic, long heads with ash-blond or golden hair and pure blue eyes; East Baltic, cephalic indices 80 or over, ash-blond or golden hair with blue or mixed eyes, red hair with blue or mixed eyes when the nasal index is 63 or higher (blond round heads with broadish noses); the Nordic Alpine blend, round heads with all other disharmonic combinations of mixed pigments and noses always with an index of 63 or more; the Dinaric mixed type, similarly round-headed, and with numerous mixed pigment combinations of hair and eyes, but with invariably narrow noses, index under 63;

the Pure Alpine type, round heads with black, dark brown, or red-brown hair and dark eyes, all with nasal indices 63 or above.

The sorted types range in number from 106 in the "Pure Nordic" to 1523 in the Nordic Mediterranean. The rigid elimination of all but purely blond long heads in the Pure Nordic selection results in a very small number. It is to be doubted that a similarly stringent selection would isolate a very large group even in Norway or Sweden. Virtually the same pigmental requirements result in a small group of East Baltic round heads, in fact, only 177 individuals. The long-headed near blonds or Predominantly Nordic group, on the other hand, number 878. Such persons are usually loosely assigned to the Nordic race.

Again, the pure brunet long heads (Mediterraneans) are comparatively few in number (252), and the pure brunet brachycephals (Alpines) are even fewer (145). The Keltic type with blue eyes and red or dark shades of hair, but long heads, includes some 531 men; the mixed pigmental round heads with long noses (Dinarics) 733; and the vast brachycephalic group with mixed pigmentation and broad noses (Nordic Alpines) numbers 1344.

Our very large series of Mexicans was eliminated from this racial sorting because of the high proportion of American Indian blood which it carries.

After sorting out these nine putatively racial types of criminals from our total series of prison and reformatory inmates of White stock, irrespective of nativity and national origin, the following procedure was adopted. Each of these nine types was compared with the total series of which it formed a part, in order to determine whether it showed metrical and morphological differences from the total series sufficient to distinguish it as a separate anthropological group, as contrasted with a random sample. The criteria of differentiation employed included all those not actually used in the arbitrary sorting process. Similarly, each racial type was compared with the total series in order to determine its degree of sociological differentiation — in marital state, previous convictions, occupation, education, and nature of offense.

Then the check sample of law-abiding civilians was similarly divided into nine racial types on the basis of the same sorting characters, and each criminal type was compared with its civilian counterpart, firstly to determine its metric and indicial differentiation, then its morphological differentiation, and finally its degree of sociological separateness. Thus we are able to ascertain concerning each racial type: (1) whether it is anthropologically and sociologically distinct from total White criminals, (2) whether it is anthropologically and sociologically distinct from the similar type sorted out of the civilian check sample. For present purposes all of these comparisons may be summarized together for each racial type.

PURE NORDIC

The Pure Nordic type is metrically differentiated by deficiency of age, of head breadth, of face breadth, of nose height, of ear breadth, of length-height index of the skull, and by excess of the relations of forehead breadth to head breadth and of jaw breadth to face breadth (fronto-parietal and zygo-gonial indices). These young Nordics also have an excess of the nasal index which may be significant (i.e. an increased breadth of nose relative to nose height). They have excesses of pinkish and ruddy skins, of thin eyebrows, of upturned nasal septa, of non-prognathous or straight faces, a deficiency of prominent jaw angles, of pronouncedly worn teeth, and an excess of individuals who have lost no teeth. The dental features mentioned are doubtless related to the very young average age of this small group.

The general picture of this type is of course extremely

fair pigmentation and blue eyes with a very narrow and not very long squarish face, a short and almost snub nose, without jaw projection and frequently weak-chinned, slightly narrow-shouldered, and generally weedy. This is not a vigorous type in appearance, but rather fragile looking. It is lowest in mean age of all of the racial series, with an average of only 25 years.

Sociologically, the Pure Nordic type is distinguished by a deficiency of foreign born individuals (especially Italians), and an excess of persons of British Canadian parentage. It contains individuals of mainly Old American stock, with small percentages of British, Teutonic, and Scandinavian extractions. It is very strongly represented in New Mexico criminals and deficient in the Tennessee and possibly the Wisconsin series. Partly because of its tender age, this type has a huge excess of single men. It has no significant statistical deviations in occupation, although it ranks first in transportation and in skilled trades, last in unskilled laborers, tradesmen, and personal servants, and includes no public servants and no professional men whatsoever. In education it is undistinguished, since it ranks fourth of the nine types with a ratio of .66. However, this Pure Nordic type is remarkably differentiated in nature of crime. Its characteristic offense is forgery and fraud in which it far outstrips all other types. It is second in burglary and larceny, ninth or last in first degree murder, in second degree murder, in assault, robbery, and sex offenses other than rape, and next to last (or eighth) in rape. It does a little better in bootlegging, with sixth rank. This type is as strongly distinguished for its disinclination to commit crimes against persons as in its physical characteristics. It comes about as far from fulfilling the ideal of the lusty, red-blooded Nordic as is possible, since it is given to cheating and thieving, and abstains from use of fist and weapons. Thus we have a new conception, that of the gentle and furtive Nordic.

If we compare the criminal Pure Nordic type with its counterpart among civilians, we find many differences. The criminals are 5.75 years younger and probably smaller in most dimensions, including stature. The delinquents certainly have lower heads, shorter and broader noses, wider jaws, shorter ears, relatively greater shoulder breadth and sitting height, rounder heads, and a number of significant differences in head and face indices which suggest that, on the whole, they represent a type more transversely and less longitudinally developed. These include lower head heights relative to head length and head breadth; relatively shorter, broader faces, noses, and ears; wider foreheads relative to head breadth. The only certain morphological deviations of the Pure Nordic criminals from their civilian counterparts are more sloping foreheads and less rolled rims of the ear. These two features are perhaps indicative of a more primitive physical status on the part of the criminals.

Sociologically, the Pure Nordic criminals differ from Pure Nordic civilians in their greater proportion of Old Americans and smaller of British and (probably) of Irish descent, in their excess of widowers and of extractive workers, and in their deficiencies of public servants, professional men, and students. The civilians have ten times as high an educational ratio as the criminals.

It is clear that the Pure Nordic criminal is inferior physically and sociologically to his civilian mate. Physically he resembles more the stunted alien type than the elongated Old American type. So we have these mean, narrow blond men, who cannot live with their wives, and who, although not well educated and mainly engaged in humble occupations, tend to get into the clutches of the law by stealing, forging, and cheating. They have not the physiques to be aggressive or violent; they are, rather, sneaky.

RACIAL TYPES OF OLD AMERICAN CRIMINALS
GENERAL PROPORTIONS AND MOSAIC OF EXCESS FEATURES
PURE NORDIC

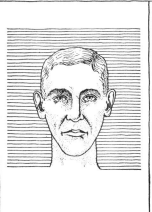

Golden, ash blond hair - low waves
Pure blue eyes
Pink, ruddy skin
Long headed
Narrow head
Narrow face
Thin eyebrows
Short, rather broad nose
Nasal septum inclined upward
Facial prognathism absent
Gonial angles not pronounced

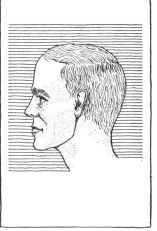

RACIAL TYPES OF OLD AMERICAN CRIMINALS
GENERAL PROPORTIONS AND MOSAIC OF EXCESS FEATURES
PREDOMINANTLY NORDIC

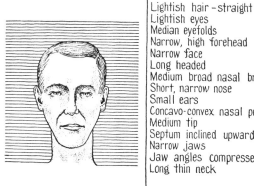

Lightish hair - straight
Lightish eyes
Median eyefolds
Narrow, high forehead
Narrow face
Long headed
Medium broad nasal bridge
Short, narrow nose
Small ears
Concavo-convex nasal profile
Medium tip
Septum inclined upward
Narrow jaws
Jaw angles compressed
Long thin neck

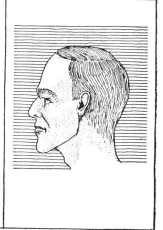

PREDOMINANTLY NORDIC

Apart from characters actually involved in the process of type selection, the Predominantly Nordic group of long-headed near blonds is distinguished by deficiencies of age (8.5 years), of chest depth, forehead and face breadth, nose height, nose breadth, jaw breadth, ear length, and ear breadth, and by taller stature and sitting height than is found in the total racial series of criminals. In proportions or indices its significant differences include diminished relative shoulder breadth and sitting height, a lowered head height relative to head length, and a relatively narrow nose. The height of the head is increased relative to its breadth; the face is broader relative to breadth of head; the ears and nose are relatively longer and narrower, the forehead broader as compared with the head and the jaws than is characteristic of the total series. Thus the Predominantly Nordic type is not only very long-headed and near-blond in pigmentation, but also tall, narrow-shouldered, long-legged and relatively short in the trunk, with elongated face and lantern jaws, but a short, rather pinched nose.

The morphological differentiae of this type include rarity of dark-skinned persons, unusual prevalence of straight hair, deficiency of thick eyebrows, and frequent high foreheads. The nose is distinguished by medium breadth of bridge and thickness of tip, concavo-convex profile, and upward inclined septum. Lip seams are likely to be absent, teeth only slightly or moderately worn, and rarely lost, excess of normal or slight overbites. The neck tends to be long and thin. These peculiarities describe an elongated and rather narrow, but possibly sinewy type.

The Predominantly Nordic type is distinguished in the following sociological characteristics from the total series of Old American criminals. It is overwhelmingly of Old American extraction, and shows small excesses of British and probably of Scandinavian elements, with most other ethnic stocks markedly deficient. This type is notably rare in Massachusetts and in Wisconsin and excessively represented in all of our other states except Arizona and Texas. The Predominantly Nordic type is definitely prison rather than reformatory, and yet is notable for its deficiency in previous convictions. In marital state it is undistinguished; in occupation notable for excesses of extractives and clerical persons, and deficiency in unskilled laborers. Actually, it ranks first in extractives, second in clerical work, and next to last in unskilled laborers and personal servants. Its sole statistical differentiation of certain significance in education is an excess of college men. It ranks fourth of the nine types in education, just above the pure Nordic type.

The only absolutely certain offense differentiation of the Predominantly Nordic type is a deficiency of rapists, in which it ranks last of all types. It ranks third in second degree murder, in forgery and fraud, and in offenses against public welfare; fourth in first degree murder and robbery; and is fifth or median type in burglary and larceny. It is sixth in sex offenses other than rape. This Predominantly Nordic type is then most distinctive criminologically in its disinclination to commit sex offenses. It is not so clearly defined in offense proclivities as the Pure Nordic type.

The Predominantly Nordic criminals are inferior in most bodily dimensions to the Predominantly Nordic civilians. Most of these deficiencies are statistically significant; practically all are logically so. The criminals, however, have broader heads, foreheads, noses, and jaws; and show, as in the case of the Pure Nordic comparisons, a greater tendency to laterality in head and face indices than do the civilians, together with much lower absolute and relative head heights. More specifically, in addition to younger age and also diminished stature, shoulder breadth, and chest dimensions, the criminals have shorter and broader faces, noses, and ears, and relatively wider foreheads than have the Predominantly Nordic civilians. In morphological features the criminals show more straight hair, more gray-brown eyes, more external eye folds, more pronounced height and slope of the forehead, more extreme deviations of cheek bone prominence, less roll of the helix of the ear, and more pronounced Darwin's points.

Sociologically, the Predominantly Nordic criminals are much more strongly Old American than their mates of the check sample. They exceed the civilians in divorced and separated men, in extractives, and in unskilled laborers, and fall below them in public servants and clerks. They are greatly inferior in education to the civilians, who have more than eight times as many well educated individuals in proportion to illiterates and the unschooled.

This Predominantly Nordic type of criminal is almost the most distinctively Old American. It shows the same biological and sociological inferiority to the civilians of that type as was manifested by the Pure Nordic type. It is, on the whole, a youthful type, the third youngest in comparison with its civil counterpart of our series (mean age 27.9 years). Although it is again a rather tall, narrow type, it gives the impression of greater physical vigor than characterizes the Pure Nordics, and it is certainly more versatile, criminologically speaking.

KELTIC TYPE

The Keltic type was so named because the combination of dark hair and blue eyes with long narrow heads, and redheadedness, in general, are very characteristically present among the inhabitants of Scotland and Ireland of Gaelic speech, a language belonging to the Keltic Indo-European group. It may be noted that these pigmentation combinations are also frequent among the Welsh and the Bretons, who likewise speak Keltic languages.

Our Keltic type of Old American criminals is older by one year than the average of the entire series, is taller, heavier, longer in the body, and larger in head circumference, but it is deficient in breadth of forehead, face, nose, and jaws. It has a head which is high relative to its breadth, an elongated narrow face, and jaws which are compressed relative to breadth of the face. Nose and ears are relatively longer and narrower than in the total series. The head is low in comparison with its length and the shoulders narrow relative to stature. So we have another tall, narrow, angular type, with a horse face, a long, pinched nose, and constricted brows.

In addition to blue eyes combined with dark or red hair, these Keltics are notable for deeply wavy hair, ruddy skins, thin nasal tips, absence of jaw protrusion, and multiple loss of teeth.

The Keltic type is characterized ethnically by a significant excess of persons of Old American parentage and by a dearth of the foreign born. Its predominant extractions are Old American, Irish, and Scandinavian, and it is very poor in other national strains. This type is outstandingly represented in Kentucky and North Carolina and deficient in Tennessee and Texas. It is disproportionately strong in reformatory inmates. It has a marked excess of married men and of extractives. Actually, in occupations the Keltic type ranks second in extractives and in transportation, third in the professions and in personal service, but low in factory, trade, and clerical work. It is rather poorly educated, ranking sixth of the nine types (ratio .43).

Criminologically, the Keltic type is notable in its conformity to popular impression. It ranks first in assault just as in red hair, first in sex offenses other than rape, first in offenses against the liquor laws (versus public welfare), second in first degree murder, third in burglary and larceny, and low in rape (seventh) and in robbery (eighth). On the whole, this type specializes in crimes against persons, if it can be said to specialize. It bats a generally high average.

When this Keltic type is compared with its civilian check sample, it is noted that most of the body and head dimensions of the criminals are smaller, slightly and insignificantly in the former case, markedly in head height and head circumference. The criminals are especially shorter in nose and in ear, but they have broader foreheads and noses, and probably broader jaws and ears. The height indices of the criminal heads are notably lower; the nasal, ear, and forehead indices are higher. The Keltic criminals have more straight hair than the Keltic civilians, more blue-gray eyes, more external eye folds, more extreme deviations of forehead height, more sloping foreheads, excess of median or pointed chins, more pronounced and also more compressed cheek bones, and less rolled ear rims.

The Keltic criminals are much more strongly Old American and less Irish than the Keltic civilians; they are far oftener married than are the civilians, although they are of about the same mean age. This difference is, incidentally, contrary to the general run of criminal-civilian contrasts. The criminals also show the usual excess of extractives and unskilled laborers, and deficiency of public servants and clerks over the civilians. This occupational difference is partially due to the larger proportion of rural residents among the criminals, as contrasted with the almost exclusively urban character of the check sample. Possibly this matter of rural or urban residence also accounts to some extent for the vast disparity between the educational qualifications of the Keltic criminals and the Keltic civilians. The criminals rank sixth in education among the criminal types, the civilians second in their group. The civilians are more than fifty times as high in educational ratio as are the criminals.

The physical disparity between Keltic criminals and

RACIAL TYPES OF OLD AMERICAN CRIMINALS
GENERAL PROPORTIONS AND MOSAIC OF EXCESS FEATURES
KELTIC

Dark hair or red hair - deep waved
Blue eyes
Ruddy or pale skin
Long headed
Face relatively long and narrow
Nose relatively narrow
Nasal tip thin
Loss of many teeth
Jaws compressed
Facial prognathism absent

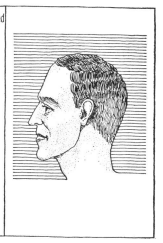

RACIAL TYPES OF OLD AMERICAN CRIMINALS
GENERAL PROPORTIONS AND MOSAIC OF EXCESS FEATURES
ALPINE

Dark curly hair
Dark eyes
Dark skin
Round headed
Relatively broad forehead
Thick eyebrows
Low, broad nasal bridge
Nasal index over 63
Short, broad face and nose
Thick nasal tip
Pronounced facial prognathism

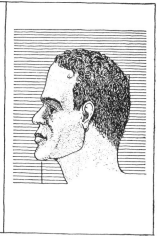

Keltic civilians is similar, but of less magnitude than those of the types previously discussed. Sociological differences, however, are enormous, possibly because of the specialization of recently immigrated Irish civilians in certain urban occupations.

ALPINE TYPE

The Alpine type was selected to include round heads with somewhat broad noses and of purely brunet pigmentation of hair and eyes. Consequently, the head is short and broad and the nose is broad (but not significantly short). This Alpine type is deficient in stature and in trunk length (sitting height), and is also low in head circumference and in face height. It has excesses of forehead and of face breadth, of sitting height compared with stature, and of head height expressed as a percentage of head length. It falls significantly below the total series in the cephalo-facial index (relation of face breadth to head breadth), in the breadth-height index of the head, in the upper and total facial indices, and in the relation of forehead breadth to face breadth (fronto-parietal index). These excesses and deficiencies describe a squat, bullet-headed, short and broad-faced type, with a relatively broad forehead and a relatively high brain case.

In the soft parts this type exhibits unduly large proportions of dark skins, curly hair, thick eyebrows, low, broad, and probably concave, blunt-tipped noses, and facial prognathism. It has a dearth of long, thin necks and creates, by the description of its outstanding differences from the total series, a slightly Negroidal impression.

The Alpine type is composed principally of native Whites of foreign parentage and of foreign born. It is deficient in Old American stock and has excesses of Italians, men from the Balkan states, French Canadians, Spanish and Portuguese, Polish-Austrians, and persons of Near Eastern origin.

It is strongly represented in criminals from Massachusetts and Wisconsin, and deficient in those from Kentucky. Occupationally, it shows a dearth of extractives and a surplus of unskilled laborers. Although many of its occupational distinctions are not statistically certain because of the small size of the group, it is extremely differentiated in its vocational rankings. Thus it ranks first in factory operatives, personal servants, professional men, and public servants, but last in extractives, transport workers, and skilled tradesmen. It is second in unskilled laborers and semi-professional men, but eighth, or next to last, in trade and in clerical work. It is an urban class, evidently drawn from a wide economic range. It is poorly educated, ranking last in this category (educational ratio .29), not because of its low percentage of well educated men, but because of its great number of illiterates and persons who have received no formal education. Its outstanding offense is armed robbery, in which it ranks easily first, but it is last in forgery and fraud. It ranks second in sex offenses other than rape, but only fifth in rape. It is low in murder, but high in assault. It takes fourth place in burglary and larceny.

The Alpine type shows the usual size inferiority when it is compared with its civilian check sample. It is particularly deficient in shoulder and chest breadths and in head dimensions. The criminal forehead, however, appears to be broader, the nose shorter, and the total face height probably shorter. The criminal ear is shorter and broader; the relative shoulder breadth of the criminals is greater; the head rounder, the face and nose relatively wider. Thus the criminals resemble the general type of the foreign born rather than that of the Old Americans.

The Alpine type criminals have straighter hair than the civilians, less dark brown hair (and probably more red-brown and black hair), less of dark brown eye color and more of light brown, more extreme deviations in both directions of forehead height, more pointed chins, and more prominent cheek bones.

Sociologically, the Alpine criminals diverge from the check sample in their ethnic composition, which is far more strongly Old American, British, Teutonic, and Portuguese, as contrasted with Near Eastern, Italian, and Irish elements in the civilians. The occupational status of the criminals is again much lower, as is indicated by a great excess of unskilled laborers. Extractives are disproportionately high in the criminals, and students and factory operatives very low. The civilian Alpines rank eighth in education as against ninth in the criminals. The former have only a little less than six times as high an educational ratio as the latter.

EAST BALTIC TYPE

The East Baltic type, as previously mentioned, consists of round heads with ash-blond or golden hair combined with blue or mixed eyes, or red hair combined with blue or mixed eyes when the nose is at least moderately broad. This is a very young group, almost seven years below mean age, and, on the whole, rather undersized. Its head, of course, is shorter and broader than average, and the upper face is shorter. The forehead and face are excessive in breadth, as are also the jaws. The relation of forehead to head breadth is lowered, the length-height index of the head is increased, and the breadth-height diminished. The forehead and face are narrow relative to head breadth, and both upper and total face dimensions are relatively short and broad.

Morphologically, this type shows excess over the total series of criminals in ruddy skins as contrasted with pale and swarthy, a surplus of low waved hair, a deficiency of the internal or so-called Mongoloid eye fold, a diminished eyebrow thickness, excess of concavo-convex nasal profiles, of teeth which are only slightly or mediumly worn, and of persons who have lost no teeth. These dental characteristics are doubtless dependent upon the tender age of the group.

The East Baltic type is disproportionately low in foreign born, but seems to run rather high in native born of foreign parentage. Its definite excesses in ethnic extraction are Russian and Polish-Austrian, which is in accordance with expectation, since these countries fall, in part, within the area of concentration of the so-called East Baltic race. This type is deficient in Italians and probably in Scotch and in French Canadians. It cannot be said with certainty to have been derived, disproportionately, so far as this criminal sample is concerned, from any state, although it is possibly significantly strong in Tennessee. It tends to be found in excess in reformatories, partly because it is our second youngest type (mean age 26.25 years). Partly for this reason also it shows a marked excess of unmarried men. Because of the small size of this group (only 177 members), we cannot be sure of the validity of its occupational diversification. It ranks first in trade, has no professional men or public servants, and is next to last in transportation and semi-professional pursuits. It is third in unskilled laborers and third in factory workers.

Its educational excesses and deficiencies fail to attain statistical validity, but, on the whole, it is well educated as criminals go, and takes second rank in the ratio of the highly schooled to the illiterate and the unschooled. Criminologically, these little round-headed blonds are quite distinctive. Their most notable offense excess is burglary and larceny, in which they take first ranking. They are third in rape, but last in bootlegging, and next to last in second degree murder, assault, and forgery and fraud. In robbery and sex offenses other than rape they rank seventh, and in first degree murder sixth. Evidently this type, like the blond Pure Nordic type, is averse to crimes against the person, but it lacks the Pure Nordic talent for forgery and fraud and is even more thievish.

The East Baltic type of criminals shows the usual tendency toward size inferiority when it is compared with its civilian check sample, although the age disparity between the two groups is insignificant. These criminal metric inferiorities attain statistical signficance in chest depth and head height, nose height and ear length, and are probably good in a number of other measurements. On the other hand, the criminals have definitely broader foreheads than the civilians. Indicially, the East Baltic criminals differ from similar civilians in relatively greater shoulder breadth, relatively lower heads in relation to length and breadth, in shorter and broader upper faces, noses, and ears. Morphologically they differ from East Baltic civilians in deficiency of blue eyes and excesses of gray-brown and (probably) green-brown shades, in their large proportion of high foreheads, in the excess of pronouncedly sloping foreheads, and in the lesser roll of the rims of the ear.

The East Baltic criminals are far more Old American and Teutonic in extraction than are the civilians of that type; they are far stronger in unskilled laborers and extractives. Naturally they are strongly deficient in public servants when compared with the check sample, perhaps because public servants, when criminals, usually evade conviction, but, more likely, because we have so many firemen in the civilian check sample. The East Baltic criminal type is also deficient in students as compared with the civilian check sample. These East Baltic criminals show absolutely large, though statistically dubious, excesses of persons in the lower educational categories, and deficiencies in the eighth grade and in college men. Yet they rank second of the nine criminal types in education. But the civilian East Baltics are easily first in their series, since they include no illiterates whatsoever, and no persons who have not attended school.

DINARIC TYPE

The pigmentally mixed, round-headed Dinarics, with their long noses, are older than the series mean, but are below standard in weight, height, chest depth, head circumfer-

RACIAL TYPES OF OLD AMERICAN CRIMINALS
GENERAL PROPORTIONS AND MOSAIC OF EXCESS FEATURES
EAST BALTIC

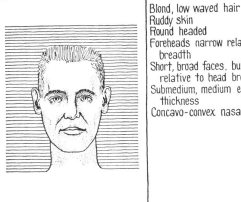

Blond, low waved hair
Ruddy skin
Round headed
Foreheads narrow relative to head breadth
Short, broad faces, but narrow relative to head breadth
Submedium, medium eyebrow thickness
Concavo-convex nasal profile

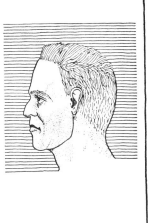

RACIAL TYPES OF OLD AMERICAN CRIMINALS
GENERAL PROPORTIONS AND MOSAIC OF EXCESS FEATURES
DINARIC

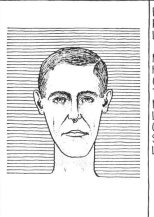

Round heads, mixed pigmentation
Pale white skin
Long narrow noses (nasal index under 63)
No eyefolds
High narrow nasal bridges
Convex nasal profile
Thin tips
Nasal septum inclined down
Loss of many teeth
Compressed jaw angles
Slight facial prognathism
Long thin necks

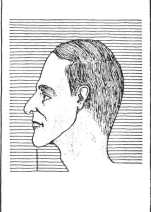

ence, and ear length. They show excesses of face breadth, upper and total face height. In body indices they display deficiencies of relative shoulder breadth and relative sitting height. Their faces are narrow relative to head breadth, as are also their foreheads, and their jaw breadths are constricted in relation to the total breadth of the face. They show head height excessive relative to head length, but deficient in relation to head breadth. Both total and upper face length are excessive relative to facial breadth. You must picture this group as men somewhat below average criminal stature, with narrow chests and slender builds, with high, short heads, broad long faces, and very long noses.

The morphological differentiae of the Dinaric criminals include excesses of pale white skin and deficiency of ruddy skins, absence of eye folds, high narrow nasal bridges with convex nasal profiles, thin tips directed downward, slight facial prognathism, compressed jaw angles, teeth with no wear, many teeth lost, undershot jaws, and long thin necks.

In nativity the Dinaric type is outstanding for dearth of Old Americans and excess of first generation and foreign born. Its predominant extractions are Teutonic, Polish-Austrian, French Canadian, Scotch, and Near Eastern, in the order named. This criminal sample was derived in disproportionate numbers from Massachusetts and Wisconsin and is notably poor in delinquents from Kentucky, North Carolina, and Tennessee. It has a probably valid excess of widowers. The Dinarics have significant occupational excesses of semi-professional men and clerks. They rank first in these two categories, second in professional men and in public servants, third in skilled trades. In other occupations their place is mediocre except in unskilled laborers, in which they drop to seventh place. The Dinarics are the best educated of all of our criminal types — an interesting fact in view of their predominantly foreign origin.

The outstanding offense proclivities of the Dinarics are an excess of rape and a deficiency of second degree murder, with a probable excess of forgery and fraud. This type ranks second in forgery, in rape, and in offenses against public welfare. It is third in sex offenses other than rape, seventh in both classes of murder, sixth in robbery and in burglary and larceny. Here, again, we have a type well differentiated in its preference for sex offenses and for the more sophisticated and profitable crimes of a gainful nature. The Dinarics appear to be further notable for a superior occupational and educational status to those enjoyed or endured by other racial types of criminals.

When we compare the criminal Dinarics with the civil Dinarics, we note that the convicts are definitely younger, lighter, smaller in chest diameters and probably in shoulder breadth, lower in head height, smaller in head circumference, narrower in face, jaws, and nose, and shorter in the ears. However, they are quite as tall as the civilians and have even greater sitting height. They possess just as long and broad heads, broader foreheads, longer upper faces, and probably longer noses. The criminals have absolutely and relatively greater sitting heights, lower heads in relation to height and breadth, and less round or brachycephalic heads. Their upper faces and noses are relatively narrower and longer, their ears much shorter and broader, and the relationships of forehead breadth to face and head breadth are also greater in the convicts.

The criminal Dinarics represent physiognomically a rather exaggerated type as compared with the civilians who fall in the same racial classification. They are, as it were, cadaverous caricatures of the Dinaric civilians. The Dinaric criminals, when compared with their civilian racial check sample, have more straight hair, more reddish-brown hair, less dark brown hair, more mixed eyes and fewer of the pure shades, more internal epicanthic and external eye folds, more extreme variations of forehead height, and more sloping foreheads. In the criminal Dinaric nose the septum is oftener inclined upward; the chin form is more frequently pointed or median, and the cheek bones compressed. Finally, slightly rolled ear rims and prominence of Darwin's point on the ear are significantly commoner in the criminals.

The criminal Dinarics are far more Old American in extraction than is their civilian check sample and also have more Teutonic elements, fewer Near Eastern, Italian, and Irish strains than the civilians. The criminals are less often married, but more frequently divorced or separated. The occupational contrasts lie in the great excesses of extractives among the criminals and a smaller excess of unskilled laborers and skilled tradesmen, together with a great dearth of public servants, students, and persons alleged to have engaged in trade. The criminal Dinarics have the unique distinction of being a tiny bit better educated than the civilian Dinarics — the only instance of this sort which occurs in our entire survey. The criminal Dinarics rank first of all racial types in education, but the civilian Dinarics last. The probable reason for this discrepancy is the recent immigrant origin of many of the civilian Dinarics as contrasted with the strong Old American strain in the criminals. The civilians have had less time to profit by the educational opportunities which this country affords.

NORDIC MEDITERRANEAN TYPE

The Nordic Mediterranean type is long-headed with darkish but mixed pigmental characters of hair and eyes. It differs from the total series in its excess of stature, of sitting height and of head circumference, in the narrowness of its forehead and face, in the extreme length of both the upper segment of the face and the total face, in the decreased breadth of the jaws, and in the large dimensions of its ears. It is also, of course, much longer and narrower of head. In index relationships it is differentiated by relatively narrow shoulders, a broad face relative to head breadth, heads low relative to their length, faces long in comparison with their breadth, relatively broad short ears, broad foreheads relative to breadth of head, and hinder angles of the jaws broad in comparison with the breadth of the face across the cheek bones. The Nordic Mediterranean is thus a somewhat narrow-bodied, lantern-jawed type, displaying rather primitive features in the excessive breadth of the face relative to that of the head.

This type of long heads also has an excess of dark skin and of low waved hair, of eyebrows which are medium or thick as contrasted with thin. It is outstanding in low foreheads, high broad nasal bridges which are straight in profile, pronounced lip seams, medium or marked facial prognathism, pronounced wear of teeth and undershot jaws.

The Nordic Mediterranean type is very strongly Old American in extraction. Its only other possible excesses in ethnic strains are Scotch and Italian. It is deficient in Scandinavians, Teutons, Polish-Austrians, and Russians. It is notably strong in Kentucky and North Carolina, curiously weak in Tennessee and New Mexico. It is also deficient in Wisconsin, and possibly in Massachusetts, but these paucities are only to be expected from the character of the immigrant stocks in the two northern states. This type is essentially prison rather than reformatory and seems to be oftener married than most other criminal types. Its only statistically valid occupational difference from the total series is a deficiency of clerical workers, in which it ranks last. It takes second place in skilled trades and third in transportation, fourth in extractives and unskilled laborers. It has an excess of illiterates, and is only the seventh in educational ranking. The Nordic Mediterranean type is the most replete with murderers, since it ranks first in first degree and second in second degree. It is not very high in any other offense, nor very low, except that it ranks next to last in burglary and larceny. We must consider that this is a mainly rural type in which opportunities for gainful offenses are limited.

When we compare the criminal Nordic Mediterraneans with their civilian check sample in physical features, we find the former to be younger, lighter, smaller in chest and shoulders, lower in head and smaller in head circumference, with shorter faces, shorter and broader noses, and shorter ears. However, the criminals have broader foreheads and probably broader ears than the civilians. The former have relatively greater sitting heights, and facial breadths greater relative to head breadth. Their heads are proportionately lower, faces shorter and relatively broader, noses and ears shorter and broader, and the relation of forehead breadth to face and head breadth is greater.

Morphologically, the criminal Nordic Mediterraneans differ from similar civilians in having more straight hair, more black and red-brown hair, more gray-brown and fewer green-brown eyes, more epicanthic and external eye folds, more extreme variations of forehead height and more sloping foreheads, more median chins, more compressed and more flaring cheek bones, more slightly rolled ear helices, and more Darwin's points.

The criminal Nordic Mediterraneans are much more strongly Old American than the civilians and have notably fewer Irish, British Canadian, English, and Welsh strains. They are much less frequently married and oftener divorced and (probably) widowed. The criminals are excessively enrolled in the extractive occupations and in unskilled labor and show a great deficiency of public servants, students, and clerks when compared with the Nordic Mediterranean civilians. They are also far less well educated, in fact roughly one-sixth as far advanced in educational attainment as measured by our ratio.

RACIAL TYPES OF OLD AMERICAN CRIMINALS
GENERAL PROPORTIONS AND MOSAIC OF EXCESS FEATURES
NORDIC MEDITERRANEAN

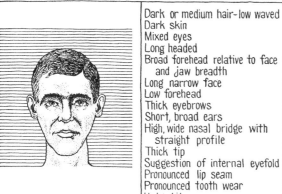

Dark or medium hair-low waved
Dark skin
Mixed eyes
Long headed
Broad forehead relative to face
    and jaw breadth
Long narrow face
Low forehead
Thick eyebrows
Short, broad ears
High, wide nasal bridge with
    straight profile
Thick tip
Suggestion of internal eyefold
Pronounced lip seam
Pronounced tooth wear
Under-bite
Medium or pronounced facial
    prognathism

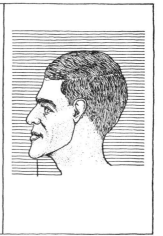

RACIAL TYPES OF OLD AMERICAN CRIMINALS
GENERAL PROPORTIONS AND MOSAIC OF EXCESS FEATURES
PURE MEDITERRANEAN

Dark, low waved hair
Dark eyes
Dark skin
Long heads
Narrow foreheads but broad relative
    to head and jaw
Long narrow faces
Thick eyebrows
High, broad, nasal bridges
Long, broad noses
Slight facial prognathism
Short, thick necks

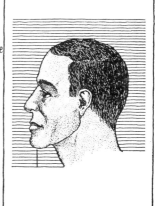

I am disposed to think that the designation, Nordic Mediterranean, for this type is a misnomer. I doubt that it is due to a cross of the above racial types. It is probably rather the survival of an Upper Palaeolithic, tall brunet, long-headed race, sometimes called Atlanto-Mediterranean — a more primitive stock than either the classical Mediterranean or Nordic races.

PURE MEDITERRANEAN TYPE

The Pure Mediterranean type consists of long heads with very dark hair and eyes. It is notably short-statured and underweight, deficient in sitting height, in head circumference, in forehead and face breadth, and in ear length. Its head is also excessively long and narrow, since it is selected partly on the basis of the low value of the length-breadth index of the skull. The face is long, the nose long and broad, and the jaws narrow. The Pure Mediterranean type has a surplus of head heights low relative to head length, but high relative to head breadth. The face is broad relative to the head breadth, but in itself narrow and long. Again, the forehead is absolutely narrow, but broad in comparison with the breadth of the brain case.

These brunet dolichocephals show, of course, an excess of olive and darker skins, and also of low waved hair and thick eyebrows. Low foreheads and high, broad nasal bridges are in evidence. The type has a deficiency of men whose teeth are unworn, and undue proportions of slight facial protrusion or prognathism. It also displays a somewhat incongruous surplus of short, thick necks.

The Pure Mediterranean type is disproportionately weak in Old Americans and has a large excess of the foreign born. The predominant strain of the latter is Italian, with a strong representation of Spanish and Portuguese and individuals of Near Eastern descent. Polish-Austrians are notably deficient, as are probably Teutons and Scotch. Massachusetts and New Mexico are the leading contributors to the criminal sample of this type, which is also strong in Colorado. Texas, Kentucky, and Tennessee yield low quotas of the Pure Mediterranean criminals.

This group has an excess of previous convictions which is probably valid, a definite dearth of married men, and a surplus of widowers. Its leading occupation is unskilled labor, in which it ranks first of all racial types. It is second in personal servants, and has no professional men. It ranks last in factory operatives and next to last in extractives and skilled tradesmen. In transport workers it is seventh. It is then an urban type of rather humble occupational status. Nevertheless, it is third in trade and public service, and fourth in clerks. While the Pure Mediterranean type has no certainly valid statistical excesses in education, it ranks next to the last in this sociological category.

The outstanding offense of this racial type is rape, in which it ranks first. However, it is also first in second degree murder, third in first degree murder, and second in assault and robbery. In spite of its preeminence in rape, it ranks eighth, or next to the bottom, in other sex offenses. It is last in burglary and larceny — the most common category of offense — and next to last in versus public welfare crimes. It is very low in forgery and fraud, ranking seventh. The Pure Mediterranean type is then outstanding for crimes of violence against persons and for its disinclination to commit crimes against property, except armed robbery. Its criminological differentiation is as clean cut as that of any other racial type.

The Pure Mediterranean criminals differ metrically from the same type of civilians in much the same manner as most criminal types diverge from civilian types. The criminals manifest generally small and statistically uncertain inferiorities of size and weight, but are significantly low in head height, length of ears, and nose height. However, they conform to other racial types in exceeding the civilians in forehead breadth, nose breadth, and jaw breadth. The head height relative to breadth and length is apparently lower in the criminals; the face, nose, and ears shorter and broader; and the relation of forehead breadth to face and head breadth higher. Morphologically the criminals display more straight hair, more red-brown hair, probably more black hair, and less dark brown hair than the civilians, more internal and external eye folds, higher and more sloping foreheads, more pointed chins, more pronouncedly flaring cheek bones, and less roll of the helix of the ear.

The sociological comparison of Pure Mediterranean criminals with the same type in civilians indicates that the former include a far greater proportion of Old Americans and an excess of Scotch. The type, as compared with civilian Mediterraneans, is definitely low in Near Easterners, and probably in Italians.

Maritally the Pure Mediterranean criminals differ from their check sample in their deficiency of single men. The usual occupational differences are to be noted, caused in part, no doubt, by the predominantly urban character of the civilian check sample. Thus the criminals are far stronger in unskilled laborers and extractives, much weaker in trade, public service, factory operatives, students, and skilled tradesmen. There are also great contrasts in educational qualifications. The civilians have about seven times as high an educational ratio as the criminals.

NORDIC ALPINE TYPE

The Nordic Alpine type includes, by the sorting criteria, round heads of mixed pigmentation and relatively broad noses. It is above mean age and average weight, but short in stature and in trunk length, and deep in the chest. The head is short, broad, and rather high, and probably significantly low in girth. The face, forehead, nose, and jaws are broad, but facial and nose lengths are short. The shoulders are slightly narrower relative to stature than is the case in the total series; the head is high with reference to its length, but low in comparison with its breadth. Jaw breadth expressed as a percentage of face breadth is low, as is also forehead breadth in relation to total head breadth.

Morphologically this mixed Nordic Alpine type shows a dearth of very dark skins and a surplus of external folds of the upper eyelids. The broad nose is of medium height and frequently concave in profile. The nasal tips are commonly thick, but there is an excess of downward inclined nasal septa. Facial prognathism or protrusion is absent in a disproportionately large percentage of cases, and the hinder angles of the jaws tend to be flaring. Markedly worn teeth, excess of slightly undershot jaws, and necks both slender and thick are also features of the Nordic Alpine type.

The Nordic Alpine type is composed of a disproportionately large number of first generation Americans and foreign born. Apart from its deficiency of Old Americans, it is probably unduly low in English, Welsh, Scandinavians, and Scotch. Its strength is in persons of Polish-Austrian, Russian, Teutonic, French Canadian, Jewish, and Balkan descent. Massachusetts, Texas, and Tennessee are the states which exceed their quota in this criminal type, while Kentucky, North Carolina, Colorado, and New Mexico fall short of their proportional representation. This type of criminal, the oldest of our series, tends to be found in prisons rather than in reformatories. It has no certain marital distinction, but is above average in the percentage of single men.

Occupationally, the Nordic Alpine type is certainly differentiated only by a deficiency of extractives. Its highest ranking is second place in trade and its lowest seventh in personal service. It has the lowest educational rating of all types, although it falls below the Pure Mediterraneans only to a trifling extent. Again this mixed Nordic Alpine type shows no statistically certain offense differentiae. It ranks third in robbery; fourth in assault, forgery and fraud, rape, other sex offenses, and versus public welfare. It sinks to fifth in first degree murder and sixth in second degree, and is seventh in burglary and larceny. On the whole, this mixed type is the least differentiated by nature of offense.

The Nordic Alpine criminals are younger by 3.5 years, lighter by 5.5 pounds, and in many dimensions smaller than the civilians of the same type. The criminals are no shorter, but are smaller in chest and brain case measurements, except forehead breadth, in which they are possibly significantly larger. All of the criminal face measurements are also slightly lower, but the deficiency attains significance only in nose length. The criminals also have much shorter ears. In indices the Nordic Alpine criminals show probably lower relations of head height to other head dimensions, much shorter and broader noses and ears, broader foreheads relative to face and head breadth. These deviations follow the general trend of criminal-civilian difference. Morphological differences, from the point of view of the criminals, are: more straight hair, more light brown hair and less of the darker shades of brown, more gray-brown and blue-gray eyes, more external eye folds and fewer individuals with no folds, lower and more sloping foreheads, less rolled ear rims, and more pronounced Darwin's points on the ear.

The criminal Nordic Alpines have been derived from Old American stock to a greater extent than are the civilians, and the former also include deficiencies of Irish and Near Easterners. Single and divorced men are greatly in excess among the criminals. The criminal type also shows the usual surplus of extractives and unskilled laborers, together with the natural deficiency in public servants and students. An excess of transport workers among the criminals is a further significant occupational difference. The criminals are, of course, distinctly inferior in educational attainment

RACIAL TYPES OF OLD AMERICAN CRIMINALS

GENERAL PROPORTIONS AND MOSAIC OF EXCESS FEATURES

NORDIC ALPINE

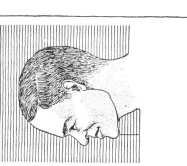

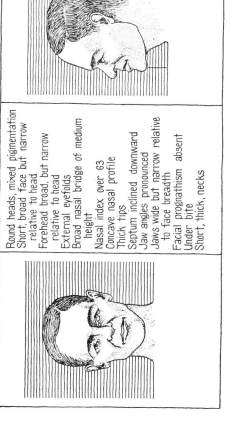

Round heads, mixed pigmentation
Short, broad face but narrow relative to head
Forehead broad, but narrow relative to head
External eyefolds
Broad nasal bridge of medium height
Nasal index over 63
Concave nasal profile
Thick tips
Septum inclined downward
Jaw angles pronounced
Jaws wide but narrow relative to face breadth
Facial prognathism absent
Under bite
Short, thick, necks

to the civilians. The latter have more than twice as high an educational ratio as the criminals.

GENERAL TRENDS OF METRIC AND INDICIAL DIFFERENCES
BETWEEN RACIAL TYPES IN CRIMINALS AND IN CIVILIANS

If we take the nine racial types of criminals, each in comparison with its similar civilian type, we find that the measurements of the criminals fall below those of the corresponding civilians, to an extent which is significant statistically, in 33.9 per cent of cases. In 8.5 per cent of cases the criminal dimensions are significantly larger than those of the civilian racial types. The remaining 5 6 per cent of dimensions show differences which are not statistically certain. In the great majority of these the criminals are smaller than the civilians. In seven of the nine pairs of racial types the criminals are younger than the civilians (in three cases only is the difference certainly significant). Also in weight seven of nine criminal types are inferior, but again only three of the differences are of certain significance. In height, further, seven of the criminal groups are inferior, but in this instance no single difference is statistically significant. In shoulder breadth all of the nine criminal types show minus deviations, but only three are significant. All of the criminal types are deficient in chest breadth, in five cases significantly so. A similar condition obtains in chest depth. In sitting height, head length, and head breadth there are no certain trends of deviation, since the criminals sometimes surpass the civilians and about as often fall below them. Head height and head circumference show a virtual unanimity of criminal inferiority. Not all of the deviations are statistically significant, but all point in the same direction. All of the criminal types have broader foreheads than the corresponding civilian types, although this difference may have been slightly exaggerated by a personal equation which developed in the taking of this measurement. On the whole, however, I believe the criminal superiority in this dimension is valid. In seven of the nine types criminals also have broader faces, but the only significant difference statistically is in the opposite direction. Total and upper face heights of criminals are also lower in seven of nine cases, but in two pairs of cases only are these inferiorities statistically dependable. On the other hand, criminals have certainly shorter noses in eight of nine pairs of types, and in six cases the criminal nose is broader than the civilian nose (four of which are significant). There are also seven of the nine pairs in which the criminals have broader jaws. All criminal types have shorter ears than the civilians, but here again I am afraid that the probable criminal inferiority has been exaggerated by personal equation.

In indices, or relations of one measurement to another, the criminal trend of difference from the civilian is in the direction of greater criminal transverse diameters relative to vertical diameters. The criminals have greater sitting height relative to stature (four significant differences). Relative to stature, shoulder breadth of the criminals is usually greater. The relation of head height to head length and head breadth is commonly less in the criminals than in the civilians. In eight of the nine pairs, criminals have relatively shorter and broader faces, and in three of these cases the differences are statistically reliable. The nose is relatively shorter and broader in eight of nine criminal groups when compared with the civilian types. The relation of forehead breadth in the criminals to breadth of face and breadth of jaws is generally elevated, but again these differences may not be wholly dependable because of suspected personal equations in the measuring of forehead breadth. The Dinaric criminal type diverges from its civilian check sample in a generally contrary and opposite direction to that displayed by the other types. This perversity of the criminal Dinaric deviations may be due to the fact that this particular racial type is rather too much of a miscellany in pigmentation (i.e. it includes too many pigment combinations) and should be resolved into two or more types. The actual ethnic extraction of our criminal Dinarics is rather different from that of the civilian check sample.

MORPHOLOGICAL DIFFERENCES

In observed morphological characters of the soft parts, aside from those actually used in sorting out the nine different types, the criminals differ from the civilians of the same type in a minimum of 17 per cent of subcategory features found in the Pure Nordics and in a maximum of 70 per cent of variations of total features in the Nordic Mediterranean type comparison. The general trend of these differences suggests that the criminals usually have straighter hair, more of the mixed patterns of eye color, more of the various kinds of skin folds of the upper eyelids, lower and more sloping foreheads, more pointed chins, more extreme variations in the projection of the cheek bones, ears with less roll of the helix or rim, and more frequent occurrence of the cartilaginous nodule on the ear rim which is called Darwin's point — the vestige of the free tip of the mammalian ear.

The racial type deviations of criminals from civilians suggest stunted growth and inferior development of the former in most cases, but they also indicate quite as clearly a diminished criminal adaptability. The morphological trends are not so unequivocal, but, on the whole, they point toward a condition on the part of the criminals which appears more primitive, but probably is to be interpreted as the pseudo-primitiveness of degeneracy. There can be no doubt that each criminal racial type is biologically inferior to the same type as exemplified in the civilian check sample.

SOCIOLOGICAL DIFFERENCES

The differences between the criminal and civilian racial series in proportionate representation of the several types, in ethnic extraction, and in general sociological characters

are conditioned by so many factors that they are often difficult to interpret. First of all, if we compare the percentages
of the nine racial types in the civilian series of 815 individuals and in the criminal series of 5689 individuals, respectively, we observe certain striking inequalities. For example,
the civilian series includes 10.19 per cent more of Dinarics
and 7.79 per cent less of Nordic Alpines. Slight excesses of
Pure Nordics, Alpines, and Pure Mediterraneans are found
among the civilians, and slight excesses of Predominantly
Nordics, Keltics, East Baltics, and Nordic Mediterraneans
in the assemblage of criminals. But it would be unsafe to
assume that these differences mean that one or another type
is necessarily more or less criminalistic, for the reason that
the criminal series is drawn from the population of ten
states, largely rural, whereas the civilian check sample is
predominantly derived from urban Boston. The racial
composition of urban Boston among the law-abiding populations probably differs somewhat from that which would
be found in an absolutely representative civilian sample
gathered from all of the states studied in the survey.

Again, in the matter of ethnic derivations and extractions,
it has been stated repeatedly that this or that criminal racial
type is much more strongly Old American than is the same
type in the civilian check sample. Actually the entire criminal racial series is 69 per cent Old American, whereas the
native Whites of native parentage in the civilian racial series
comprise only 36 per cent of their series total. Consequently, any statement that a racial type is more largely
derived in the criminal sample from Old Americans has
no inevitable criminological significance, because of the
disparate derivations of the total series. These difficulties
of interpretation pervade the sociological comparisons of
criminals and civilians. Although it may be asserted that
the nine criminal types are vastly inferior in sociological
status to the corresponding civilian types, it is probable that

some of the differences are conditioned by the matter of urban or rural residence.

An even more interesting and important question is the extent to which criminological differences within the racial types series of delinquents may be effected by the varying nativity compositions — Old American, first generation American, or foreign born — of the nine types. When we compare first generation Americans with foreign born of the same ethnic derivation — both criminals — we find that the children of immigrants tend in most cases to diverge from the violence offenses, which are prominent among the foreign born, toward acquisitive crimes. Thus it might be contested that racial offense differences may be in part attributable to the varying nativity compositions of the several racial types. This matter is one which will require a careful examination in the second large volume of our technical series, which will include all discussions of first generation and foreign born criminals and of race in all White criminals. At the moment it may be stated that certain racial types within the criminal series are virtually identical in nativity composition. For example, the Pure Nordic and Keltic types are composed of practically the same proportions of Old Americans, native born of foreign parentage, and foreign born. Nevertheless, these two types differ profoundly in offense rankings, since the Keltics are very high in murder, assault, and other sex crimes, whereas the Pure Nordics are last in all of these offenses. In acquisitive offenses the two types are closely similar only in their low percentages of commitments for robbery (almost identical), and in their high rankings in burglary and larceny. In the latter category the Nordics rank second and the Keltics third, but the Nordics far outstrip the Keltics in actual percentage of individuals convicted of this type of offense (difference 7.06 per cent).

As another example we may select the Dinaric and Nordic

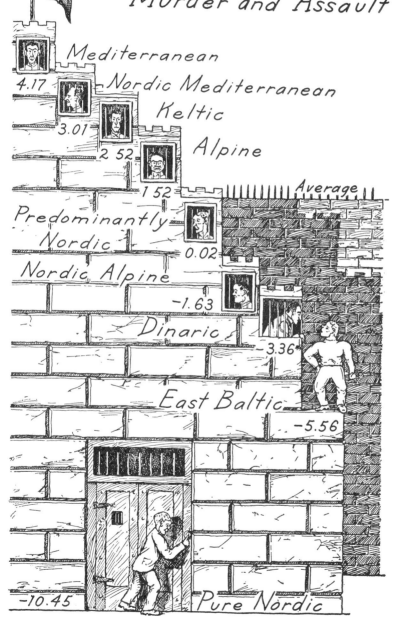

OFFENSE RANKINGS
OF RACIAL TYPES
Murder and Assault

Mediterranean

4.17

Nordic Mediterranean

Keltic

3.01

Alpine

2.52

1.52

Average

Predominantly
Nordic

0.02

Nordic Alpine

−1.63

Dinaric

−3.36

East Baltic

−5.56

−10.45

Pure Nordic

Alpine types which are again of virtually identical nativity composition. These two types rather resemble each other in murder and assault, although the Dinaric type is consistently somewhat lower in ranking. The Nordic Alpine type markedly exceeds the Dinaric in robbery, whereas the positions are reversed in the case of forgery and fraud, and rape.

In sociological categories other than offense, the two pairs of criminal types selected for practical identity in nativity composition are similarly divergent, each racial type from the one with which it is matched in nativity. Thus the Pure Nordic and Keltic types are occupationally dissimilar, and rank respectively fourth and sixth in educational ratios with .66 and .43. The Pure Nordics tend to be much better educated. The Dinaric and Nordic Alpine types differ from each other occupationally particularly in the primacy of the former in semi-professional and clerical occupations, and educationally in the substantial superiority of the Dinarics. The Dinarics rank first in educational ratio (.78) and the Nordic Alpines fifth (.48). Physically, of course, these two types are both very composite, both brachycephalic and of mixed pigmentation, but the Dinaric has a long narrow nose, and the Nordic Alpine has a short broad nose.

In the main, there seems to be no valid reason for attributing racial offense differences to this matter of disparity of nativity composition, and the same holds true for most other sociological categories. One might consider that the types most overloaded with the foreign born would be likely to have the poorest educations, and this is true in the case of the Mediterranean and Alpine types, which are most strongly foreign born in derivation. However, the Dinaric type, which ranks fourth in foreign born members, outstrips all of the others in educational ranking.

One could as reasonably attribute the general sociological differences between the first generation Americans and the foreign born of the same ethnic antecedents to differences in

OFFENSE RANKINGS OF RACIAL TYPES

Burglary, Larceny, Fraud

1 Nordic

2 East Baltic

3 Nordic

4 Predominantly Dinaric/Keltic

5 Alpine

6 Nordic-Alpine

7 Nordic-Medit.

8 Alpine

9 Nordic-Medit.

racial composition between the groups, as to assign differences between the racial types to disparities of nativity. When we find trends of difference between comparable native born of foreign parentage and foreign born of the same antecedents, we not unreasonably tend to attribute these differences to change of environment and nativity. When similar differences occur between racial types, since we are studying racial types, the differences ascertained seem to be racial. Both environmental and hereditary influences operate continuously upon any group. Differences between native born and foreign born of the same stocks are examined mainly on the basis of a classification which is set up on criteria of environmental change. Differences between racially selected groups are explored from the point of view of varying hereditary physical complexes. Each yields its own substantially valid results, but in each case the interpretation of the results is complicated by at least some minor influence of the etiological factor which we are for the moment attempting to exclude, and consequently are neglecting.

CONCLUSIONS ON RACIAL TYPES IN CRIMINALS

The principal importance and interest of this sub-investigation of our survey — this wheel within a wheel — may now be recapitulated. Most laymen and many anthropologists talk about "race" emotionally, without having any clear conception of what they mean by the term. They do not even realize that race is a matter of physical heredity. It is a rallying cry of bigots, of ignoramuses, of evil men who utilize its symbolism to arouse mass hatreds for the perpetration of social injustice. To no one is this prostitution of science more utterly detestable than to the physical anthropologist who has devoted a large part of his career to the classification and analysis of the physical characters of races. It is a notorious fact that nations are not synonymous

OFFENSE RANKINGS
OF RACIAL TYPES

Robbery

Nordic

Keltic

Dinaric

East
Baltic

Predom.
Nordic

Nordic
Med.

Nordic
Alpine

Mediter-
ranean

Alpine

with races. All nations consist of racially mixed peoples. The Germans are not a pure race; they are not a race at all, but only a hash of racially mixed Whites. They are no more Nordic than are the Finns. The term Aryan does not connote race nor physical characteristics of any sort. It is purely linguistic, and languages are learned, borrowed, and swapped about, irrespective of the physical heredity of the speaker. It is wholly possible on philological grounds that the American Negro has as much right to call himself an Aryan as has any Italian or German. The so-called Aryan languages were imposed upon a non-Aryan speaking population in Italy late in the Bronze Age and there is good evidence in favor of the view that Germanic was a language learned by a non-Aryan people. All of the trash about Nordics and Aryans which has been trumpeted by the dictators of Fascist states and by their kept professors can be dismissed as barefaced lies, which no one with a knowledge of anthropology and with the slightest rudiment of scientific judgment believes. I trust that I have made clear my position in this matter.

In this investigation, almost, if not quite for the first time, a very large body of White adult males has really been divided into racial types according to the combinations of alleged racial characters actually exhibited by individuals. If the types so distinguished are not in reality "racial types" they are, at any rate, physical types, within each of which the individuals so resemble each other that any student of zoological classification would declare them to be closely related by reason of descent. The object of this sorting into racial types was primarily to ascertain whether the types so delimited were differentiated criminologically. The answer is flatly "yes." These putative racial physical types are as distinct from each other sociologically as physically. Now of these nine types, those theoretically the most pure are the Pure Mediterranean, the pure Nordic, the Alpine, and the East Baltic. The others are frankly composite: Predominantly Nordic, Nordic Alpine, Nordic Mediterranean, Keltic, and Dinaric. They are supposed to be either secondary races, or merely types resulting from the mixture of two of the primary White races. Now the remarkable result of this investigation is that the "pure" racial types are those which are most sharply delimited in their criminal proclivities, and often also in their educational attainments and in their choice of occupations. Further, the ethnic extractions of these purer racial types are, for the most part, restricted to the nationalities which in the European homeland are supposed to cluster about the focus of distribution of that particular racial type.

Thus the blond, long-headed Pure Nordic type is principally British and Scandinavian, ranks first in two occupations and last in several others, is an easy leader in forgery and fraud, a strong second in burglary and larceny, and last or next to last in all crimes against persons. Again, the brunet, round-headed Alpine type is largely composed of Italians, Spanish, Portuguese, French Canadians, and Central or Southeastern Europeans. It also ranks first in four occupations and ninth or last in two others. It is the most poorly educated type and ranks first in robbery but last in forgery and fraud. The blond, round-headed East Baltic type is particularly strong in Russians and Polish-Austrians, ranks first in trade, but has no professional men nor public servants, takes first place in burglary and larceny, and is notably low in offenses against the person, except rape.

The frankly composite or mixed racial types also have their sociological differentiae, but they are not in general so extreme. It can scarcely be argued that the criminological unities displayed by the various racial types are really due to their national compositions, because each racial type includes, in addition to several nationalities, a strong and often preponderating nucleus of Old Americans, although the latter are most characteristically concentrated in certain of the mixed racial types.

On the whole, I think it may be stated that criminological differentiation according to these sorted racial physical types is more clear cut than that which is based upon nationality alone. In other words race, if it is race, seems to be a stronger determinant of nature of crime than nationality. However, to this generalization, at least one exception must be made. Italians as an ethnic or national group are more strongly differentiated in their criminal proclivities than any physical type which we have been able to sort out by racial criteria.

In general, also, racial differentiation in choice of offense seems to supervene body build differentiation. But here again exceptions must be made in the cases of the extreme body build types, such as the short-heavy which is so remarkably addicted to sex offenses, and so strongly averse from murder, the tall-slender which is non-sexual and given to homicide and robbery, and the short-slender which is specialized in burglary and larceny. But these body build types, although distributed sporadically in the extraordinarily mixed Old American stock, and therefore seemingly due to familial or individual causes, are probably in the last analysis the result of the segregation of racial characters.

We found initially, among the Old Americans, a very strong criminological and physical diversification by state of birth or incarceration. The state differentiation, both sociological and anthropological, is probably quite as strong as, if not stronger than, racial type differentiation. It is due to several factors: inbreeding and local variation, state mores and state idiosyncrasies of criminal law and justice, rural or urban character of the population, the personal equations of the two observers who have studied the various states, and, finally, the ethnic and racial blends which have entered into the composition of the prison population of each state. But this thread of racial heredity is clearly discernible in

OFFENSE RANKINGS OF RACIAL TYPES

SEX

Dinaric · Mediterranean · Alpine · Nordic Alpine · East Baltic Keltic · Nordic Mediterranean · Predominantly Nordic · Pure Nordic

+2.65 +2.27 +.72 +.56 +.53 +.16 −.30 −3.02 −3.97

Average

state physical differentiation and it may constitute a vital criminological determinant. Race, after all, is nothing other than the generalized hereditary background of physical characters, and possibly of mental and temperamental characteristics — the large nexus of features from which special variations are chosen by familial heredity and by other factors to constitute the individual combination which makes the personality.

Now, however repugnant it may be to sociologists and to emotional protagonists of democracy and equality, this body of evidence suggests, if not proves, that race is definitely associated with choice of crime, and with sociological status. There is, however, no implication whatsoever that these racial differences in criminal propensities are evidences that one race is superior to another, or that various races may be graded qualitatively — as good, bad, or indifferent — on the basis of the amount of antisocial behavior which their members exhibit. On the contrary, these data seem to me to prove that crime is not due to race, but merely varies in conformity with racial predilection. Every race is criminalistic, and within every race it is the biologically inferior — the organically unadaptable, the mentally and physically stunted and warped, and the sociologically debased — who are responsible for the majority of the crimes committed. Each race has its special abilities and its quota of weaknesses. Each produces its pitifully few men of genius, its hordes of the mediocre, its masses of morons, and from the very dregs of its germ plasm, its regiments of criminals.

CHAPTER VIII

THE CRIMINAL AND CIVIL INSANE:
THE HIERARCHY OF DEGENERATION

You are, no doubt, familiar with the remark which the social reformer, Robert Owen, made to his business partner: "All the world is queer save thee and me, and even thou art a little queer." If this saying was originally intended to be humorous, it has now lost that rich incongruity which is the essence of humor, and has become something in the nature of a valid sociological generalization, if not an eternal verity. It contains the implication that sanity is relative to the individual, behind the devastating statement that most people are crazy. The problem of the insane of modern populations is such that the egotistical yet naïve statement of the uplifter ceases to be a joke. One of the most acute problems of higher education is that of the psychotic student; mental disease is present and recognizable in every social and economic class. Alfred Korzybski in his work, "Science and Sanity," emphasizes the malignant rôle of language in creating misunderstandings of the meaning of words ("semantic" difficulties) which result in psycho-physiological disturbances in the human organism. He attributes these semantic difficulties in part to the Aristotelian logic which has impregnated Indo-European languages and syntax, with artificial abstractions and categorizations in which body is separated from mind, thoughts from emotions, speech from other sorts of motor actions, et cetera. Korzybski points out that the misunderstandings of these highly complex linguistic usages actually set up in individual organisms muscular tensions and colloidal disturbances which short-circuit the brain — cut out the participation of the cerebral cortex from the processes of muscular response to nervous stimuli, thus reducing the unfortunate human individual to an animal dependent upon and controlled by simple reflexes through the thalamus. Thus a great many persons from their youth upward have been so continuously frustrated by their sheer inability to grapple with the intricacies of language and semantics that their attempts at adjustment have resulted in the mental state which we call insanity. They have acquired their own individual meaning of meanings, and so they are crazy. There is a great deal of truth in this suggestion and explanation, but behind them there is implied the hypothesis that those men who are licked by linguistic difficulties owe their defeat to the fact that they are inferior organisms, unable to cope with the demands for the most intricate type of conditioned responses continually made upon them by modern civilization.

And now, lest I involve you and perhaps myself in semantic difficulties and frustrations by a further exposition of the etiology of insanity, I will state simply that a part of the survey which I am summarizing deals with the anthropological status of the insane, whether criminal or civil. It is our purpose to ascertain whether the criminal insane of a given race and nationality are physically and sociologically different from the civil insane of the same ethnic origin, if and how the insane criminal differs from the sane criminal, and the same in the case of the sane and insane civilians. This is a large order which we cannot hope to fill adequately. We can only offer samples.

Our data relating to insane Whites were gathered principally in Massachusetts institutions and by one observer only. About 1500 male insane were studied, of whom approximately 700 were criminal insane and the rest civil insane. These numbers would appear to constitute adequately large series, but unfortunately they have to be divided into 24 subgroups according to nativity and parentage, criminal or civil classification. The totals of these subgroups range from 10 to 300. Many of them are far too small for elaborate statistical treatment. Life is so short and crime is so long that we cannot elucidate here all of the gruesome details of resemblance and difference between native born and foreign born, civilian and criminal insane, in the case of British, Irish, French Canadian, Italian, Polish-Austrian, Teutonic, Near Eastern, and Spanish-Portuguese stocks, respectively. Of course the few groups of adequate size have been subjected to all of the standard statistical processes. But in order to utilize as far as permissible the wretched little groups, ranking tables listing means and percentages of various characters for each of the 24 groups have been drawn up. These ranking tables include 9 criminal subgroups of the insane and 15 civil subgroups. Of these 24 subgroups, 11 are native born of certain ethnic parentages, and 13 are foreign born. A perusal of these tables permits one to appraise the general trend of differences not only between criminal and civil insane, but also between the native born of any ethnic parentage and the foreign born of the same parentage, and between first generation Americans as a whole and those of alien birth. When evidence is drawn from multiple pairs of samples, even when many of them are quite small, the results of universal trends of difference are reliable, in spite of their statistical inadequacy. However, in the case of the native born Whites of native parentage, the groups are large enough for the usual statistical treatment involving the calculation of probable errors of differences, and this procedure has been followed.

Not very much can be done with the details of mental classification in these Old American insane groups, since in both criminals and civilians Dementia praecox is the predominant disease. This diagnosis applies to 57.6 per cent of criminal insane and to 55.7 per cent of civil insane. It is of some interest to note that 8.85 per cent of the civilians are classified as epileptics, but only 2.94 per cent of the criminals. Alcoholic psychoses account for 7.65 per cent of criminals, but only 1.97 per cent of civilians. Mental deficiency is a diagnosis which covers 18.8 per cent of the criminal insane and only 8.8 per cent of the civil insane.

The study of the offenses committed by insane criminals is not particularly profitable, because the largest offense group is miscellaneous or undefined. The criminal insane are apparently often committed on the basis of mental condition and generally delinquent behavior, rather than because of any specific criminal acts which they may have performed. Nature of offense and previous convictions are frequently unreported by our field observer.

OLD AMERICAN INSANE — CIVIL AND CRIMINAL

We may first consider summarily the detailed comparison between 170 Old American criminal insane and 300 Old American civil insane. In the case of these native Whites of native parentage we are also able to deal with two disease subgroups as compared with the total series — Dementia praecox and mental deficiency. Sex offenses are very characteristic of the deficient group (25 per cent), whereas the Dementia praecox patients are fairly well distributed among the various offense classifications. Forgery and fraud and offenses against public welfare are virtually unrepresented in the Old American insane. The marriage rate of insane criminals is only about half as high as in the insane civilians, but part of the disparity is presumably due to age, since the civilians average nearly 12 years older than the criminals.

Illiteracy is much higher in the insane criminal series than in the civilians, and it is higher in the deficient subgroup of criminals than in the Dementia praecox subgroup. The civilians are, on the whole, vastly better educated than the criminals. The ratio of the well educated to the illiterate is more than eight times as high in the civilians (.50) as in the criminals (.06).

Insane criminals seem to have been derived in greater proportion from urban areas than are the civil insane, since the former show nearly 13 per cent more of unskilled laborers (criminals 42.6 per cent, civilians 29.7 per cent) and the latter nearly 10 per cent more of extractives (criminals 13 per cent, civilians 22.8 per cent). The general occupational status of the civilians is also much higher than that of the criminals. Just as the sociologically inferior are selected for delinquency in the sane population, so in the insane the criminal is more ignorant and of a humbler occupational status than the civilian.

The mental disease subgroups of the criminals — Dementia praecox and mental deficiency — are not anthropometrically differentiated from the total insane criminal series of which they form a part, although the mentally deficient subgroup shows many suggestions of undersize. But the total Old American criminal insane series is distinct in measurements and indices from the corresponding civil insane series. The criminals are nearly 12 years younger and have narrower foreheads and probably smaller head and face measurements, shorter trunks, possibly shorter stature, but deeper chests. The criminals have relatively longer and narrower ears and relatively narrower foreheads.

However, the insane Old American criminals differ even more remarkably from the total series of presumably sane Old American criminals. The insane are pronouncedly smaller in most bodily dimensions, but they are superior to the sane criminals in head height, nose length, and ear measurements. In indices the insane show proportionately higher heads, much longer and relatively narrower noses and ears, and foreheads which are relatively as well as absolutely more constricted. The civil insane differ just as tremendously from the sane civilian check sample gathered in Massachusetts, and in very much the same way. They are much older, shorter, and lighter than the civilians, have smaller chests, narrower shoulders, shorter trunks, smaller heads, faces, and ears. They are more long-headed than the sane civilians, have narrower faces relative to head breadth, and absolutely smaller and relatively shorter and broader ears.

Of the numerous morphological differences between criminal and civil insane, both Old American, a few of the more striking may be mentioned here. Moles and tattoo marks are much commoner among the criminals (in each case reported nearly eight times as often). The latter are also more pallid than the civilians, perhaps because they are more closely confined. The criminals have darker hair, and more hair of fine texture than have the insane civilians. Whether in the criminal or in the civil series, Dementia praecox patients tend to have lighter hair than their total series, and lighter eyes. But eye color, contrary to hair color, seems to run darker in the civil series than in the criminal series. Low and slanting eye slits are considerably commoner among the criminals than among the civilians. Thin and non-concurrent eyebrows which are in excess among the criminals are perhaps to be ascribed in part to the younger mean age of the insane delinquents. More extreme variations of height and slope of the forehead seem to characterize the criminals as contrasted with those who are law-abiding, though crazy. The criminals have higher bridged noses with more compressed nasal wings and more frequently drooping tips. The delinquents also have thinner integumental lips with less marked lip seams, fuller cheeks, teeth more worn and more frequent loss of many teeth, commoner edge-to-edge bite, more high, narrow palates, and more mouth-breathers. The civilians have less protruding occiputs than have the criminals and more

OLD AMERICANS
CRIMINAL AND CIVIL INSANE
MOSAIC OF DIFFERENCES

CRIMINAL INSANE

12 years younger
Absolutely and relatively
    narrower foreheads and ears
More moles
Darker hair
Low and slanting eye slits
Thinner eyebrows
Higher nasal bridges, more
    compressed wings and drooping
    tips
Fuller cheeks
Thinner integumental lips, less
    marked lip-seams
More mouth-breathers
More protruding occiputs
Less crown flattening

Criminal

Civil

Criminal

Civil

frequent flattening of the crown of the head (lambdoid flattening).

On the whole, the Old American criminal insane, although younger than the civilians, seem to represent a physically inferior sample, and also present a number of differences which suggest a distribution of racial blends and constitutional types which may diverge from those prevalent among the civil insane of similar ethnic antecedents. Physically and sociologically the Old American insane criminals are at the bottom of all of our Old American series. This bottom is very low and slimy. It is thickly populated with human creatures who ought not to exist.

OLD AND NEW AMERICAN INSANE — CIVIL AND CRIMINAL

We may now proceed to consider the results obtained by ranking 24 groups of the insane, criminal and civilian, according to nationality and parentage. A study of the mean age of groups in relation to marital status shows that there is no close relationship between the two. All civilian groups, except the small sample of first generation French Canadians, show higher marital rates than the criminals of corresponding ethnic origin. Foreign born groups generally show higher percentages of married men than do the native born of foreign parentage. Notable in the rankings are the high marital rates of Polish-Austrian and Italian criminal insane. In percentage of married men the French Canadian civil insane lead with 48.7, closely followed by the Irish civil insane with 42.9 per cent. The Old American civil insane are in ninth place, the criminals in fifteenth place. At the bottom of the groups represented by fairly adequate numbers of individuals are the first generation British criminals with but 8.9 per cent of married men. One of the few pleasing findings of this survey is that all of the insane, criminal or civil, have very low marriage rates when compared with the males of the general population. It is to be

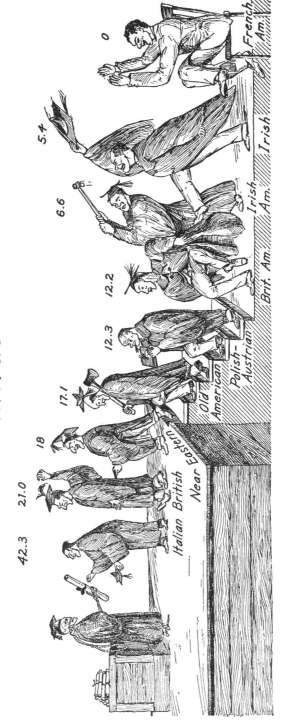

OFFENSE RANKINGS OF THE INSANE

Murder

42.3 21.0 18 17.1 12.3 12.2 6.6 5.4 0

Italian British Near Eastern Old American Polish-Austrian Brit. Am. Irish Am. Irish French Am.

hoped that this means relatively few offspring of insane parents who are law-abiding and still fewer fathered by insane criminals. However, all persons do not provide themselves with marriage certificates before they reproduce their kind.

Nine ethnic groups of insane criminals provided a basis for ranking by nature of offense. The offense categories are combined murder, assault, combined robbery, burglary and larceny, combined sex offenses, and drunkenness (which may be considered a weakness rather than an offense). The Italian insane far outstrip all other groups in combined murder (42.3 per cent) and in assault (14.1 per cent). They also rank second in combined sex offenses, but last in drunkenness and next to last in offenses against property. The native born of French Canadian parentage are easy leaders in combined burglary, robbery, and larceny (33.3 per cent), and also in combined sex offenses (20.8 per cent). They are, moreover, second in assault (8.3 per cent). However, they commit no murder (on the basis, of course, of our small sample). The foreign born Irish rank easily first in drunkenness (23 per cent), and are followed at a distance by the native born of Irish parentage (13.2 per cent). On the other hand, the Irish are last in crimes against property and next to last in combined murder. None of the other groups of the criminal insane have any particular distinction in offense ranking. It is clear, however, that the native born of foreign parentage are particularly addicted to crimes against property, whereas the foreign born lead in crimes of violence. The insane Italian criminals manifest the same preference for murder and other crimes against the persons which makes the Italians outstanding among the sane criminals. The Italian insane are by far the lowest in ill-defined and miscellaneous offenses.

In these insane groups the native born of foreign parentage are much better educated than the foreign born, and, irrespective of nativity, the criminal insane are vastly

OFFENSE RANKINGS OF
INSANE CRIMINALS
Robbery, Burglary, Larceny

inferior in education to the civil insane. A table giving the rankings based upon percentage of illiterates and those who can read and write but have never attended school shows the first nine places occupied by the foreign born. The lowest four ranks in educational inferiority are occupied by first generation Americans of foreign parentage. The Near Eastern group of criminal insane ranks first in ignorance with 88.3 per cent of illiterates or unschooled, while the first generation of civilians of Near Eastern parentage ranks last or twenty-fourth in educational inferiority. Of course, individual comparisons of the group rankings are rather misleading, since many of the groups are quite small. Old American criminal insane take fourteenth rank in educational inferiority and Old American civilians twentieth place.

The outstanding occupational difference between criminal and civil insane is that the civilians have been engaged much more largely in the extractive, rural occupations, whereas the criminals are predominantly unskilled laborers, probably of urban residence. The civilian insane are much higher in factory workers than the criminal insane, but lower in transportation and in personal service. Presumably the former generally enjoy a higher occupational status than the latter. An interesting table ranks the various groups according to percentage of unskilled laborers and compares their ranking in inferiority of education. The seven ranking groups in unskilled labor fall within the first eight places in proportion of educational inferiors. Incompatibilities between educational qualifications and percentage of unskilled laborers are sometimes found. In the civil insane of the Irish, British, French Canadian, Teutonic, and Near Eastern groups, and in the British criminal insane, the native born of foreign parentage exceed the foreign born in proportion of unskilled laborers, although the first generation in this country has almost invariably enjoyed better

CALLIPYGE LA CHAUDE IN
PERILS OF PULCHRITUDE
AND THE 57 RACKETTES

4 British

7 British-American

9 Irish-American

8 Near-Easterner

5 Irish

2 Italian Irish

3 Old American

1 French-American

6 Polish-Austrian

educational advantages. The highest proportion of unskilled laborers is found among the Irish criminal insane
(61.1 per cent), and the lowest in French Canadian civilians
(17.95 per cent).

Metric Differences

The manifold differences in anthropometric measurements and indices between these 24 separate groups of the
insane, civilian and criminal, of various nationalities and
parentage merit here only the barest summary. The civil
insane groups are generally older than the criminal insane,
and the foreign born groups are older than the native born
of the same ethnic stock. The age disparity is usually greater
between civilians and criminals of the same parentage than
between foreign born and native born of the same nationality. This generalization suggests that the younger mean ages
of the criminal insane are related more closely to the age
incidence of criminality than to place of nativity.

The criminal insane are commonly heavier than the civil
insane of the same ethnic origin, and the first generation
born in this country is usually inferior in weight to the
foreign born of similar antecedents. Stature rankings seem
to depend upon race and nationality more largely than
upon nativity and criminal or civilian status. The tallest
groups are Old Americans, British, Irish, Scandinavians,
and Teutons, whereas the lowest rankings are occupied by
Italians, Portuguese, French, et cetera. The insane, of whatever nationality and parentage, tend to be shorter than the
sane of similar origin.

There is a marked tendency for the criminal insane to
exceed corresponding civil insane groups in chest dimensions. The foreign born tend to have bigger chests than the
native born of the same nationality. The civil insane usually
surpass the criminal insane in sitting height and the first
generation Americans have greater sitting heights, as a rule,

OFFENSE RANKINGS OF CRIMINAL INSANE

Alcoholic Psychoses

(1)
Irish
23.%

(2)
Irish–American
13.2%

(3)
Near
Eastern
10.3%

(4)
Old American
10.%

(5)
French-American
8.3%

(6)
British-American
6.1%

(7)
British
5.3%

(7)
Polish-Austrian
5.3%

(9)
Italian
5.1%

than the foreign born of the same ethnic origin. Head length is distributed mainly on racial lines, but in head breadth the civilian insane tend to surpass the criminal insane of the same nationality, and the native born of foreign parentage often have narrower heads than the foreign born of the same nationality. These trends are discernible in addition to the usual racial differences. The criminal insane have definitely greater cranial circumferences than the civilian insane in most pairs. In facial breadth (bizygomatic diameter) the principal distinction is between the native born of foreign parentage and the foreign born, the latter usually displaying the larger means. Of course, the stocks which are round-headed regularly have broader faces than the dolichocephals, irrespective of civilian or criminal status. The tendency toward diminution in head breadth and in face breadth in the first American born generation of European nationalities is clearly shown also in the groups of sane criminals and sane civilians. Nose breadths are larger in eight pairs of the criminal insane than in the civil insane of the same stock, and tend uncertainly to be somewhat smaller in the native born of foreign parentage than in the foreign born. The first American generation also has invariably narrower jaws. The criminals tend to have longer and narrower ears than their civilian mates.

The native born of foreign parentage in most of the groups have shoulders which are narrower relative to their stature than have foreign born of the same nationality. In relative sitting height the criminal insane fall below the civilians, and the first generation Americans usually, but not invariably, exceed the foreign born.

There is a very clear trend of criminal insane toward relatively longer and narrower heads than are found among the civilian insane of like origin. This is true of five ethnic pairs, but the difference is reversed in two others. Correspondingly, the criminals have longer and relatively narrower faces than the civilians (seven pairs of groups) and the same distinction holds good when the native born of foreign parentage are compared with those of their nationality born in Europe (six pairs). The native born of foreign parentage rather consistently show a reduction of the breadth-height index of the nose (nasal index) as compared with foreign born of the same nationality. The ear index is lower in all of the criminal insane than in the civil insane with whom they are compared — i.e. the ear of the insane criminal is relatively longer and narrower. The native born of foreign parentage, finally, seem usually to exceed the foreign born in the relation of forehead breadth to jaw breadth.

Group Differentiation

A few of the ethnic pairs of insane groups are of sufficient size so that it is possible to apply the statistical tests which determine whether they are, in the sum total of measurements and indices, anthropometrically distinct from each other. Thus it is possible to say that native born insane criminals of British parentage do differ significantly from British born insane criminals in that they are younger, have narrower chests, shorter heads, smaller head circumferences, diminished forehead breadths, and proportionately longer and narrower faces. In the first generation stock of British parentage the criminal insane also are physically differentiated from the civil insane. The criminals have deeper chests, longer faces, narrower foreheads, longer ears absolutely and relatively to their breadth, and jaws which are narrower in relation to forehead breadth. However, the British born insane criminals are not clearly distinguishable from the insane civilians of the same origin except in three metric features, and the American born insane criminals of British parentage are scarcely distinct in measurements and indices from the Old American insane criminals.

The native born insane criminals of Irish parentage differ from the foreign born Irish insane criminals in very much the same way as do the corresponding British groups. But the first generation Irish-American insane criminals also are anthropometrically distinct from the Old American criminal insane. The Old Americans tend to be somewhat smaller in most dimensions and especially to have shorter faces and noses, greater relative sitting height, and heads higher in relation to their breadth. Further, the Irish-American insane criminals are different also from insane civilians of the same antecedents. The criminals are younger, have longer faces, relatively and absolutely broader shoulders, reduced relative sitting height, probably deeper chests and narrower ears. Finally, the foreign born Irish insane criminals are not certainly distinguishable from insane Irish civilians, probably because of the small size of the samples which we have for study.

We have for further comparison groups of civil and criminal insane, one or both, of French Canadian, Italian, Polish-Austrian, and Near Eastern stocks. The grim business of comparing each criminal group with each civil insane group, and the foreign born with the native of foreign parentage, has been carried out to the bitter end whenever the samples were large enough, but we have already washed enough dirty linen of the insane of various nationalities, and I do not suppose that you could abide the sight of all of it hung out to dry at once. Differences between civil and criminal insane of the same national origin, and between the first generation and the foreign born, are much alike in these various groups. Perhaps most consistently the criminal insane diverge from the civil insane in the deeper chests, longer and narrower ears, and lower relative sitting height displayed by the felons.

Morphological Differentiation

We must plough on through the qualitative, morphological differences which distinguish our 24 groups of insane by comparable pairs. The following distinctions seem to present themselves in so many cases as to warrant brief mention to the surfeited reader. Moles and tattoo marks are much more frequently reported among the criminal insane than in the civilian insane. The former may possibly be considered stigmata of degeneracy; the latter certainly as marks of stupidity. The criminal insane invariably show more thick head hair than the civil insane, but this is probably due in part, if not wholly, to the fact that the civil insane are generally older. The criminal insane also appear to show larger proportions of men with light skin color than the corresponding civil insane. However, the criminal insane are presumably more closely confined than the civil insane and have less opportunity to become tanned. Darker hair seems to characterize the criminal insane as contrasted with civil insane of the same ethnic origin. Naturally, racial differences are everywhere to the fore in such a character, and, as a matter of course, we find the Teutonic groups, for example, high in blondism and the Spanish-Portuguese groups very dark in hair color. It is a rather curious fact that the criminal insane of most ethnic stocks seem to show earlier graying of the hair than the civil insane of the same stock. This may be due in part to the darker hair color of the criminals. Gray hair is more easily discernible against the darker shades of hair color.

The iris of the eye displays many variations of pattern as well as of color. A mixed eye in anthropological terminology is one in which the periphery of the iris is of some clear and usually rather light shade, whereas specks, spots, or zones of yellow, brown, or orange pigment tend to be concentrated around the pupil. This superficial pigment usually radiates out from the pupil. Such eyes are called rayed eyes. However, not infrequently the heavily pigmented part of the iris is a more or less sharply defined band around the pupil, while the peripheral zone is very light — gray, green, blue, or beer-colored. Such eyes are called zoned eyes. Both rayed and zoned eyes commonly occur in persons of medium or mixed pigmentation, as contrasted with the almost solid brown, homogeneous irides of very dark persons and the pure blue or gray eyes of blonds or persons with fair skins. Both of these varieties of mixed eyes are commonly described by laymen as "hazel," but that term is more properly applicable to a clear, light reddish-brown eye, and although used by Shakespeare, should be avoided by persons who have never seen a ripe hazel nut. At any rate, there is a very peculiar difference between many of our ethnic pairs of civil and criminal insane in that the civilians seem commonly to have many more of the zoned eyes and the criminals of the rayed eyes. Unless this phenomenon is due to an aberration of the observer, which seems doubtful, the implication may be that the mixed eyes of the criminal insane tend to be darker than those of corresponding civil insane, since the raying usually carries the superficial pigment further out into the periphery of the iris. A rayed eye may be lightly pigmented or very heavily pigmented. A zoned eye is usually nearer light than dark. Low palpebral openings or eye slits are more common in the criminal insane than in the civil insane of the same stock (8 pairs). More frequently also in the criminals the outer corner of the eye opening is depressed, so that the eyes appear to slant downward and outward, the opposite from the Mongoloid slant. Eyebrows are less often thick and concurrent and more limited in lateral extension in most of the criminal groups as contrasted with civilians of the same stock, but this difference may be due in part or wholly to the greater age of the civilians.

The prominence just above the root of the nose and between the eyes is called glabella. This elevation, which over-
lies the central portion of the frontal sinus and was called by
phrenologists the "bump of God-fearingness," seems frequently more prominent in many of our criminal insane
groups than in their civilian insane check samples. Nearly
all of the criminal insane groups seem to show excesses of
high foreheads over the civil insane — a rather inexplicable
fact which, nevertheless, agrees with an apparent superiority
in the criminals of head height, as measured with a head-
spanner. On the other hand, depressions of the root of the
nose (nasion depressions) appear to be more marked in the
civilian insane, who also have excesses of broad nasal roots
in seven of eight paired groups. Higher but wider nasal
bridges are recorded among most of the criminal groups in
comparison with the civil insane. Elevated or snubbed nasal
tips are more frequent among the criminals, but it is a well
known fact that the tip of the nose tends to become depressed
with age, and our civilians are usually older than our criminals. The criminal groups almost invariably show more
compressed or narrower nasal wings (alae) than do the
comparable civilians.

The circular muscle which surrounds the mouth like a
draw-string may be thick and well developed or thin. The
development of this muscle conditions the thickness of the
integumental lips, which are those portions of the lips
above and below the membranous lips. The integumental
lips are those parts upon which males sometimes grow
moustaches and goatees, the membranous lips those parts
upon which females usually smear paint. Now our criminal
insane invariably have excesses of thin integumental lips
over the comparable civil insane. The civilians also show a
stronger development of the raised white line at the bound-
ary between the integumental and membranous lips, which
is called the lip seam. I really have no explanation for these

curiously consistent differences which run contrary to age change, since the civilians are usually older than the criminals. Older persons more frequently have lost their teeth. When this happens the jaws shrink, the membranous lips roll inward, and the lips appear thinner and the lip seams less prominent. A thin, straight mouth line used to be regarded as an evidence of strength of character, but it is usually rather an indication of store-teeth.

Anthropologists call a pointed chin a median chin, because it has but one median bony eminence on the lower border of the jaw. A bilateral chin is a square chin, with an eminence on each side separated by a cleft or a dimple. Median chins are almost invariable in females; bilateral chins are almost exclusively male, but many males also have the weaker pointed type of chin. Curiously, nearly all of the civilian insane exceed the criminal insane in their proportions of the median or pointed chins. All of our insane groups tend to have excesses of thin cheeks. However, the civil·insane rather consistently surpass the criminal insane in the proportions of cheeks recorded as thin.

Another very strange finding is that civilian insane groups are usually less wrinkled than criminal insane groups, although the latter are invariably younger. There are also some ethnic differences in wrinkling. All Irish groups tend to show a great profusion of wrinkles, whereas wrinkling is at a minimum in Spanish, Portuguese, and Near Easterners. In pronounced wear and loss of teeth ethnic factors tend to override sociological differences. Irish, for example, usually have wretched teeth, whereas Italians and Spanish-Portuguese tend to have excellent teeth which are harder and resist wear.

The study of the morphology of the ear, a reduced and degenerative feature in man and in many of the lower primates, reveals few consistent trends of difference between criminal and civil insane of the same ethnic origin. Actual caliper measurements indicate that the criminals quite commonly have longer and relatively narrower ears than the civilians, a condition opposite to that found in the comparisons of sane criminals with sane civilians. In one morphological point only do the civilian insane appear to show a rather consistent trend of difference from criminal insane. The antihelix is the inner cartilaginous rim of the ear which borders posteriorly the concha, or shell of the ear, from which the auditory passage opens. A pronounced development of the antihelix is a progressive or possibly a degenerative feature in man. It is, at any rate, incompatible with the slightly rolled rim, or helix, and the Darwin's point upon this rim — both of which features are reminiscent of lower mammalian conditions. It is remarkable then that the first 14 of 24 rankings in prominence of antihelix are held by civilian insane groups and that each civilian group exceeds in development of this feature its criminal counterpart. Marked protrusion of the ears seems generally characteristic of our insane groups, but there is no clear trend of difference between the criminal and civil insane.

Finally, the criminal insane consistently surpass the civil insane of the same national origin in proportions of long, thin necks. This may be, in some measure, an age difference.

Now at this point I wish to interject a discussion of the reality and significance of the mass of rather confusing physical differences between insane criminals and insane civilians which I have been describing. First there arises the question as to the reality of these differences. Are they actually valid and of criminological significance, or may they be due to the accidents of small samples, or to variations of anthropometric technique and inconstancy of morphological judgment on the part of the field worker who made the observations? It may be stated at once that the odds are enormously against the hypothesis that the differences are statistically specious. Many of them have been safeguarded by the use of the standard statistical checks, and nearly all of them here stressed are manifested independently by so many pairs of ethnic groups that they are certainly not fortuitous.

We have then to consider the spectre of personal equation. Fortunately all of the measurements and observations upon the insane were taken by the same anthropologist within a short period of time. This man was already an experienced and careful observer, and it is incredible that he should have changed his measuring technique and his subjective standards of morphological judgment in moving from the Bridgewater to the Taunton asylum. I am willing to admit the possibility that some slight and unconscious shift in the qualitative and quantitative grading of features may have had the effect of overemphasizing certain differences, but I cannot think that these differences are nothing more than figments of an erratic anthropological imagination. Besides, you must know that the vast majority of measurements and morphological observations show no significant differences between criminal and civil insane, or between native born and foreign born of the same nationality, and, consequently, have gone unmentioned here. It is only in relatively few cases that these startling differences manifest themselves. Again, it should be noted that nearly all of the ethnic differences which an experienced physical anthropologist would expect to find, for example, between Italians and English, are accurately realized in these samples, although I have not discussed them here because they are irrelevant to our primary interest. Finally, the differences between first generation Americans of a specified ethnic parentage and the foreign born of the same parentage are in the main those which accord, not only with our own numerous findings in other parts of this survey, but also with the results of previous anthropological investigators, and with our own data gathered in other surveys by quite different field workers.

Consequently, I am disposed to believe that the results here briefly described are valid. I have "harped" upon this subject in these lectures, because it has demanded my very careful consideration and has caused me no little worry for years. I consider myself a fairly cautious, critical, and even suspicious appraiser of the quality of field data gathered by anthropometrists, and my public may be assured that I am even less anxious to make a fool of myself by accepting results based upon faulty material than I am to foist pseudofacts and erroneous conclusions upon gullible laymen. I am not grinding any personal axe, because I know that if I were, it would inevitably fall upon my own neck, which although naturally short and thick, by all anthropological standards, is in this survey most precariously out-stuck.

Assuming then that these physical differences which have been found to obtain between criminal and civil insane of the same ethnic antecedents are valid, what do they mean? I do not think that they are explicable by any single cause. I offer as a first tentative and partial hypothesis the suggestion that, within these various ethnic mixtures, certain specific physical combinations, selected from the mélange of racial characters, for unascertained reasons may be persistently associated with tendencies in the mentally diseased to commit various antisocial acts, particularly crimes of violence. Perhaps a clearer way of putting it would be to say that certain blends of racial features occur more frequently in the insane who commit crimes than in the insane who have not been convicted of infractions of the law.

If there is any merit in this suggestion, it ought to be brought out by the next step of our investigation, which is the sorting of the insane into racial types by the use of combinations of conventional racial characters occurring in individuals — a process which yielded rather illuminating results in the case of sane White criminals and civilians.

RACIAL TYPES OF INSANE — CRIMINAL AND CIVILIAN

It may be recalled that nine pure and mixed racial types were sorted out by the use of combinations of head form, hair and eye color, with the supplemental use, in some types, of the nasal index and of stature. Now the rarest racial type in all of our series is the Pure Nordic, which is long-headed and has ash-blond or golden hair with pure blue eyes or pure gray eyes. This type occurs in only 2.58 per cent of our total sane civilian check sample, in 1.59 per cent of sane Massachusetts criminals, but is represented by too few individuals for tabulation in our racial type series of 617 insane criminals from Massachusetts. Another rare type is the East Baltic which consists of blond round-headed men, with broad noses and eyes which are usually blue or blue-gray. This type is found in 2.45 per cent of the total civilian check sample, 3.64 per cent of sane Massachusetts criminals, and again is absent, or exists in too few numbers for statistical treatment, in the Massachusetts insane criminals. Other types which show a deficiency of representation in the criminal insane of Massachusetts as compared with the sane criminals of the same state are the Predominantly Nordic near-blond long heads, who include only 4.70 per cent of the insane criminals but 6.61 per cent of the sane Massachusetts criminals, and the Nordic Alpine type of pigmentally mixed but rather lightish round heads with broad noses, who comprise only 21.39 per cent of the insane, but 28.93 per cent of the sane Massachusetts criminals. Thus the criminal insane of Massachusetts show a total deficiency of 5.3 per cent of pure blond types as compared with the sane criminals of the same state, and a further deficiency of 9.45 per cent of medium pigmented or near-blond types.

The racial types which are markedly in excess in the Massachusetts insane criminals as compared with sane criminals from the same state are the Keltic with 13.78 per cent,

5.12 per cent more than in civilians, and the Dinaric, which comprises 22.85 per cent of the insane criminals and 8.04 per cent less of the sane. The Keltic type is long-headed with dark hair and blue eyes, or red hair and blue eyes. The Dinaric is round-headed with many combinations of medium to dark pigmentation, but always with a long and narrow nose. Other types are represented in the insane criminals about in the same proportions as in the sane, although the pure brunet, round-headed, broad-nosed Alpine type comprises 5.51 per cent of the insane series, which is nearly two per cent more than in the sane criminals.

Now let us consider the sociological and physical characteristics of those racial types which are over-represented in the insane Massachusetts criminals as contrasted with Massachusetts sane criminals. In both of these groups the leading extraction is Irish, followed closely by Old American (possibly also of Irish extraction). The Keltic group of insane criminals is 37.66 per cent Irish and the Dinaric group 18.98 per cent. However, the Keltic group includes 10 different ethnic extractions and the Dinaric, which is extremely diversified, 14 ethnic extractions. This Keltic type of insane criminals ranks first in commitments for alcoholism and alcoholic psychoses and is last in Dementia praecox. In offense ranking it is first in drunkenness, but last in robbery and in sex offenses. Occupationally it leads in skilled trades and in transportation, but is very low in personal service (sixth). Half of its members are unskilled laborers. Educationally it is in the middle position.

Physically this Keltic type is notable for its very long, high, and narrow heads; narrow foreheads, faces, noses, and jaws; long ears; tall stature and sitting height; and relatively narrow shoulders. This type is supposed to include red hair, but curiously only 5 of the entire 617 insane criminals used for racial sorting and but one of the Keltic type have red hair. Hair color is almost invariably dark brown or black;

eyes, of course, light. This type leads all others in proportions of rayed irides, is very low in eyebrow concurrency, has the maximum proportion of low foreheads, and the second highest percentage of sloping foreheads. It ranks high in high, broad nasal bridges (first), thin membranous lips (first), bilateral chins (third), wrinkles (first), poor teeth (caries first, multiple losses first), and long, thin necks (first). Now all but one of these physical features are among those in which the criminal insane exceed the civil insane. The civil insane have not been sorted for racial types, owing to the immense labor involved in this process, but it is possible to isolate the racial differences between the insane criminals and the insane civilians by considering, as we are doing, the gross differences between the two total series in the light of the racial excesses over sane criminals and civilians displayed by the insane criminals.

The Dinaric type, which is heavily in excess among the insane as contrasted with the sane criminals of Massachusetts, ranks second in combined murder and in robbery, and third in sex offenses. It also holds second place among all the criminal insane in proportion of factory workers. It is close to the ranking Predominantly Nordic type in excellence of education, and ranks first in the diagnosis of Dementia praecox, but sixth or next to last in the mentally deficient. The outstanding physical characters which it contributes to the complex of the criminal insane are round heads, especially long and narrow noses, narrow chests, and long broad faces. On the morphological side this type in the criminal series has a rather high proportion of dark hair (77 per cent) and all shades of eye color, with the intermediate green-brown predominating. Noses of high convex bridge with compressed alae are characteristic. The Dinaric type then contributes to the excess of dark hair which the total criminal insane display as contrasted with the civil insane, and also to the long faces and long, narrow noses. It further has the least protrusion of the back of the head (occipital protrusion) and the most flattening of the crown (lambdoid).

Actually, the strongest numerical element in the criminal insane is the Nordic Mediterranean type, although its occurrence (24.96 per cent) is about the same as that in the sane Massachusetts criminals. In this type Old American derivations (26 per cent) slightly exceed the Irish extractions (24 per cent). It includes slightly more than 15 per cent of Italians and scatterings of several other ethnic stocks. The Nordic Mediterranean type ranks second in sex offenses, and third in murder, assault, and drunkenness. It is second in unskilled laborers and personal servants, low in extractives and factory workers (sixth in each). This type is next to the bottom in Dementia praecox, but second in mental deficiency and in miscellaneous phychoses. Educationally, the Nordic Mediterranean type is in third place among the seven racial types of insane criminals. It is of intermediate pigmentation, usually with mixed eyes and darkish hair, and it is dolichocephalic or long-headed. It contributes to the insane criminals' narrowness of forehead, face, nose, and jaws, and is especially shallow of chest. It is the second most tattooed of all the racial types among the criminal insane (20.86 per cent). Over 88 per cent of its members have dark hair. Eyes are usually mixed (predominantly green-brown) and irides zoned. The nose is remarkable for low ranking in elevation of tip and for excess of compressed alae. It has the highest percentage of normal bites (slight overbites), also of underbites, and ranks first in attached ear lobes. This numerous physical type then emphasizes darkness of hair and mixed character of eyes, together with narrowness of face and forehead and a few other features.

The Nordic Alpine type is deficient in the criminal insane as contrasted with the sane criminals, but nevertheless contributes 21.39 per cent to the insane criminal series. Its leading extraction is Polish-Austrian (23.6 per cent), followed by Irish (18.9 per cent). It is the most diversified of all types in its extractions, since it includes representatives of fifteen ethnic groups. This type ranks first in robbery and second in burglary and larceny. It is also second in drunkenness. The Nordic Alpine type has round heads, mixed pigmentation, and rather broad noses. Most of its bodily proportions are those which tend to be less common in the criminal insane than in the civil insane and the sane criminals. Thus it accentuates shortness and breadth in head, face, and body, rather than vertical extension and lateral compression. Although the sorting criteria for this type include the medium shades of hair color, the actual sample of the criminal insane runs heavily to dark hair (black 12.12 per cent, dark brown 63.64 per cent). The eyes are of mixed or light shades. In the general assemblage of the criminal insane this type also reinforces the prevalent condition of heavily worn teeth with frequent multiple tooth loss. The Nordic Alpine type leads all of the rest in percentage of tattooed men, and exhibits a number of physical differentiae which need not be listed here.

The Pure Alpine racial type in the criminal insane includes 5.51 per cent of the series (an excess of 1.79 per cent over its occurrence in the sane criminals of Massachusetts). Of these Pure Alpines, 30.6 per cent are Italian, 18.2 per cent French Canadian, and 12.1 per cent of Near Eastern and Eastern European birth or extraction. This type is last in murder, in burglary and larceny, and low in other offenses except assault, in which it takes second place. It leads in factory operatives and personal servants and is last in extractives. It is also last in unskilled laborers, in skilled tradesmen, and considerably the lowest in educational attainment. It is mainly composed of urban dwellers of recent immigration. It is second in Dementia praecox (70.6 per cent) but ranks low in other categories of mental disease.

This Alpine type contributes no physical features which tend to characterize the insane criminals as a whole, except dark hair.

The Pure Mediterranean type, with 6.81 per cent of the total series, is just within its quota as defined in the sane criminals of Massachusetts. Of these Mediterraneans 35.7 per cent are Italian, 19 per cent Portuguese, and the rest distributed through 8 extractions. This type leads in married men, ranks first in murder, first in assault, last in drunkenness, and next to last in every other offense. It has the highest percentage of mental deficients found in any type and the lowest of alcoholics. It ranks next to the top in extractive workers and next to the bottom in educational attainment. The Mediterranean type has very dark hair, skin, and eyes, and is long-headed and undersized. It adds to the dominance of dark hair among the criminal insane, but otherwise is unimportant in giving physical tone to the group, although, of course, it shows many distinctive metric and morphological features.

It is now apparent that the distribution of racial types among the criminal insane in Massachusetts is somewhat different from that among the sane criminals and, by deduction, different also from that of the civil insane of Massachusetts. As contrasted with the sane criminals the insane show marked excesses of the Keltic and Dinaric types, virtually complete absences of the Pure Nordic and East Baltic types, and deficiencies of the Predominantly Nordic and Nordic Alpine types. Pure Alpine types are also in slight excess among the criminal insane. Now the most striking physical difference of insane criminals from the sane and from the sane civilians lies in scarcity of the blond-haired races among those which are both criminalistic and insane. As a matter of fact, ash-blond and golden hair are extraordinarily rare among both the civil and criminal insane, but the civilians have much higher proportions of light brown or near-blond hair. Among 716 criminal insane there are only 5 blonds and 3 redheads; in 792 civil insane 6 blonds and 2 redheads. But a check sample of 815 sane civilians yields 41 pure blonds, and the Massachusetts sane criminals used for racial sortings number 1317 and include at least 69 with pure blond hair and pure light eyes, not counting the blonds who may have mixed eyes. Blondness is not confined to any one racial type, but it seems to be almost non-existent in the insane of our samples, whether civil or criminal. But the latter are characterized not alone by almost complete absence of blond hair and by strong deficiencies of the near-blond and medium shades, but also by enormous excesses of black and dark brown hair.

There are two extraneous factors which might operate speciously to decrease the percentages of ash-blond, golden, and red-haired individuals in the insane. The first of these is the possibility that the observer responsible for the field data on all of the insane was unduly chary in rating hair color as golden or ash-blond in contrast with light brown. If this were the case, the comparatively small percentages of men with strictly blond hair might well have been absorbed into the near-blond categories, and this would account for the complete absence of the Pure Nordic and East Baltic types. An extensive checking of this observer's records with those of the other principal observer shows that the man who studied the insane was indeed a little low on blond and red classifications and rather high on light browns. But his personal equation is not enough to account for the dearth of these hair shades in the insane, since he found them about three times as plentiful in comparable sane criminals.

The other possibility is that the insane groups, civil or criminal, are too old to include any sizable proportion of pure blond racial types, since these groups in the sane criminals and civilians are considerably the youngest racial types. It is indeed true that the civilian insane are considerably older than the civilian sane, and the criminal insane slightly older than the sane criminals, but the civilian sane are older than the criminal insane and yet show fair samples of the Pure Nordic and East Baltic types. On the whole then, in spite of racially irrelevant factors which may contribute to some extent to reduce these types in the insane, I think that there can be little doubt that the dearth of pure blond racial types in the Massachusetts insane is a reality.

The difference between the criminal insane and the civil insane in hair color is not open to the question of personal equation of the observer because both series were recorded by the same anthropologist. The civil insane have much more of the medium and comparatively light hair. There is no escaping the conclusion that men who in addition to being insane are criminalistic are derived to a disproportionately large extent from the very dark haired races. They are also selected particularly from types which have long narrow faces and noses, especially the Keltic and Dinaric types.

Now a close inspection of the offenses committed by the same racial types in insane and sane criminals, respectively, indicates that there is some consistency of racial specialization in type of crime, regardless of mental status. Thus the Pure Mediterranean type is first in murder, first or second in assault, and very low in burglary and larceny, whether sane or insane. The Pure Alpine type is low in murder but very high in assault in both mental classifications. But there are also some marked contradictions in offense rankings between insane and sane of the same racial type. For example, the Predominantly Nordic group of sane criminals ranks last in rape, but easily leads in this offense among the insane.

Insane criminals commit slightly less murder, rape, and other sex offenses than do the sane groups, considerably more assault and arson, but far less of all other specified offenses. Forgery was committed by but one of 617 insane criminals among the racial type series, but by 10.53 per cent of the sane. On the whole, it appears that mental status, whether sane or insane, affects very little the amount of crime committed against persons, but very markedly the amount committed against property.

Among the criminal insane all of the dark haired long-headed types, which are Mediterranean or mixed Mediterranean, lead in proportions of mentally deficient individuals. These are the Pure Mediterranean, Nordic Mediterranean, and Keltic types. The Keltic type far excels all others in alcoholism and alcoholic psychoses. The two round-headed dark haired types — Dinaric and Alpine — greatly exceed others in Dementia praecox. The Pure Mediterranean type with its primacy in mentally deficients is also first in murder and assault, and the Nordic Mediterranean type, second in mental deficients, is third in murder and third in assault. The Dinaric type, which is first in Dementia praecox, is second in murder, fourth in assault, second in robbery, and third in combined sex offenses. But the Alpine type, second in Dementia praecox, is last in murder, second in assault, and fifth in combined sex. The Keltic type, so notable for alcoholic psychoses, is outstanding in offenses only in that it is last in robbery and last in sex. It therefore does not seem that that type of mental diagnosis particularly influences choice of offense, although it is closely associated with specific racial types. Thus we are left with the conclusions that it is particularly the dark haired races who combine insanity with criminal propensities and that they are particularly prone to commit crimes against the person, with the possible exception of the Keltics who are preternaturally addicted to drunkenness. In this connection it is perhaps illuminating to note once again that the Pure Nordic and East Baltic blonds, who among sane criminals are extremely low in offenses against the person, but lead

respectively in forgery and fraud, and in burglary and larceny, are not found at all among the criminal insane.

The very ticklish subject of nationality in connection with
insanity must be dealt with here even if it provokes squirm-
ings and recriminations. In the Keltic and Dinaric racial
types, which are excessively represented among the criminal
insane, the Irish form the largest ethnic contingent, and are
closely followed by the Old Americans. In the Nordic
Mediterranean type, which is numerically the strongest, but
is not disproportionately represented, the Old Americans
have a slight advantage over the Irish. The Italians are
enormously preponderant in both Pure Mediterranean types
and Pure Alpine types, and are a strong third in the very
numerous Nordic Mediterranean type. The Portuguese are
an easy second in the Pure Mediterranean type, and the
French Canadians in the Alpine. The total of Old Americans in the smaller criminal insane series used for racial
sorting is 21.42 per cent, of Irish 20.74 per cent, of Italians
11.64 per cent. In the 7 racial types the Irish take two firsts
and three seconds, the Old Americans two firsts and two seconds, the Italians two firsts. The Polish-Austrians lead in
one insane criminal racial type — Nordic Alpine.

In the total assemblage of the criminal insane studied in
Massachusetts, the Irish lead numerically with Old Americans in second place. However, in the civil insane the Old
Americans are far in the lead, with the British second and
the Irish a rather poor third. Two stocks — the Teutonic
and the Spanish Portuguese — contribute fairly sizable samples to the civil insane but have no criminal insane, or too
few for group study. Foreign born constitute 46.4 per cent
of the criminal insane, but only 35.4 per cent of the civil
insane. The native born of Irish parentage form 35.3 per
cent of the native born criminal insane, whereas the foreign
born Irish comprise of the foreign born criminal insane only
22.7 per cent. The British, Irish, and French Canadians are

the only stocks in which the first American born generation contributes more heavily to the ranks of the criminal insane than the foreign born.

If we compare the racial types which are excessively represented among the insane criminals — Keltic, Dinaric, and Alpine — with the same racial types in the sane criminals, we are struck by the magnitude and consistency of the metric and indicial differences. The insane are always older and much smaller in all dimensions except chest depth, head height,[1] nose height, nose breadth, and ear length. The insane are relatively broader shouldered, very slightly rounder headed (except the Keltics), probably relatively higher headed, have proportionately longer faces, noses, and ears, narrower foreheads in relation to head and face breadth, and narrower faces in comparison with the greatest breadth of the head. Indeed these generalizations are approximately applicable to the whole body of the criminal insane as compared with sane criminals.

Given a criminal diathesis or propensity, there can be no doubt that within each racial type certain specific subtypes are selected for insanity. Longer and relatively narrower noses and ears in the insane may be due in part to their higher mean age, but other differences cannot be thus explained. The size depression of the insane is such as to imply definite inferiority of biological status.

Just as sane criminals tend to be younger than random samples of sane civilian males drawn from the same ethnic stocks, because crime is very largely a phenomenon of youth, so the criminal insane are younger than the civil insane. Nevertheless, the insane criminals are older than the sane criminals, because the age incidence of insanity is apparently later than that of criminality.

---

[1] Apparent superiority of the criminal insane racial types in head height may be due to a shift in techniques and instruments between the measurement by Observer B of the civil and criminal insane series.

All of the insane, whether criminal or civil, are undersized and apparently represent stocks which are inferior physically to the sane, whether of law-abiding or antisocial status. The criminal insane apparently represent exaggerations of the types of the civil insane, which are due not only to overrepresentation of certain racial combinations, but also to accentuations of the features which generally characterize the insane. I am inclined to deduce from our evidence that criminality and insanity are quite independent functions of the human organism, and that the former is not usually the result of the latter.

As we go from sane civilians to sane criminals, and thence to insane civilians and finally to insane criminals, we descend rapidly in occupational status, educational attainment, and physical condition, as well as in mentality. Both crime and insanity appear to be manifestations of inferior human organisms, and when they occur together in the same individuals, you have nearly plumbed the bottom of human degradation, short of complete idiots. A society which palliates crime and cherishes criminals, which fosters the insane and turns them loose to breed, bids fair to evolve into a pandemonium of morons, imbeciles, and idiots, ruled by the insane and by criminals. If these be the offspring of democracy, the end of human liberty is imminent. I think that such a vile parturition is likely to produce those microcephalous Siamese twins, the Isms — Fasc and Commun.

CHAPTER IX

NEGRO AND NEGROID CRIMINALS:

RACE MIXTURE AND CRIME, SOCIOLOGICAL UNITY AND PHYSICAL DIVERSITY, OFFENSE DIFFERENCES IN PHYSIQUE

THE most underprivileged human group in this country is that great body of descendants of the reluctant colonists and unwilling emigrants from Africa. The American Negro is not much farther than two generations from slavery and between four and ten generations removed from primitive African culture. If then, as Lombroso thought, criminal behavior is a primitive or atavistic phenomenon — a reversion in modern society to types of action which are customary among savages — we ought to find among the Negroes a purer distillation of criminality associated with primitive physical characters than among the more sophisticated and possibly more degenerate Whites. Quite apart from any such hypothesis, if culture promotes physical differentiation a comparative lack of the latter between the law-abiding and the criminalistic Negro ought to be manifest, since in all American Negroes European culture is a comparatively recent and, to some extent, an involuntary acquisition. Furthermore, inbreeding has not proceeded so far in the Negro as to afford full opportunity for the segregation of inferior, degenerative types, such as undoubtedly have been produced in copious numbers among the Whites. There ought then to be less criminal specialization of various physical types, just as there is less economic and social differentiation in the Negro population. We might expect among the Negroes a predominance of the simple, brutal offenses against persons, together with plain

theft and robbery. However, more or less similar findings
might be predicted from the hypothesis that general environmental depression of any social group results in a
profusion of criminal acts, quite irrespective of biological
status. The population on the lowest economic level would
show the least occupational and educational differentiation
and have the least diversity of criminal opportunity. Consequently, a predominance of the less "cultured" offenses
and a lack of correlation with physical type might be expected among the Negroes, without reference to any fanci-
ful theory of the atavistic or primitive character of crime.

However, the Negro crime situation is not so beautifully
simple as it would have been if White masters had been
less promiscuous with their female slaves. Even in Africa
race mixture between Negroes and Whites has gone on from
prehistoric times, and quite apart from miscegenation there
are distinct racial types among African Negroes. Consequently, before the imported Negro slaves received any
adulteration of White blood from the European colonists
they were already radically diversified and, to some extent,
mixed. The blending of different African strains and the
incessant seepage of White and Indian blood into the American Negro have brought about a multiplication of physical
types through purely biological causes, which is hardly less
marked than that among the Whites with their racial and
ethnic heterogeneity and their constant accretions of immigrants from many parts of the world. The proliferation
of Negroid physical types through race mixtures has been
accompanied also by a considerable social and economic
differentiation. To some extent, those with White blood and
physical features approximating those of Europeans have
been favored in education, in occupation, and in social
status, although they do not like to admit it and are none
the happier for it. Fewer obstacles have been placed in the
path of the mixed blood than in that of the individual who

displays a full development of Negro physical characters. Social selection and racial discrimination have operated to create the impression that the Negroid, or mixed blood, is more capable and more intelligent than the pure Negro, whether or not that is actually the case. Criminal opportunity is likewise much more diversified for the mulatto.

Under these circumstances, it is important to study the differences in criminal activity between the more or less pure Negroes as a group and those which almost certainly have infusions of White or Indian blood. No distinction of this sort is usually made in the reports upon prisoners compiled by the Bureau of Census. Consequently, we are almost completely in the dark as to differences in criminal propensity displayed by the various groups of this extremely heterogeneous colored population. In the case of Whites, we are given, at any rate, some information by state and government compilations of statistics in regard to the crimes committed by groups of diverse nativity and national descent. But all of the crimes committed by persons who are nearly White are charged to the account of the Negro. A spurious racial classification, based upon social discrimination, befuddles information concerning the nature and extent of antisocial behavior in this great segment of our population.

Our Negro and Negroid material in the prison and reformatory group consists of approximately 4100 records gathered in ten states. We have a very large sample from Missouri, a state unrepresented in our studies of White criminals. The vast majority of our Negroes and Negroids come from North Carolina, Kentucky, Tennessee, Missouri, and Texas, since the Negro population of Massachusetts, Wisconsin, Colorado, New Mexico, and Arizona is comparatively small.

All of our field data pertaining to Negroes were gathered by two observers. These were instructed to classify as Negro

only such individuals as seemed to them to show a full development of Negro physical characters, including woolly
or frizzly hair, broad, flat noses, and facial protrusion or
prognathism. We did not insist upon black skin color, as
contrasted with very dark brown shades, because it is by no
means certain that pure Negroes always have black skins.
On the contrary, the African evidence suggests that very
dark brown shades are, on the whole, more characteristic
of the unmixed Negro. Some of the blackest skinned Afri-
cans show in other features clear evidence of admixture of
non-Negroid blood. In our classifications any combination
of several physical features of distinctly non-Negroid appearance was considered justification for relegating its pos-
sessor to the mixed or Negroid category. Thus if the hair
was merely curly and not woolly or frizzly, if, in addition,
the nose was high and narrow, the lips were thin, and the
facial profile was straight instead of convex, the owner was
classified as Negroid rather than Negro. However, a single
character which deviated from the Negro norm was not
usually considered as justification for a Negroid classification of any individual. Thus there appear in our Negro
series occasional individuals who are aberrant in hair form,
eye color, or some other feature. After all of the records
were completed, one of the two observers went through the
individual records and photographs of the other, checking
and correcting certain erroneous or dubious classifications.
No attempt was made to secure genealogical information
concerning the proportions of White blood alleged to occur
in the prisoners. Such information is sufficiently dubious,
even when collected from the most highly intelligent and
cooperative persons. It is, moreover, of little use when it
is available. Of what value, for example, is the fact that
Great-uncle Abimelech Prism married for his third wife
Prunella Popp, and had by her thirteen children who died
in infancy? Such really important items as the fact that

Uncle Abimelech had woolly hair and that Aunt Prunella was a platinum blond are seldom found in genealogies. As a result of this selection, we have one group of 766 prisoners whom we call Negroes and another of 3325 designated Negroid. Thus the apparently full-blooded Negroes constitute only 18.7 per cent of the total colored criminals. Now, without question, many of these so-called Negroes, if not the most of them, carry small portions of White blood. On the other hand, it is improbable that many of the Negroid group are in reality full-blooded Negroes, although some of them, no doubt, have no more White blood than certain who have been classified as Negroes. The Negroid group has a wide range of physical attributes, from almost completely Negro to near White. It would be easy enough to subdivide it into at least three groups grading toward the completely White combinations of features, but this task has not been undertaken because of the excessive labor which it would involve. This is primarily a study of criminal anthropology and not of race mixture.

DISTRIBUTION OF NEGROES AND NEGROIDS

Texas contributes more than one-quarter of both colored criminal series (Negroes 25.33 per cent, Negroids 26.74 per cent). Missouri follows closely in the Negroid series with 24.09 per cent, but only yields 15.67 per cent of the full-blooded Negroes. Kentucky provides more than one-fifth (20.37 per cent) of the Negro series and about the same (21.14 per cent) proportion of the Negroids. Tennessee's contribution to the Negroes is again about one-fifth (20.63 per cent), but it yields a considerably smaller quota (12.93 per cent) to the Negroids. North Carolina has furnished 10.84 per cent of the Negroes and a slightly smaller proportion (8.39 per cent) to the Negroids. The other five states are responsible for insignificant quotas, totalling about 7 per cent in each series.

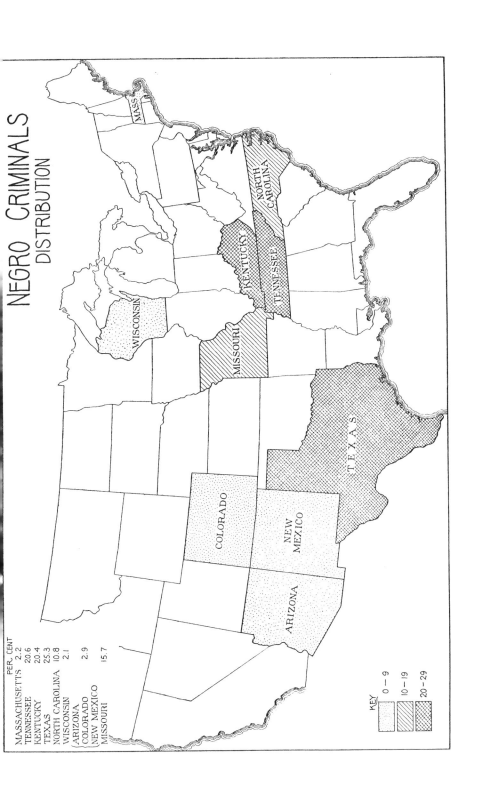

NEGRO CRIMINALS
DISTRIBUTION

	PER CENT
MASSACHUSETTS	2.2
TENNESSEE	20.6
KENTUCKY	20.4
TEXAS	25.3
NORTH CAROLINA	10.8
WISCONSIN	2.1
ARIZONA	
COLORADO	2.9
NEW MEXICO	
MISSOURI	15.7

KEY
0 — 9
10 — 19
20 — 29

MASS.
NORTH CAROLINA
KENTUCKY
TENNESSEE
WISCONSIN
MISSOURI
TEXAS
COLORADO
NEW MEXICO
ARIZONA

Thus the putatively pure Negroes are drawn in a somewhat excessive proportion from Tennessee (excess over
Negroids 7.70 per cent) and in lesser excess from North
Carolina (excess 2.45 per cent). Missouri is the state which
is overbalanced with Negroids (excess over Negroes 8.42
per cent). However, the discrepancy in derivation between
the two series is, on the whole, so small that even if a state
differentiation of Negro and Negroid physical types existed,
it could be disregarded in physical comparisons of the total
series.

SOCIOLOGY OF NEGROES AND NEGROIDS

We may first consider the comparative sociology of these
two series of colored American delinquents. The Negroes
have 31 per cent of recorded previous convictions, whereas
this figure rises to 38 per cent in the case of the Negroids.
This latter figure is still one per cent less than the previous
convictions of Old Americans. However, the Old American
figure is enhanced either by the excessive criminality or the
more complete records of Massachusetts and Wisconsin, two
of the states which contribute very small samples to the
Negro and Negroid series. In some of the states we have
studied, illiteracy is so widespread that one is inclined to
suspect that the dearth of criminal records may be due to
the scarcity of people who can write.

The percentage of single men among the Negroes (52.37)
considerably exceeds that of the Negroids (44.28), and the
Old American criminals fall about midway between the
two colored groups in percentage of the unmarried (48.63).
In both colored classes the burglary and larceny group leads
in celibacy, as is ordinarily the case among the White criminals. However, the Negro group with a mean age of 29.85
years falls below the average age of the Negroid series by
more than one and one-half years (Negroid mean 31.45
years), so that some of the Negro deficiency in marriage may

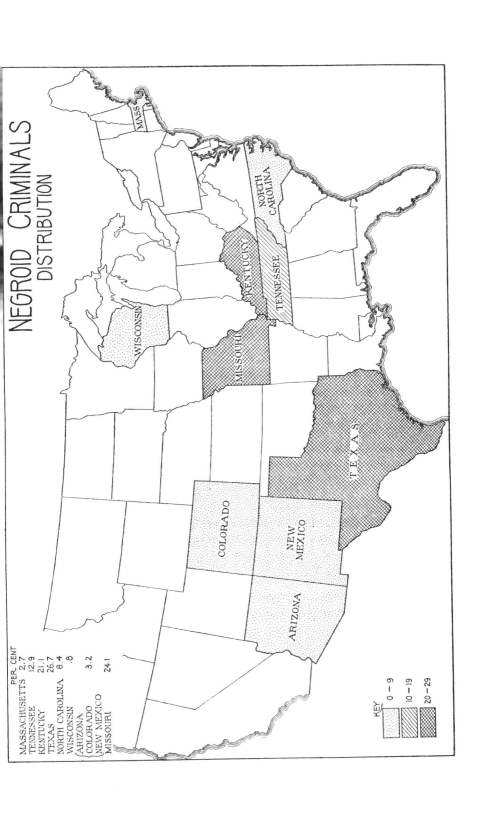

NEGROID CRIMINALS
DISTRIBUTION

	PER CENT
MASSACHUSETTS	2.7
TENNESSEE	12.9
KENTUCKY	21.1
TEXAS	26.7
NORTH CAROLINA	8.4
WISCONSIN	.8
ARIZONA	
COLORADO	3.2
NEW MEXICO	
MISSOURI	24.1

KEY

0 – 9
10 – 19
20 – 29

be due to this age factor. I think, however, that one reason why burglars seem commonly to be bachelors is that wives do not like to have husbands who have to be out at night, and that thieves are not satisfactory family providers because most of them spend so large a portion of their time as unwilling guests of the state.

The differences in distribution of offense between Negroes and Negroids are almost negligible. The full-blooded group has about one and one-half per cent more of first degree murder and about the same amount less of second degree murder, but these differences may well be due to accidents of sampling. Larceny is 4.67 per cent more common in the Negroes than in the Negroids. The latter make up their deficiency by slightly exceeding the Negroes in assault, robbery, and forgery and fraud. The two groups commit about the same percentage of rape (Negroes 4.31 per cent, Negroids 4.54 per cent). Other sex offenses are very rare in both groups (Negroes 0.65 per cent, Negroids 1.05 per cent). I am very much intrigued by the apparent rarity of sex offenses in these colored delinquents, because one has the impression that eternal vigilance and frequent lynchings are the price of honor among southern White women. Unless nearly all Negro rapists are shot, hung, burned at the stake, or all three, it seems necessary to conclude that the perils of female chastity have been exaggerated. Of course, it may be that rape of a Negro by a Negro is not considered a crime for a Negro. The Negroids are slightly higher in offenses against public welfare (Negroes 2.87 per cent, Negroids 4.66 per cent), possibly because they have had superior educational advantages.

We reach the important conclusion that the more nearly pure Negroes are scarcely differentiated in type of offense committed from the group which has perceptible proportions of White blood. The aggregate of percental differences in offense distribution between the two series is

RANKINGS IN MURDER

5
Native White
Foreign Parentage
12.8%

1
Negro
30.6%

2
Negroid
30.4%

4
Old
American
22.1%

3
Foreign White
24.9%

about 12. In other words, the average difference between the proportion of offenses committed respectively by Negroes and Negroids in ten pairs of offense categories is only 1.20 per cent. Evidently, then, our selection of the supposedly pure Negroes from the total colored criminal population has little significance in the matter of nature of crime.

Both Negroes and Negroids are slightly higher in first degree murder than Old American Whites, and very much exceed the latter in second degree murder. In fact both Negroes and Negroids surpass all of the three main White series — native of native parentage, native of foreign parentage, and foreign born — in both classes of the lusty crime of homicide. The native born Whites of foreign parentage are considerably the lowest in murder, apparently because they are so busy with more lucrative crimes. Robbery is slightly more frequent in our colored series than in the Old Americans and the foreign born Whites, but less common than among the native born Americans of foreign parentage. Both groups of African descent somewhat surpass the Old American Whites in burglary and larceny, and the pure Negro group ranks first of all parentage groups in this category of offense, slightly exceeding the amount committed by first generation American Whites. Both Negroidal groups are well below the Old Americans and the New Americans in forgery and fraud, but equal the amount committed by foreign Whites. The Negroidal groups commit about the same amount of rape as do the Old American Whites, somewhat less than the New American Whites, and not much more than one-third of the amount committed by foreign born Whites, who seem to regard America as a land of special opportunity in this respect. In sex offenses other than rape the colored groups are far below the three White series, either because of moral superiority or because what is a crime for Whites is a mere peccadillo as between Negroes. In offenses against public welfare the Negroidal series are

RANKINGS *in* BURGLARY
AND
LARCENY

2
Native White
Foreign Parentage
43.7 %

1
Negro
43.9 %

3
Negroid
39.2 %

4
Old American
38.3 %

5
Foreign White
32.8 %

below Old Americans and foreign born Whites. The Negroids commit more offenses of this sort than first generation Whites and the Negroes less. Both Negroes and Negroids are at the bottom in arson and miscellaneous offenses. I do not know to what extent the total tally of Negroid offenses may be diminished by possible tendencies of southern courts to neglect prosecution of crimes committed by Negroes

RANKINGS IN RAPE

1
Foreign White
12.5%

2
Native White
Foreign Parentage
6.2%

3
Old American
4.7%

4
Negr.
4.5%

5
Negro
4.3%

against Negroes, or to overlook petty offenses against the property of Whites, on the ground that these are a part of Negro traditional *mores*.

The Negroes and Negroids are also closely similar in occupation. In both, the leading category of employment is unskilled labor (Negroes 36.65 per cent, Negroids 35.33 per cent), then extractive (Negroes 21.38 per cent, Negroids 19.38 per cent), and in third place personal service (Negroes 18.59 per cent, Negroids 18.83 per cent). The mixed Negroid group is slightly lower in extractives (2 per cent), and in unskilled laborers (1.32 per cent). In some of the higher grades of occupations — factory, transportation, trade — the Negroids enjoy a very slight superiority, but the num-

bers of either group engaged in semi-professional, professional, clerical, and public service vocations are negligible.
This circumstance, of course, gives them little chance at
embezzling, defrauding, forging, and other genteel criminal
pursuits. On the whole, it may be said that the Negroids
tend to be a little above the Negroes in occupational level,
but the differences are hardly more than were found in the
distribution of offenses.

In comparison with the Old Americans both Negroes
and Negroids are occupationally inferior. The Old Americans include less than one-half as many unskilled laborers,
proportionately, as are found in either Negroid group, and
more than a ten per cent excess of extractives. The Whites
have not much more than one-third of the proportions of
personal servants found in the other two series, but nearly
twice as many factory workers. In all of the higher occupations the Old Americans are substantial leaders, usually with
two to three times the proportions of either Negroes or
Negroids. However, the Negroids definitely exceed the
Old Americans in transport workers, and the Negroes also
are slightly higher than the Whites in this category. It is a
matter of some satisfaction to me that this survey was made
in the years when most persons worked instead of merely
drawing pay through the W.P.A. I suppose that now-a-days
a study of employment could be made, but hardly one of
occupation.

The slight superiority which the Negroids show over the
full-blooded Negroes in occupational status becomes more
definite in educational attainment. The Negroes have an
insignificantly higher proportion of illiterates (Negroes
19.52 per cent, Negroids 19.19 per cent), but in the category
of persons who can read and write but have never attended
school there is an excess of 3.34 per cent of full-blooded
Negroes (Negroes 8.18 per cent, Negroids 4.84 per cent).
Through the sixth grade the proportions of Negroes exceed

those of Negroids, but thereafter the Negroids show consistent and marked superiority. The ratio of the well educated to the illiterate and unschooled is .10 in the Negroes and .15 in the Negroids. However, our Old American criminals, though in general wretchedly educated, far surpass both of the colored series, for their ratio of men who have reached the last two years of high school or have gone farther to the illiterate and unschooled is .54.

This raises the interesting question as to whether a well educated criminal is preferable to a felon who is ignorant and illiterate. Ought we to point with pride to the probability that we have the best educated criminals in the world, and should we endeavor to teach our criminalistic illiterates how to read and write so they can have a broader scope for their talents than unprofitable murder, unsatisfactory rape, and cheap thievery?

In the almost total lack of offense differentiation between the supposedly full-blooded Negroes and the mixed-blood Negroids, and in the very slight occupational and only moderate educational superiority which the latter enjoy, we encounter an extraordinarily interesting sociological phenomenon. The easiest way of explaining the paucity and relative insignificance of these differences between the group we have labelled "Negro" and the one designated as "Negroid" would be an assumption that our anthropological criteria of racial purity or hybridization in the Negro have broken down, and that all we have done is to select arbitrarily a subgroup with darker skins, woollier hair, et cetera, which is really no more purely Negroid racially than the larger residuum which we have assumed to carry White blood. If we have been totally erroneous in our choice and application of criteria of physical distinction between pure Negroes and Negroids, it would be natural that we should find no sociological differences between the two series. Therefore we must find out whether our supposed Negroes are anthropometrically distinct from our alleged Negroids in physical characters other than those used for separating the two groups.

PHYSICAL DIFFERENTIATION OF NEGROES AND NEGROIDS

Now it may be stated at once that our Negro group is overwhelmingly differentiated in measurements and indices from the larger Negroid series. The supposedly pure Negroes are younger, shorter, inferior in weight, and in every other measurement except shoulder breadth and nose breadth. In the latter they significantly exceed the mixed-bloods. In indices or proportions the two groups also show some interesting differences, although they are not of great magnitude. The Negroes have relatively lower sitting height, much broader noses in relation to nose length, shorter and relatively broader ears, wider foreheads relative to face breadth, and narrower jaws relative to face breadth. The head of the pure Negro is also slightly more dolichocephalic.

A few of the more important morphological differences between the full-blooded Negro group and the mixed-blood emphasize their anthropological distinctness. The mixed-bloods have slightly thicker head hair, better developed beards, and heavier body hair. The Negroids also have thicker eyebrows. Internal epicanthic or Mongoloid folds of the upper eyelids are also far commoner among the Negroids. The mixed-bloods also have higher foreheads, less depressed nasal roots, more pronounced lip seams, far more square chins, more projecting cheek bones, more prominent jaw angles, longer and more frequently attached ear lobes, more markedly rolled ear rims, more prominent antihelices (the inner fold of the ear), and ears which are more frequently protruding. The neck of the Negroid is oftener short and thick and the shoulder slope less pronounced. Most of these morphological differences between Negroids and Negroes are in the nature of convergences of the mixed-bloods upon racial features more characteristic of Whites or Indians.

From this brief summary of differences in soft parts between our supposedly pure Negroes and mixed Negroids I have omitted, of course, such features as hair form, pigmentation, shape of nose and lips, prognathism — i.e. the characters used for distinguishing the groups. Naturally in these sorting criteria the full Negroes show more nearly typical racial development. There is then no question of the anthropological differentiation of the two groups. However, an inspection of the distribution of grades of these racially diagnostic characters shows that the vast majority of our Negroid or mixed group are, in reality, much closer to the Negro racial type than to the White type, and probably carry much more Negro blood than White blood. Let us take, for example, pigmentation. Only 8 of 3325 Negroids have white skins (0.24 per cent). Only 1.41 per cent have skins light enough to be classified as olive. On the other hand, 31.16 per cent of the Negroids have dark brown skins and 3.37 per cent black skins. In other words, more than one-third of our Negroids are sufficiently dark-skinned to be accounted in this feature pure Negro.

If we take hair color, we find that only 17.05 per cent of the Negroids have shades lighter than black, including three-quarters of one per cent of white or gray hair. Further, less than 13 per cent of the Negroids have eye color lighter than dark brown. Finally, only 7 per cent of the Negroids have hair which is not either frizzly or woolly. It therefore appears that our Negroid group includes very few men indeed who have a strong preponderance of White blood. Quadroons and octoroons probably are extremely rare in this series. My rough guess is that the average amount of Negro blood in the Negroid group may be as much as six-eighths and that in the Negro group it may amount to seven-eighths, or fifteen-sixteenths.

NEGRO AND NEGROID CRIMINALS

MOSAIC OF GENERALIZED FACIAL AND CRANIAL DIFFERENCES

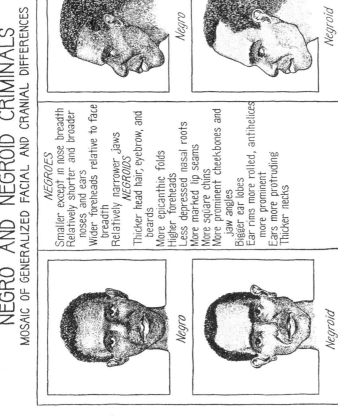

NEGROES
Smaller except in nose breadth
Relatively shorter and broader noses and ears
Wider foreheads relative to face breadth
Relatively narrower jaws

NEGROIDS
Thicker head hair, eyebrow, and beards
More epicanthic folds
Higher foreheads
Less depressed nasal roots
More marked lip seams
More square chins
More prominent cheekbones and jaw angles
Bigger ear lobes
Ear rims more rolled, antihelices more prominent
Ears more protruding
Thicker necks

Negro

Negroid

Negro

Negroid

If our principal concern were the study of the relation of race mixture to crime, we should proceed to dissect our large Negroid series into two or three subseries, according to the probable proportions of White blood as indicated by physical characters. This method would undoubtedly yield some definite and perhaps regular regression of sociological characters upon degree of mixture. It is apparent that such a subdivision of the Negroid series would clarify some of our anthropological and sociological questions, and it is proposed to carry it out before publishing in detail the volume relating to this material, of which the present discussion is only a preview. But it is quite obvious that no processes of sorting or subdivision by the use of racial characters would establish any very marked correlation with nature of offense. There is no such thing as a purely Negro crime, nor a distinctively mulatto crime, nor a characteristically White crime. There are two clear reasons for the comparative lack of criminological differentiation between Negroes and Negroids. The lesser of these is that our Negroid series is so heavily Negro, as contrasted with White, in its ensemble of physical characteristics that it is overweighted with the same racial characters which are found in a degree only slightly more accentuated in our supposedly pure Negro series. Both are "tarred with the same brush" and nearly equally so. Much more important is the fact that the term "Negro" in this country delimits socially a section of the population of the United States and restricts it to certain classes of occupations and certain economic levels, quite irrespective of the amount of White blood which may be included in the individual blends. Any person who has the minimum of Negroid physical characters which enable him to be identified as of partially African blood is thereby relegated to a sphere of life in which economic opportunity is meager and from which it is impossible to escape. Social mobility is very small, save within the limits of the arbitrarily defined "Negro" group. This cramped and depressed Negro environment restricts the scope of their criminal activities. Equality of criminal opportunity is not vouchsafed to the delinquent of African ancestry, however fractional his Negro heredity.

PHYSICAL DIFFERENTIATION BY OFFENSE GROUPS

Under these circumstances it is hardly to be expected that Negroes and Negroids will display the amount of physical differentiation by offense groups which we have found to exist among the White Old American criminals. Social mobility and diversification of economic status are prerequisites for offense differentiation in antisocial activity. When two series, Negro and Negroid, in spite of their physical divergences are not socially well distinguished and are practically identical in distribution of offenses, the prospect of nature of offense being associated with physical type is rather dim.

OFFENSE DIFFERENTIATION OF NEGROIDS

Nevertheless, first degree murderers (281 in number) are significantly differentiated from total Negroid criminals in their bodily measurements. They average nearly six years older and two pounds heavier, have wider shoulders, broader chests, possibly broader heads, and certainly greater head circumferences. Their noses are longer and broader than the total series of Negroids, their jaws wider, and other facial dimensions are probably slightly larger. Superiority in ear dimensions is also suggested. However, in indices or proportions of the head and face, the first degree murderers do not differ from a random sample drawn from the total series. A preliminary survey of the comparative morphology of the soft parts in the first degree murderers gives the following tentative differences from the entire series — tentative because as yet the statistical validation of these deviations has not been completed. The first degree murderers have in general scantier head hair and more abundant beard and body hair, possibly as a consequence of their superior mean age. They differ in skin color and hair color from the total Negroids only in a trifling excess of lighter shades, but more of them have woolly hair as contrasted with frizzly hair and the lesser grades of hair curvature. They also show a slight excess of thin eyebrows. Low and narrow foreheads seem to occur with slightly more than average frequency. The bridge of the nose is oftener high and less frequently broad than in the series as a whole. Associated with this is a slightly more frequent convex nasal profile. A downward inclination of the nasal septum and a rarity of septa deflected to the left also characterize the first degree murder group to a greater extent than the total series. The integumental lips of this group are oftener thick, and the lip seam more frequently absent or poorly developed. Prognathism, on the whole, is slightly less developed than in the total series. These murderers also seem to excel in prominence of chin and, especially, of cheek bones. More of them have full cheeks and flaring jaw angles, and, undoubtedly in connection with their superior age, they lead in wrinkling of the cheeks. Pronounced wear of the teeth and excess of multiple tooth loss and caries are also attributable, perhaps, to age superiority. But an excessive proportion of marked overbites cannot be caused by age difference. High, broad palates (according to one observer) are unusually common in this offense group. With the overbites and the form of palate are associated a small excess of mouth-breathers. A slightly greater prevalence of large ear lobes and of the type which is free rather than attached, a definite excess of slightly rolled helices or ear rims, and slight surplusage of short thick necks and square shoulders complete the tale of the probable morphological distinctions of the first degree murderers. Very few of these differentiae are quantitatively large in this offense group.

Inspection of the sociological characters of first degree

murderers first shows that they are derived in disproportionately large numbers from the states of Kentucky, Tennessee,
and Texas. They are very low in previous convictions, are
deficient in single men, are unduly high in widowers (11.15
per cent) and those who have been divorced or separated
from their wives. Occupationally, the first degree murderers
are notable only for a considerable excess of extractives and a
slight deficiency of unskilled laborers and personal servants.
They also show a definite inferiority in education to the
Negroid criminals as a whole.

Taking them by and large, the first degree murderers,
within their total group, are much more clearly distinguished in the sum total of physical and sociological features
than might be expected. Evidently they are not only older
and more robust men, but also more largely derived from
the rural areas and, in general, more ignorant than the total
Negroids. A similar trend of difference was manifested by
the first degree murderers among the Old Americans. There
are uncertain indications that first degree murderers, as a
group, carry slightly less Negro blood than is found in the
total Negroid series.

The second degree Negroid murderers (729 in number)
are also clearly distinguished from the total series in their
measurements. They too are larger than the run of the
mill of this criminal series. Specifically, they are 2.6 years
higher in mean age and have bigger chests, but shorter
heads and noses, broader faces and jaws. Yet they also fail
to achieve distinction from the total group in indices or
proportions of the head and face. The distribution of skin
tints suggests a slightly greater prevalence of lighter pigmented individuals among the second degree murderers.
They also have small excesses of curly and frizzly hair as contrasted with the woolly variety. Green-brown eyes are possibly unduly common. Conspicuous in this group are high
and broad foreheads and also those of pronounced slope.

They lead in depth of depression of the nasal root, which is often low. Broad nasal bridges are slightly deficient, but both concave and convex noses occur oftener than in the series at large. Square chins are in excess as are also prominent cheek bones. The group is rather high in wrinkling, in wear of teeth, dental caries, and multiple tooth loss. Edge-to-edge bites are commoner than is ordinary. The rim of the ear seems somewhat better rolled than in first degree murderers or in the total series, and marked development of Darwin's point occurs less often. Long, thin necks are slightly in excess.

These second degree murderers include unduly large quotas from Tennessee and North Carolina. They have the smallest percentage of previous convictions in the series (22.46), and are very high in married men (55.96 per cent as contrasted with 48.32 per cent in total Negroids).[1] Second degree murderers follow the occupational peculiarities of the first degree murderers in excess of extractives and deficiencies of personal servants, but they are also high in unskilled laborers. On the whole, this group is even more depressed educationally than the first degree group. It has 23.41 per cent of illiterates, 6.79 per cent who lack formal education but are able to read and write, 39.61 per cent who have never gone farther in school than the first to fifth grades.

Second degree murderers as a group seem to display the common anthropological and sociological features which we have found in all murderers. They are older, larger, more rural in residence, more depressed in occupation, and more ignorant than total criminals of their series. But they have, in addition, certain peculiar and differentiating features. Notable in this group is the evidence of slightly more White admixture than is found in Negroid first degree murderers.

---

[1] I suppose that one reason why murderers have so few recorded previous convictions is that if one begins his criminal career with murder he is likely to remain a first offender, simply because he may be kept in jail "for good."

The small offense subgroup of 81 assault prisoners shows a great many minor metric deviations which suggest that it is undersized, but statistically they are insufficient to establish the certainty that this group differs anthropometrically from a random sample of the total series. Consequently it need not detain us further here.

The 374 robbers in the Negroid series do, however, attain a modest statistical differentiation from the total series. They are over two years below mean age and broader in shoulder, shallower in chest, wider in head, and deficient in head circumference. Further, they are almost certainly lighter, and possibly taller and longer of face than the total series. Probable, but not certain, statistical differentiations in indices are a narrow face and forehead relative to head breadth, and an elongated and relatively narrow upper face.

The robbers rate very high in prevalence of medium amounts of head hair and in medium yellow-brown skin color. They rank first in the darkest shades of brown eye color (90.62 per cent), and are high both in yellow pigmented sclerae, or whites of the eye, and in those which are clear or unpigmented. Eye folds of the upper lids are rare and heavy eyebrows are slightly in excess. This group is highest in approximate verticality of the forehead and shows an unusual prevalence of medium height, but pronounced breadth, of the nasal root. The nasal bridge also is notable for excess proportions of medium height and of pronounced breadth. The data suggest that the tip of the nose is likely to be thin in this group oftener than in the total series of Negroids. Upward inclinations of the nasal septum are at the maximum of the series (68.36 per cent) — a figure more than 6 per cent above the series average. Pronounced thickness of the membranous lips is also a leading feature of the robber group. Associated with this lip thickness is great development of the lip seam. Feeble chin prominence is more marked in this group than in any other offense class.

This feature is associated with a high frequency of pointed chins. The robber group again is one of those which features projection of the cheek bones, perhaps because it is also rather conspicuously thin-cheeked. The robbers are one of the least wrinkled offense subgroups, are lowest in heavy wear of the teeth and in multiple dental caries. The slight overbite which is normal is excessively present. Ear lobes are small in unduly large proportions and especially frequent in their soldered or attached category. These features of nose and teeth are certainly attributable in part to the comparative youth of this offense class. A well rolled helix or rim of the ear is commoner than ordinary among the robbers, and the inner ridge of the ear or antihelix is often well developed. Short thick necks are at the maximum of the series. Some of the physical differentiae of the robbers appear to be due to their lower average age. In general they give the impression of a physically distinctive group.

This robbery group is extremely high in Missouri Negroids (excess of 20.29 per cent), and may perhaps owe some of its physical peculiarities to that fact. It is high in previous convictions (43.1 per cent) and in unmarried men (49.46 per cent). Occupationally, the robbers are far the lowest in extractives, somewhat high in unskilled laborers, and definitely in the lead in transport workers. In their sociology they singularly resemble the robbers of the pure Negro series. The Negroid robbers are comparatively very low in illiteracy, and have the fewest proportionately of those who can read and write but have not attended school. Yet they show a large excess of persons who have not gone beyond the fifth grade and are slightly deficient in most of the higher educational categories.

As among the Old American Whites, so in the Negroids, the robbers tend to be a predominantly urban group, but of much lower educational status than the Whites. It is worthy of mention here that Missouri, which furnishes 24.09 per cent of our Negroid criminals, contributes no less than 44.38 per cent of the robbers. Probably an apposite fact is the existence in Missouri of two large cities, St. Louis and Kansas City, with heavy Negro and Negroid populations. The physical characteristics of the robbers suggest a thoroughly hybridized Negroid group in which Negro blood predominates, but body build and facial characteristics recall the weedy modernized types found in the Old Americans of the present generation and in the American born children of European immigrants.

The enormous burglary and larceny group of 1303 individuals is clearly distinguished from the total Negroid criminal series by size inferiority. The mean age is three years below that of the entire series and nearly every bodily dimension shows a deficiency which is certainly, or very probably, significant. The thieves and burglars show slight and insignificant superiority only in head height. Probably the head heights relative to length and breadth are superior in this class of criminals, and there are strong indications of relatively longer and narrower faces, broader foreheads with reference to jaw breadth, and relatively wider ears.

In the larceny group head hair is a little thicker, beard and body hair a shade more sparse than in the total Negroid series, again probably because of the lower mean age of the thieves and burglars. No peculiarities of hair form are discernible. Although this group ranks first in percentage of black skins, it is probably not differentiated in general pigmentation. Internal epicanthic or Mongoloid folds of the upper eyelids are somewhat in excess. Low foreheads are commonest in this category. Pronounced depressions of the nasal root are perhaps unduly common and very broad nasal bridges are more frequent than in any other group except the robbers. Concavo-convex noses are at the series maximum and the septum of the nose tends preferentially to be inclined upward. This group has the highest occurrence of deflections of the nasal septum. It is very high in thickness of the membranous lips and leads both in pronounced alveolar and total facial prognathism, or protrusion of the jaws. Submedium chin projection is in excess, and median or pointed chins are highest of the total series. Cheek bones are of medium prominence in a very large excess of the thieves and burglars. Jaw angles are infrequently pronounced and often little developed. Wrinkling of the cheeks is less common than in the total series, tooth wear is less, caries rather fewer, and number of teeth lost is significantly diminished. These latter differentiae are probably due to low average age. The group displays no distinctive features of the ear. The physical characteristics of the thieves and burglars suggest a possibly heavier preponderance of Negro blood than is characteristic of the total Negroid series.

The burglary and larceny group of Negroids is derived from all of the ten states in approximately the same proportions as they contribute to the entire series. This group leads all others in previous convictions and has the largest proportion of single men. It is low in extractives, and slightly high in unskilled laborers, personal servants, and transportation workers. It cannot be stated that the thieves and burglars are below the general level of Negroid criminal education. On the contrary, they are rather deficient in illiterates and slightly high in men who have reached the first two years of high school.

In this criminal offense group we have very similar characteristics to those isolated in the Old American thieves and burglars: deficiency in body size so marked as to suggest degeneration or stunting, better than average criminal educational attainment, but low occupational status, low marriage rate, and high frequency of previous convictions.

The group of forgery and fraud criminals (184 in number) is barely distinguishable in metric features from the total series, since it displays but two certain excesses — in head circumference and in shoulder breadth — and is undifferentiated in indices. However, since this group always represents the aristocracy of delinquents, it is worth while to investigate such morphological and sociological characteristics as may confirm or refute its lack of anthropological distinction.

The forgery criminals are somewhat high in sparse head hair and in abundant beard and body hair, although these excesses run counter to the fact that they are a year younger than the total series. They show excesses of medium red-brown and dark brown skin color. They are high in all of the varieties of hair form which are non-Negroid, and low in proportion of frizzly hair. They also show a moderate surplus of dark brown hair. Light brown eyes and green-brown eyes occur more frequently than in the total Negroid series. Internal epicanthic folds of the eyelid are unduly common. Low foreheads are rarest in this group, and narrow foreheads are not recorded, although pronounced forehead slope is in excess. Depressions of the nasal root are generally pronounced. The nasal bridge is prevailingly of medium height, but sometimes low. Broad nasal bridges are least common of any offense group (save the inadequate arson offenders). Concave and straight nasal profiles are slightly in excess. Various degrees of elevation of the nasal tip, as contrasted with depression, are more frequent than in most other offense series. This group is also somewhat high in flare of the nasal wings. A very strong prevalence of downward inclined septa is at variance with the characteristics of the nose previously described as present in excess. Deflections of the nasal septum are fewer than average. These fraudulent criminals lead in thinness of the integumental lips, although pronounced membranous lip thickness predominates. The lip seams appear to be less prominent than in most other groups. The development of facial and alveolar prognathism or jaw protrusion is not distinctive, but chin prominence is unusually marked. Outstanding malars are also notably in excess. This group, further, is high in cheek fullness and in projection of the jaw angles. It is low in loss of teeth and especially high in marked overbites. Mouth-breathers are more than ordinarily common. Ear lobes are rarely large; Darwin's point on the rim of the ear is perhaps to be seen in pronounced development more often than one would expect, while protrusive ears are also a little commoner than average. These fraudulent criminals have the least facial asymmetry and are finally characterized by a slight excess of pronouncedly sloping shoulders. In their physical characteristics they suggest more White and possibly more Indian admixture than is found in other Negroid groups.

A remarkable feature of the distribution of the forgery and fraud group is that it is heavily overloaded with Texans, as is also the corresponding group of the Old American White criminals. Texas contributes nearly 43 per cent of the group, although its general quota among the Negroids is less than 27 per cent. It is thus possible that the physical characteristics of this group are somewhat influenced by a local Texan type, perhaps blended with Mexican, and that its morphological characteristics reflect too strongly the personal equations of the anthropologist who worked in Texas. Previous convictions are high in this fraudulent group, and the proportion of married men is in excess by more than 5 per cent. This class of criminals leads all of the Negroids in factory workers and is proportionately low in extractives, in unskilled laborers, and in transportation employees. The few members of the higher occupations, semi-professional, professional, and clerical, represent more than the expected quota of this comparatively small group, but these fraudulent criminals also lead in personal servants. It is very clear that this group is considerably the best educated of all offense categories of the Negroids. It contains from two to three times as many men, proportionately, in all educational grades from the first two years of high school upward, and is deficient in the illiterate and the very poorly educated.

On the whole, the fraudulent criminals are better differentiated sociologically than physically. They are obviously an urban class, and perhaps owe some of their anthropological distinctiveness to the wider range of physical combinations which occur in the mixed city populations.

There are only 151 Negroid rapists (possibly because so many of them are lynched), but rape is the sort of crime which is likely to involve a fairly rigid anthropological selection. Accordingly, the fact that rapists are remarkably distinct from total Negroid criminals in their bodily measurements and indices need occasion no surprise. Rapists are significantly older (excess 2.10 years), shorter in stature, smaller in head breadth and head circumference, and longer in the nose than their fellow convicts. In all probability they also have deeper and narrower chests, shorter heads, shorter faces, and longer ears. Their relative sitting height is high as in most short men; the upper face is notably short and broad; it is probable that they are more dolichocephalic or long-headed, have wider faces relative to head breadth, and relatively longer and narrower ears than the total series. Of course long noses and long ears are found in increasing numbers in older men. Men convicted of rape are likely to be above the mean age of criminals because they are usually in jail for a long time, but these Negroid rapists are by no means a group of old men.

The rapists have a high proportion of well developed beards, but are otherwise undistinguished in hair quantity. In skin color they have an excess of light yellow-browns and are somewhat deficient in blacks. They have a possibly significant surplus of red-brown hair. Light brown and green-brown eyes are extraordinarily common. The white of the eye is clear, as contrasted with speckled or yellow, in an unduly high proportion. Rayed irides are quite unusually prevalent. Median and external eye folds are possibly unduly common. Thick eyebrows occur oftener than in any other group (15.89 per cent). The data on brow ridges and the glabella (the bump over the root of the nose) suggest underdevelopment. High foreheads are slightly more than average in occurrence and low foreheads comparatively rare. The nasal root seems to be more than ordinarily broad, but there is great variation in this feature. There is a small excess of convex noses and the nasal tip tends to be depressed. Deflections of the nasal septum are less than ordinarily prevalent. The only distinctive lip feature is a slight excess of prominent lip seams. The minimum percentage of prognathism (jaw protrusion) is found in this offense group. Square chins are commonest of all groups among the rapists. Cheek bones are compressed in an excessive percentage and the cheeks are below average fullness. Jaw angles tend to run to extremes of projection and compression. Pronounced tooth wear, many dental caries, and multiple tooth loss are high, perhaps in conformity with age superiority. A slight or normal overbite is unusually predominant. The helix of the ear tends to be heavily rolled, the antihelix slightly more than ordinarily well developed. Ears are rather frequently projecting. There is an unusual scarcity of facial asymmetry.

It is a rather curious fact that unduly large proportions of the rapists come from Massachusetts and Wisconsin, states which yield very small quotas of Negroids. New Mexico and Arizona furnish more than their share to this offense group, as does also North Carolina. Kentucky is notably deficient in rapists and to a lesser degree Tennessee is below par in this offense. Previous convictions are quite extraordinarily rare among the Negroids convicted of rape. They are not matrimonially distinguished except in small excesses of bachelors and widowers. They are a little high in extractives, in factory workers, and in personal servants. Education is only slightly below the average of the total Negroid series (a condition quite similar to that prevalent among Old American rapists).

It is sufficiently clear that these rapists, although a selected and distinctive physical group especially characterized by small and narrow heads, short broad faces, and long and comparatively narrow noses and ears, are by no means a closer approximation to a pure Negro type than is found in other Negroid offense groups. On the contrary, they seem more mixed with White blood than is ordinarily the case among our Negroid offenders, and they are by no means so depressed sociologically as are Old American White rapists. (Perhaps among Negroids rape is an indication of a certain kind of social ambition.)

One of the very smallest offense groups is that of the sex crimes other than rape. It contains only 35 men and would not be worth discussing were it not for its quite extraordinary metric distinctiveness. It is the second oldest and considerably the shortest group, with notably narrow forehead, short face, and high relative sitting height. It is notably low in the relationship of forehead breadth to head and face breadth, and of jaw breadth to face breadth. In the present summary the morphological variations in this tiny group may be neglected, because the numbers of individuals involved are so small that one distrusts the significance of excesses and deficiencies. Other sex offenders always seem to constitute a very miscellaneous group of dirty old men. Massachusetts and North Carolina are unpleasantly conspicuous for their excesses of these offenders. Their previous convictions are frequent (44.83 per cent), and they are possibly excessive in their percentage of widowers. Unskilled laborers and professional men are alike in excess, and this group far outranks all others both in its proportion of illiterates and of men who have attended college. However, only two of 35 have had this latter privilege. But there are only 36 college men among our entire series of 3304 Negroids.

The group of persons convicted for offenses classified as versus public welfare totals 155 men. Most of such offenses are violations of liquor laws. The records were gathered during the hey-day of prohibition. Almost 66 per cent of these bootleggers are Texans, although Texas contributes slightly less than 27 per cent of the entire Negroid criminal series. These liquor offenders are the tallest and heaviest of our series and are 4.3 years above mean age. They exceed the total series in shoulder breadth and in chest depth, in sitting height, head circumference, jaw breadth, ear length, and probably ear breadth. They have probably broader foreheads and faces and possibly somewhat lower heads and shorter faces than the group at large. None of the deviations in proportions are statistically certain, but there are strong suggestions of diminished height indices of the head, relatively broad faces, and slightly longer and narrower noses than are usual among the Negroid criminals.

The versus public welfare offenders are high in sparsity of head hair, but at the same time curiously high in poorly developed beard and body hair. In adult males the amount of head hair and body hair usually varies inversely. A medium red-brown shade of skin color is considerably in excess, while dark brown hair color attains its maximum of the series with nearly 19 per cent. Black hair is at the series minimum (75.2 per cent). This group is also very high in gray-brown and green-brown eye color, which of course indicates White admixture. Whites of the eye speckled with yellow pigment are excessively present. Zoned, speckled, and diffused irides are all commoner than in most Negroid offense groups. Skin folds of the upper eyelids are rarer than in any other group, and the height of the eye opening is most frequently pronounced. Upward slanting eyes slits attain a maximum. Heavy brow ridges are a notable feature of these bootleggers, and, in association, the eminence above the root of the nose is most highly developed. Foreheads are often very broad. The depression of the root of the nose is considerably less than in any other offense group, although the height of the nasal root itself is frequently below average. Narrow nasal roots are more common than in any other group, but, at that, only total 8.39 per cent. The nasal bridge is prevalently of medium height, and very wide bridges are not quite so common as in most other groups, although, because these men are Negroids, the actual frequency of wide nasal bridges is nearly 70 per cent. Straight noses are in slight excess and also concavo-convex noses, while concave noses are somewhat deficient. The nasal tip is commonly very thick and is oftener elevated than depressed. The greatest predominance of flaring nasal wings (98.06 per cent) is recorded. The nasal septum is excessive in proportion of downward inclinations and is not so often deflected as in most other groups. This group runs rather high in integumental lip thickness, and like every other Negroid offense group, contains a vast majority of persons with thick membranous lips; yet thin lips and lips of medium thickness are commoner than average and the very Negroidal lip seam is oftener absent or more poorly developed than in any other group. On the whole there are proportionately more individuals with no prognathism or jaw protrusion than would be expected, while strongly jutting chins are found in an excess of more than 15 per cent over the average of the series, which is 29.11 per cent. Square chins are unduly common, while the malars or cheek bones stand out more often than in any other group and in quite an excessive percentage (56.77 per cent). Cheek fullness tends to be pronounced and jaw angles are flaring in the maximum proportion among Negroids. Wrinkling is somewhat excessive, perhaps on account of high average age, and multiple caries of the teeth also reach a maximum. Marked overbites are highly prevalent. High, broad palates are notably common, and ear lobes are frequently large. A very slight roll of the ear rim is commoner than in other groups, and this feature is naturally associated with a high average occurrence of Darwin's point on the ear border. Ears tend to run to extremes of compression and protrusion. Pronounced shoulder slope and long, thin necks are both commoner in this group than in any other, although these extreme features occur only in about one-third of the group members.

This group is lower in previous convictions than any of the offense groups with the exception of the two classes of murderers, although closely pressed by the rapists who complete the quartet of groups in which previous criminal records are rare. There are proportionately many more married men than are found in any other offense group (68.18 per cent). These bootleggers lead in extractive pursuits, are high in transportation, low in personal service, and very low in unskilled labor. On the whole they are fairly well educated, since they lead in percentages of persons who have reached the seventh and eighth grades. In the higher educational brackets they tend to be slightly deficient.

There can be no doubt that the entire anthropological and sociological complexion of this group of violators of liquor laws is colored by the preponderance in it of Negroids from Texas. Apparently these form a quite distinctive physical blend in which there is a strong indication of racial admixture with stocks carrying Indian blood — probably Mexicans. It is quite extraordinary that these colored bootleggers in their anthropological and sociological characteristics diverge from their general series in very much the same way as do the Old American White offenders against public welfare, who are to the same degree overloaded with

Texans. Both are older, taller, heavier, and more square-faced than their respective total criminal series. In each case we have a predominance of married men drawn from the extractive pursuits. There is a very strong suggestion in both groups that the members approximate more closely the norm of the non-criminal population than is the case with other offense groups. There is a possibility that the fieldworker who collected the Texas data unconsciously stressed in his qualitative observations certain recurrent physical peculiarities of the soft parts which he found in the population of that state. But his actual caliper measurements could not have been affected by such subjectivity. The forgery and fraud groups of both the Negroid and the Old American series also include unduly large numbers of Texans. In their physical and sociological peculiarities these also resemble the versus public welfare offenders, but their physical uniformity is less marked.

The last offense group of our Negroid series is arson and all other offenses. It includes only 32 men and is too small and too miscellaneous to merit discussion here. Metrically it is undifferentiated from the total series.

Of the ten offense groups of Negroid criminals, seven show overwhelming metric and morphological differentiation from the total series of which they form a part, and are equally distinctive in their sociological traits. The small assault group has enough metric peculiarities to differentiate it slightly from the entire series, but I have not bothered here to discuss its sociological and morphological features. The forgery and fraud group hardly attains metric individuality, but morphologically and sociologically is sufficiently well defined.

The Negroids seem to show almost as much offense group variation in measurements and in morphological and sociological traits as do the Old American offense groups, but in indices — ratios of one measurement to another — which express bodily proportions in contrast with gross size, they are apparently not so differentiated as are the Old American Whites. I think that the reason for this is the unifying effect of a heavy preponderance of Negro blood. In spite of the varying degrees of White admixture in the Negroids, they are not so racially diverse as are the Whites. Consequently, it is astounding to find the offense subgroups so well differentiated. I think that we must admit also the possibility of the formation of local state types among the Negro and Negroid population, although no statistical corrections have been made for this factor as yet. My assumption has been, and still is, that homogeneity of environment and of racial antecedents is so much more marked among the Negro population than among the Whites that a serious investigation of state types and an elaborate process of statistical correction for unequal distribution of these state types in the offense subgroups is unnecessary.

NEGRO OFFENSE DIFFERENTIATION

Among the pure Negro offense groups the first degree murderers are differentiated from the total series by a considerable number of significant deviations in measurements and indices. Notably the first degree murderers are 4.20 years above mean age and have absolutely longer and relatively narrower faces. Probably significant differences include excesses of weight, chest depth, and of height and breadth of the nose, a deficiency of head length, rounder heads, and an elevated relation of jaw breadth to face breadth.

The first degree murderers (only 76 men) show slight excesses of persons with scanty head hair and black hair color, and a marked excess of woolly hair form. They are somewhat high in pronounced forehead height and deficient in marked forehead slope. They include a few men with high nasal roots and bridges — uncommon in this series — and present small excesses both of concave and convex noses. Elevated nasal tips are the rule and deflections of the nasal septum are rare. Membranous lip thickness tends to be medium and lip seams more often absent or poorly developed than in the total series. Prognathism of the alveolar portion of the face is less marked than in the total group. Chin prominences are rather well developed and the flare of the cheek bones is likely to be excessive. Thin cheeks are unduly common. Moderate and marked wrinkling is characteristic. Excesses of heavily worn teeth, multiple caries, and great loss of teeth are an effect of the superior mean age of the group. Marked overbites and high, narrow palates are prominent. The ears are characterized in excess by lobes of medium size, free rather than attached, by slightly rolled helices or rims, frequent moderate development of Darwin's point, and poor development of the antihelix.

The first degree murderers of the Negro group are derived in excess proportions from Kentucky and Tennessee. They rarely have been previously convicted, and they show a moderate surplus of single men and of widowers. Their occupational excesses (always of small magnitude) include over-representation of factory workers and persons engaged in skilled trades. They fall considerably below the average of educational attainment of the series. These first degree murderers are certainly not a group in which full development of Negro racial characters is to the fore. Rather they suggest frequent but small amounts of White admixture.

Second degree murderers, an ample group of 158 men, are also anthropometrically distinct from the total series. They are older (excess 2.45 years), have broader faces and foreheads, wider jaws, and longer upper faces. The height of the head is deficient in its relation to length and breadth, the forehead wide relative to head breadth. These men have also a probably valid superiority of chest dimensions. Head and beard hair are unduly sparse, but body hair perhaps a little better developed than average. Frizzly hair, as contrasted to the woolly variety, is in moderate excess in this group. High palpebral openings or eye slits are quite notable. A pronounced development of glabella — the eminence over the root of the nose — is a feature of the second degree murderers. Forehead breadth is greater than in any other group. The slope of the forehead also tends to be marked. Both convex and concave noses are slightly in excess. Nasal proportions are not extreme, and the inclination of the nasal septum is more often downward than is the rule in the series. Membranous lip thickness tends to be pronounced, but lip seams are frequently undeveloped. Alveolar prognathism is possibly more marked than in the total series, but total facial prognathism is less developed. Chin prominences are decidedly submedium, but square chins are more frequent than in any other offense group. Malars and jaw angles tend to flare. Wrinkling is excessive, as are also dental caries and multiple tooth loss. High broad palates are the mode. Ear lobes are of medium development and usually free rather than attached, although attached lobes markedly exceed the average of the series; the antihelix is perhaps unusually well developed; ears tend strongly to be of submedium protrusion.

Second degree murderers are disproportionately derived from Tennessee and North Carolina. They are low in previous convictions and show marked excesses of married men, divorced men, and widowers. They lead easily in extractives and are slightly high in unskilled laborers but extraordinarily low in personal servants. This group is far below the general Negro criminal level of educational attainment. It includes nearly 24 per cent of illiterates.

Assault offenders number only 14 and are not worthy of discussion here. They appear to be an undersized group.

The 82 robbers of the pure Negro group are 2.3 years below mean age and are shallower of chest and rounder of head than the group at large. They are probably taller, shorter in the upper face, and show some elevation of the nasal index.

Robbers are noticeably deficient in beard quantity, but not distinguished in amount of head and body hair. They are rather high in dark brown hair and include the only person in the pure Negro series with red hair (probably erroneously classified as a pure Negro). Eyes are very dark and sclerae yellowish to an excessive extent. More of these robbers have internal epicanthic folds than would be expected from their total number. They have thicker than average eyebrow development. High foreheads are unusually prevalent and absence of forehead slope is also in excess. The group is slightly high in proportions of very broad nasal roots and convex nasal profiles. Flaring nasal wings are present in every member of the offense group. The nasal septum inclines upward oftener than in any other group and there is a very high incidence of deflections to the right. Lips are unremarkable except for excessive development of the lip seam, which reaches its maximum among the robbers (excluding the negligible arson group). Protrusion of the alveolar region of the face is pronounced in a surplus of cases. Chin prominence is often feeble and rarely pronounced. Pointed chins are more strongly predominant in this group than in any other. In flare of the hinder angles of the jaw the robbers also lead. A medium amount of cheek wrinkling is somewhat commoner than expectation, but in accordance with their low mean age, multiple loss of teeth is rare. The normal slight overbite (63.29 per cent) attains its maximum frequency in this offense category. The robbers tend to have excesses of small and attached ear lobes, also a predominance of medium to well rolled ear rims and of prominent antihelices. A pronounced protrusion of the back of the head is found in excess, and the group is also high in sloping shoulders.

The state which markedly exceeds its robber quota is Missouri (34.15 per cent as against 15.67 per cent in the total series). In the other states which furnish large Negro contingents this offense is less common than expectation. These robbers have 37 per cent of previous convictions, which is about 6 per cent above the figure for the total series. They have a low marriage rate. This group is lowest of all in the extractive occupations (7.41 per cent) and next to highest in unskilled labor (41.98 per cent). It is also high in transportation and in personal service. The robbers include the smallest percentage of illiterates (13.58 per cent) and easily surpass in their educational attainments all other offense groups except that of the fraudulent criminals.

Burglars and thieves in this Negro series number 336 individuals, which is nearly 44 per cent of the total group, the highest proportion found in any of the major series of criminals. It is interesting to note that the Negroes of this offense group show the same size inferiority which seems constantly to stigmatize this type of offender, of whatever racial origin. A great many of the metric deficiencies of this group fall short of statistical significance, but they are certainly younger (3.30 years), and have shorter faces and longer bodies (as measured by sitting height) than the group at large. Probably valid deficiencies occur in chest diameters, head circumference, face breadth, and in the facial index. However, the metric differentiae are not very marked, but only consistent in the direction of decreased size.

In hair form, hair color, and pigmentation the burglars and thieves are not distinctive. In many characters they tend to be high in the medium degrees of development. They are, however, notable for deep depressions of the nasal root, which also tends to be low to a slightly excessive degree and of pronounced breadth in about 3 per cent more than in the total series. Broad nasal bridges are also a little more common than expectation, together with concavo-convex nasal profiles. Noses, on the whole, seem to be a little coarser than in the total series and septa inclined upward are unduly frequent. Deflections of the septum are in considerable excess.

Integumental lips among the burglars and thieves are thin in an excess of more than 4 per cent over the total series proportion; membranous lips show a small surplus of pronounced thickness; lip seams are often prominent. Both alveolar and facial prognathism (of slight degree) are somewhat high; malars are compressed rather oftener than is normal for the series. Jaw angles show a smaller proportion of pronounced flare than is average for the series, and there is less wrinkling on account of the lower mean age of this offense group. For the same reason, cases of multiple dental caries and tooth loss are unusually few. The ear presents few distinctive features. Free lobes are somewhat in excess and also well rolled ear rims or helices.

On the whole, most of the excesses in this group involve 3 or 4 per cent of extreme cases, and the rest conform rather closely to the modal types of the series of which this group constitutes nearly one-half. Generally speaking, thieves and burglars seem to me to be less typical in their physical peculiarities as an offense group than is the case with the corresponding group in the Whites.

There is no marked overloading of this group by any one state, although Missouri shows an excess of about 5 per cent and Kentucky is slightly over-represented. As is normally the case in this type of offense, previous convictions attain their maximum with 41 per cent. This group also conforms to pattern in having the highest proportion of unmarried men (63.47 per cent). It has no important occupational peculiarities and is slightly above average in education. These Negro thieves and burglars impress one as rather less stringently selected for physical inferiority than corresponding White groups. Yet they are somewhat below the physical par of the series.

The forgery and fraud group of 31 men is so small that it hardly justifies statistical analysis. However, this group is always of sufficient sociological distinctiveness to justify some inquiry into its physical characteristics. Because of its small size, most differences from the total series are of dubious validity. Nevertheless, these fraudulent Negroes show the slight age (2.95 years) and greater size superiority usually associated with this category of offense. They are probably taller with larger head circumferences, wider faces, and narrower jaws than the general group. They have certainly narrower jaws and foreheads relative to face breadth than are characteristic of the general Negro series. Their relative sitting height is probably low, as is usual among the taller, long-legged men.

This group, doubtless because of its small size, barely attains anthropological distinctiveness. We may review briefly its morphological peculiarities. Head hair quantity is almost always below average in fraudulent criminals, and these Negroes are no exception. It is a curious fact that men engaged in the more intellectual pursuits appear on the whole to have thinner hair and to suffer from baldness to a greater extent than those who presumably cerebrate less actively. Apparently the mental effort demanded by the perpetrating of fraudulent crimes tends also to select these alopecious specimens of humanity. But they are remarkable for sparsity of beard and body hair — which is unusual in men above mean age. It may be an accident of sampling that this small offense group is darkest of all in skin color and has 100 per cent of the darkest eye shade. Hence heavily pigmented yellow sclerae reach their series maximum, as do also thick eyebrows. There is the suggestion of a rather poor development of glabella and brow ridges. High and markedly sloping foreheads appear to be unduly common.

Most of the nasal features are not distinctive, but a high frequency of very broad nasal bridges may be more than an accident of sampling. Lip seams may be slightly under-developed. There is a very large and rather puzzling excess of purely subnasal or aveolar jaw protrusion, accompanied by something of a deficiency in total facial prognathism. Chin prominence is strongly marked in a high percentage of cases. Cheek bones are not especially prominent, and cheek fullness is above average. Jaw angles are compressed rather than flaring. Wrinkling is slightly in excess. Teeth in this group are better than in most others, although the group is somewhat above mean age, but marked overbites occur in an excess which may be significant.

Attached ear lobes are present in a substantial surplus of cases and the roll of the helix tends to be slight. Curiously, however, Darwin's point, usually associated with slightly rolled helices, is proportionately rare. Facial asymmetry is somewhat above average and hollow temples distinctly so. Fraudulent Negro criminals are disproportionately numerous in the Texas sample (excess 19.83 per cent), whereas the large Missouri quota of 120 Negroes contains but one convicted of forgery or fraud. This group has about the average number of previous convictions and includes more than a 9 per cent excess of married men. There are few extractive workers among the fraudulent Negro criminals, and unskilled laborers are also deficient in numbers. The excesses are in transport workers and in personal servants. Education is considerably better in this group than in any other. In order to forge or to raise a check, one must at least be able to read and write, yet 5 of these fraudulent criminals are alleged to be illiterate. I suppose that it is possible for an illiterate crook to swindle persons who are also illiterate and even more stupid. None of our Negro fraudists has attended college and only one has reached the last two years of high school. But more than 19 per cent have attained the first two years of high school. These fraudulent Negro criminals are much less differentiated from the total series than are corresponding White groups, although most of their sociological and physical differences agree in direction with those found among the possibly more sophisticated Whites.

I think that we may dispose rather summarily here of the 33 rapists, to whom have been added 5 other sex offenders. Like all other groups of sex offenders studied, this Negro handful is far above mean age (excess 8.35 years), is narrow-nosed and probably relatively long-nosed. It has great sitting height relative to stature and probably a relatively narrow forehead. Undoubtedly it would be ' differentiated metrically if the sample were of adequate size.

Morphologically these sex offenders are notable for sparse beard and body hair, excesses of medium skin tints, concentration in woolly hair, no eye folds whatsoever, thin eyebrows, big brow ridges and pronounced glabella, concavo-convex noses, thick nasal tips, infrequently deflected nasal septa, thick integumental lips, prevailingly medium prognathism of both kinds, thin cheeks, pronouncedly worn teeth with frequent multiple dental loss, unusual prevalence of edge-to-edge bite, excess of high narrow palates and mouth-breathers, complete absence of the roll of the ear rim in 5 individuals (13.2 per cent), strongly developed antihelices, quite extraordinary occurrence of facial asymmetry, very hollow temporal regions.

Sex offenders are not certainly derived in excess from any particular state except perhaps Wisconsin, which seems to show a peculiar proclivity for this sort of behavior, whether in colored men or in Whites. However, Wisconsin furnishes only three of the group and Massachusetts rather outdoes itself by adding two. In the whole Negro series there are but 17 from Massachusetts and 16 from Wisconsin. Possibly these northern states are unduly finicky about sex offenses. Rapists and other sex offenders are oftener married than not, and are scattered as to occupation, with heavy emphasis upon extractives, factory workers, and personal servants. These Negro sex criminals are the most illiterate of all offense groups — an apparently ordinary sociological concomitant of rape. The mixing in of a few sex offenders who have done something other than rape adds a few well educated persons.

In spite of the insufficient numbers in this Negro sex group, the physical features suggest degeneration and abnormality, precisely as in the case of the Old Americans.

Finally, we have another small group of liquor offenders (22 men), again heavily overloaded with Texans, who also resemble the previous samples of this criminal class in being significantly older than the average (excess 8.05 years), and probably taller and heavier, broader of shoulder and deeper of chest, with certainly larger head circumferences, relatively broader and shorter noses, and probably shorter and relatively broader faces. It is hardly worth while to attempt to summarize percentages of morphological variations based upon such feeble numbers. Distributions are almost certain to be misleading. Sociologically these Negro bootleggers conform to their offense type in infrequency of previous convictions and high marriage rate, but they include more unskilled laborers and fewer extractives than is usual in these series. They have better than average educations for Negro criminals. One of them has even gone to college.

Thus we find that, taking into account the social and economic limitations of the Negro populations and the unifying influence of a common predominance of Negro blood, physical and social differentiation according to type of offense is somewhat similar in kind and somewhat less in degree than obtains among the Old American Whites. The most extraordinary discovery is that, irrespective of racial differences, rather similar anthropological types and persons of equivalent sociological status appear to exercise the same criminal preferences.

BODY BUILD

Body build as expressed by individual combinations of weight and stature was found in the Old American Whites to offer associations of great interest with type of offense and with other sociological characteristics. The same procedure of sorting for body build type was followed with the Negroes and Negroids. A three-fold division of stature was made on the basis of the mean and standard deviation of the total series. Then three groups were delimited, with the medium group including once the standard deviation on either side of the mean. The resulting three stature groups were similarly subdivided according to the mean and standard deviation of weight in each. The final result is nine groups based upon the statures and weights of each respective series. Thus we have short-slender, short-medium weight, short-heavy, medium height-slender, et cetera. These groups in the different series are directly comparable, because the constants used for dividing the native White series of native parentage were so similar to those found in the Negroes and Negroids that the curves were cut at the same intervals in all three. It is then interesting to note how the Negroes differ in body build from the Negroids, and how each diverges from the Old American Whites. Short men are commonest among the so-called pure Negroes (17.22 per cent), proportionately nearly one-third fewer in the Negroids (11.97 per cent), and only about one-half as numerous among the Whites (8.56 per cent). The Negroes pile up their excess especially in the short-medium weight group. Men of medium height and slender weight are approximately twice as common among the Whites as among either of the colored groups (Old Americans 8.90 per cent, Negroids 4.55 per cent, Negroes 3.58 per cent). All three series have nearly half of their total in the medium height-medium weight group, with the Old American Whites superior to the other two series in this body build (Whites 49.23 per cent, Negroes 47.48 per cent, Negroids 44.89 per cent). The Negroids have a substantial lead in the medium height-heavy group, with the Negroes second (Negroids 27.78 per cent, Negroes 23.41 per cent, Whites 18.64 per cent). All tall groups are proportionately more numerous among the Old American Whites, who are followed by the Negroids (talls: Whites 14.66 per cent, Negroids 10.81 per cent, Negroes 8.29 per cent). One might say that among the Negroes, apart from the always predominant medium-medium class, the typical body builds are medium height-heavy and short-medium weight. In the Negroids the medium height-heavy is even more heavily represented, but still second, and short-medium weight is a weaker third. In the Old Americans medium height-heavy is easily the second ranking type, and medium height-slender and tall-medium weight run a nearly dead heat for a bad third place. In the purer Negroes there is more emphasis upon short stature and upon heavy weight, in the Negroids upon medium stature and heavy weight, in the Whites upon tall stature and upon medium stature with slender build.

The Negroids average one year older than the Negroes and about 8 months older than the Old American Whites (Negroids 31.2 years, Whites 30.5 years, Negroes 30.2 years). In the Whites and the Negroids the heaviest body build groups in relation to stature are the oldest groups, but in the Negroes the regression is less regular, probably because the series is so small that some of the body build groups contain only a handful of individuals.

The Whites average 151 pounds in weight, the Negroes 152.4, and the Negroids 155.3. The average weight of each of the nine stature-weight classes is practically the same in the Negroes, Negroids, and Whites. On the other hand, the Whites average a little more than one centimeter taller than the Negroids, who, in turn, are about one centimeter taller than the pure Negroes. Hence the stature means of the nine Negroid types are nearly the same as those of the Whites, but the Negroes tend to average slightly shorter in most body build types. We thus reach the interesting conclusion that the Negroids or mixed-bloods, classified by body build, tend to be intermediate in stature between the Negroes and the Whites, but surpass both in weight.

The Negroes are slightly the longest-headed of the three series, with the Negroids intermediate, and the Old American Whites the most brachycephalic (Negroes 77.49, Negroids 77.70, Whites 78.57). These differences are in accordance with expectation, since Negroes are predominantly dolichocephalic, whereas the White races include perhaps more round heads. In the Whites and the Negroids there is a tendency of heads to grow slightly rounder with increase in weight in each stature class, but this trend is not clear in the Negroes, perhaps because of inadequate size of several of their body build groups.

The Negroes have relatively the longest and narrowest faces of the three series, with the Negroids again intermediate. In all groups there is to be observed the tendency of faces to become relatively broader as weight increases within the stature classes.

Of course both Negroes and Negroids have noses much wider relative to their height than the Whites possess. In the Negroes the average relation of nose width to nose height is 88.78 per cent, in the Negroids 85.30 per cent, and in the Old Americans only 66.70 per cent. Thus the Negroids are far closer to the Negroes in this racial feature than to the Whites. In all of the series the nose tends to be relatively narrower in the slender subgroups.

Hair color does not appear to be related clearly to body build type in the group of supposedly purer African descent, with the exception of dark brown hair, which is somewhat more common in the tall stature groups of Negroids. Practically all of the pure Negroes have very dark brown eyes. The lighter shades which are found among the Negroids seem to be distributed regardless of body build.

In the Old American Whites previous convictions diminish with increasing weight within the stature classes and in general with decreasing stature. In the Negroids a similar tendency is discernible, but it is in no way so regular. The small size of several of the Negro build groups defeats attempts at comparison. The Negroes have the fewest previous convictions and the Whites the most (Negroes 33.97, Negroids 36.16, Whites 39.82).

The marked associations of body build with offense found in the Old American Whites are conspicuous by their absense in the Negroes and Negroids. In the Old Americans burglary and larceny diminish with increasing stature and weight, while murder increases. No such clear regressions can be discerned in these Afro-Americans. Burglary and larceny do appear to be more prevalent in the short groups and those of medium height than in the tall classes. In the more or less pure Negro series the most characteristic body builds — apart from the ever predominant medium-medium — are short-medium weight and medium height-heavy. The short-medium weight group of Negroes is high in second degree murder, assault, and rape, and somewhat low in larceny. The medium height-heavy group is quite undifferentiated in offense. On the other hand, the second largest Negroidal group — medium height-heavy — is high in first degree murder, rape, and versus public welfare, but low in robbery and in burglary and larceny. In these Negroids robbery seems to decrease with increments of weight, but bootlegging increases with stature. Rape apparently diminishes with growing stature. The mixed-bloods appear to show resemblances to the Whites in many of these offense associations with body build. But the pure Negroes seem to have no orderly associations of body build and nature of crime. This may be due to the fact that some of the rarer body build groups in the pure Negro series contain no more than five to twenty individuals. However, I am inclined to think that the Negro confusion in the matter of body build is due rather to lack of social selection of physical types — a process which has gone a little further in the mulattoes and is much more advanced in the Old Americans.

In the Old Americans there is also a clear relation of body build to marital status. The small and scrawny men are most likely to be bachelors, and the taller and paunchier individuals are the most married. In the pure Negro group marital rates seem to increase with weight, aside from the very small short-statured subgroups. Of the three body build series, the pure Negroes have the highest rate of celibacy (49.51 per cent), the Whites are intermediate (48.51 per cent), and the Negroids are most frequently husbands (with only 43.12 per cent of unmarried men). These marriage rates accord with the mean ages of the three groups, assuming that the older the group, the more likely it is to show a high rate of marital infection. The Negroids resemble the Whites inasmuch as marriage appears to increase with added body weight, but there is no relationship between stature and matrimony. The little ones have as many wives as the big ones.

The relation of body build to occupation is also exiguous. The only clear regression is in the personal service category. In two of three stature classes personal servants diminish proportionately with advancing weight, and in general as stature increases this type of occupation diminishes. In the Negroids, as in the Whites, the percentage of extractives increases as stature rises. That is absolutely all.

Finally, the associations of body build with educational qualifications in both of these colored series seem to be absolutely nil with one exception. In the pure Negroes and in the Negroids as well illiteracy and poor educations seem to increase with weight. Generalizing, one may state that these body build groups in the Negroes and Negroids seem to have comparatively little sociological significance. This finding is of very great interest when it is considered that body build seems intimately related to every sort of sociological condition in the Old American Whites. I think that the disagreement is easily explained. The Whites are derived from a considerable array of racial strains and nationalities and are much more diversified in environment and in economic and social status. Their range of opportunities is much greater than is the case with Negroes and Negroids, both of whom tend to be fitted to the same narrow Procrustean bed. If there are preferences and capabilities associated with body build types, Negroes and Negroids have little opportunity to exercise and to utilize them. Social mobility is not granted to the colored population, and even if a man has secured a college education, he may still be forced to seek employment as a dining-car waiter. There is no social selection of body build types, or at least it is very restricted. Again, the Negro has emerged but recently from slavery and has had little time as well as negligible opportunity for sociological adjustment. He has not found himself, even in choice of crime, because he has been kept down by racial prejudice.

CHAPTER X

NEGRO AND NEGROID CRIMINALS AND CIVILIANS

SANE CRIMINALS AND INSANE CIVILIANS

CRIMINOLOGICAL AND ANTHROPOLOGICAL EFFECTS OF RACIAL DISCRIMINATION

I DO not know how many generations must still eke out their stultified existence misled by a fatuous faith in the organic implications of democracy. Whatever may be the sociological value of the legal fiction that "all men are born free and equal," there can be no doubt that the author of this phrase deserves above all other men the description *splendide mendax*, translated by the English schoolboy "lying in state." In its biological application, at any rate, this statement is one of the most stupendous falsehoods ever uttered by man through his misbegotten gift of articulate speech. Organic equality is non-existent, even in identical twins. Organisms are not alike in quality or magnitude; they are individually and collectively different. The fact that we are not skillful enough to recognize these differences and to analyze them does not justify their denial.

Differences between individuals or groups can be ascertained and appraised without the necessity of pronouncing judgments as to inferiority or superiority. These latter may be wholly subjective and undesirable. Certainly that is true of racial differences. Now there can be no doubt that the marked physical differences between the Negro and White divisions of mankind are accompanied by physiological and probably by psychological and temperamental divergences. It is sufficiently obvious, for instance, that as yet undefined anatomical and physiological qualities of the Negro organism are responsible for Negro preeminence in sprinting and jumping, that the larynx of the Negro is constructed in some peculiar way which permits or facilitates the production of a different voice quality from that ordinarily characteristic of Whites, that a certain fluidity of muscular movement and a hypersensitivity to rhythm are responsible for the racial individuality of Negro music and art, et cetera. In general, the behavior which arises from the Negro organism differs from that emanating from the Whites, either subtilely or crassly, and there is nothing invidious in the distinction.

But, when we compare convicted felons, whether Negroes or Whites, with law-abiding citizens of the same race, we are contrasting the social liabilities with the social assets, and we deliberately judge criminals to be undesirable and of lesser worth than economically efficient and socially-minded men. Thus, if we find felons to manifest physical differences from civilians, we are justified in adjudging as undesirable biological characters those which are associated in the organism with antisocial behavior. Of course size is not an infallible criterion. Bigger things are not necessarily better things, nor smaller inferior. It is the organic complex which must be estimated inferior or superior on the basis of the type of behavior emanating from such a combination of parts functioning as a unit.

COMPARISON OF CRIMINAL NEGROES AND NEGROIDS WITH CIVILIAN CHECK SAMPLES

In order to secure civilian samples with which to compare our Negro and Negroid criminals, our field observers exercised their tact and persistence in North Carolina and Tennessee. Reluctantly we had to resort to college students in order to fill out these samples. College students, of course, represent a class almost as stringently selected as criminals, and presumably from the opposite end of the social scale — Cambridge politicians to the contrary notwithstanding.

Consequently, I have deemed it advisable to compare Negro and Negroid criminals each first with a sample of non-college civilians, and then with a sample of college students. In this way we can check the anthropometric status of the delinquents against groups presumably derived both from the same approximate social stratum and from one which, even in the depressed colored population, ought to be distinctly superior mentally, if not physically.

NEGROIDS

First we may take the comparison of our 3325 criminal Negroids with 210 non-college Negroid civilians. At present these comparisons have been restricted to metric data. We at once encounter a rather astounding fact. The Negroid criminals do indeed differ profoundly from non-college Negroid civilians, but not in the direction of smaller size and presumable physical inferiority. The criminals are significantly higher in mean age (2.95 years) and are considerably heavier (5.50 pounds) and probably taller; have broader chests, greater sitting height, longer heads, wider foreheads and faces, but lower head heights, smaller head circumferences, shorter noses, and ears which are smaller both in length and in breadth. Indicially the criminals also differ widely from their civilian check sample. They have lower head heights relative to head length and head breadth; shorter and broader faces, noses, and ears. These differences suggest that the criminals represent racially a more fully developed Negro type than do the civilians, but certainly not a physically inferior type — rather the reverse.

We may consider briefly the separate offense groups of Negroid criminals, each in comparison with the non-college civilians. Both the first degree murderers and the second degree murderers exaggerate the differences between the total Negroid series and the non-college civilians. The only important difference between the two comparisons is that the first degree murderers are more markedly superior to the civilians in head length and head breadth than are the second degree murderers and fail to exhibit the general series criminal inferiority in head height (absolute) and in head circumference.

The assault Negroid criminals are also significantly older than the non-college Negroid civilians and are inferior to them in head height and head circumference, nose height, and ear length. However, in most bodily measurements the criminals insignificantly exceed the civilians. The former certainly have heads lower with reference to their breadth and their length, and shorter, broader faces. Probably the criminals are also more long-headed and their noses are broader relative to their height.

The Negroid robbers are only slightly and insignificantly older than the non-college civilians, but are larger in most bodily dimensions. They are taller, probably heavier, with broader chests, increased sitting height, and wider faces. The criminals are superior also in head length and head breadth, and probably in forehead breadth and upper face height. However, they are definitely inferior in head height and head circumference and in ear measurements. The nasal index of the delinquents is higher and the breadth-height index of the skull lower. Decreased head height relative to head length, and somewhat shorter and broader faces on the part of the criminals are strongly suggested.

The thieves and burglars among the Negroids are the same age as the mean of the non-college check sample. The criminals, nevertheless, are superior in weight, sitting height, and forehead breadth. They fall below the civilians in shoulder breadth, head height, and head circumference, and also in nose height, jaw breadth, and ear measurements. They manifest similar index divergences from the civilians to those found in the other groups, and in addition have relatively shorter and broader ears. But, as compared with this check sample, the thieves and burglars fail to show the size deficiency which this type of offender generally manifests when compared with civilians. The forgers and fraudulent criminals show practically the same array of differences from the civilians, with some minor variations which need not be detailed here.

Rapists are generally an aged and undersized group. They are 5 years older and 5.8 pounds heavier than the check sample. However, they are not significantly smaller except in those measurements in which all of these Negroid criminals seem to fall below the civilian check sample, although they are possibly shorter. In addition to the metric differences and the usual indicial divergences, the rapists are relatively narrow in shoulder, have higher sitting height in comparison with stature, and narrow ears relative to ear length. They have not the usual superiority in relative breadth of the nose, because these rapists have long and slightly pinched noses. Altogether, this group of sex offenders shows very typical differences from the non-college check sample, which are much of the same nature as those which it manifests when compared with its total assemblage of co-criminals. The sex offenders other than rapists (with an excess of 8.35 years in mean age) are inferior to civilians in head height, head circumference, and total face height. They show also a number of minus deviations in measurements which do not attain our lower limit of statistical reliability. Certain indicial divergences include diminished head height relative to length and breadth, proportionately shorter and broader faces, foreheads narrower relative to face breadth and to head breadth, and jaws especially narrow in comparison with face breadth.

The versus public welfare Negroids are more than 7 years older than these civilians and almost 14 pounds heavier. They are also taller and larger in their trunk measurements, in head length and head breadth, forehead and face breadth, and probably in jaw breadth. They fall significantly below the criminals only in head height, and insignificantly in the vertical dimensions of face, nose, and ears. They show the customary indicial deficiencies in relative head height and face height. These liquor offenders also tend merely to emphasize in their differences from the civilians the characters which distinguish them within their own criminal series.

Very similar strictures apply to the arson and miscellaneous offense group, which particularly stresses long heads and very short, broad noses. I must confess myself somewhat surprised by the virtual unanimity of these criminal offense group divergences from the non-college civil check sample. They suggest that the criminals and civilians are samples drawn from quite different populations, of which the criminals are decidedly the more Negroid, but not smaller and biologically inferior. In this preliminary analysis of the Negro and Negroid material, which has not yet been worked out exhaustively, I can only say that I seem to detect evidence either of personal equations of the observers which may enhance differences, or of divergences due to the fact that the check sample was collected in but two states, whereas the Negroid criminal series has been derived principally from five states. Nevertheless, I am confident of the general validity of these results.

However, we have another civilian check sample of Negroids consisting of 551 college students, with whom the criminals may be compared. These students are nearly ten years younger than the Negroid criminals (averages: college, 21.7 years; non-college, 28.5 years; criminals, 31.45 years). The criminals average 3 pounds heavier and have significantly larger chest dimensions, but are definitely shorter, narrower of shoulder, and deficient in every head measurement, probably in breadth of forehead, and certainly in upper facial height. However, the delinquents appear to have greater total face heights and wider noses. They manifest a formidable array of indicial deviations from the college students. These include greater relative sitting heights, greater face breadths in relation to head breadths, decreased relative head heights, relatively shorter and broader upper faces, narrower foreheads relative to face breadth, wider foreheads relative to head breadth, and wider jaws relative to face breadth. Thus the criminals appear to be shorter and somewhat rounder and heavier men, with smaller heads and wider faces. Some portion of the weight and rotundity of the criminals must be ascribed to the extra decade of mean age which they have to their credit or debit, but there are strong indications of markedly different anthropological type. Nearly all of the cranial differences here enumerated are such as indicate that the criminals represent more conservative, less adaptable types of human organisms than do the civilians. The other differences seem to be rather those of the nature which separate the middle-aged generation from the young adults of the same stock in many of the racial and ethnic groups which we have studied. We may examine the evidence further by considering the differences from the Negroid collegians of the various criminal offense groups.

The first degree murderers differ from the college Negroids in substantially the same features and in the same direction as does the total Negroid criminal series. Of course the murderers are very much older than the college students (15.55 years) — which probably accounts for the fact that their noses are both longer and broader than those of the students, instead of being merely significantly broader and dubiously longer. One or two other differences which fail to attain validity in the total series are definitely established in the first degree murderers.

The second degree murderers show almost precisely the same differences from the college students as does the other class of homicidal criminals, with the exception of nose height, in which they do not surpass the civilians, and relative narrowness and length of the total face, in which they do. The second degree murderers have smaller brain case measurements than are found in the first degree killers.

The assault criminals present a practically identical and united front of metric and indicial deviations from the civilians, except that they are not heavier than the students and, on the whole, tend to exaggerate the size deficiencies characteristic of the entire Negroid criminal group in this comparison.

The robbers are superior to the college students in total face height and probably in nose and jaw breadth, but they are shorter, narrower of shoulder, and inferior in head measurements; yet they have broader and deeper chests. They tend to be slightly less long-headed and their relative head height indices are lower than those of the civilians.

The thieves and burglars maintain the usual criminal superiority in chest dimensions, in face length and (possibly) in nose height. Otherwise they show overwhelming minus deviations in bodily measurements except weight, accompanied by the indicial differences which need not be reiterated.

The fraudulent criminals are heavier than the check sample and fail to show the usual inferiority in head circumference. Otherwise their deviations from the check sample are much the same as those of the other criminals. Very similar differences occur in the sex offenders who have committed rape, and in the versus public welfare group, which is not, however, inferior to the college students in stature and shoulder breadth. Just as each group presents its individual array of metric differences from the entire series, so it varies slightly in the direction and significance of its differences from civilians.

All ten groups are superior to the civilians in age. Four significantly exceed the civilians in weight and the others deviate in statistically uncertain amounts in both directions. Eight of the groups are definitely below the civilians in height. All of the criminals except the bootleggers have smaller shoulder breadths than the students and these deviations are statistically valid in three groups. Every criminal group is characterized by pronounced superiority of chest depth, and in six groups the larger chest breadths of the criminals are statistically reliable. Sitting height is significantly less in three criminal groups and is in no case higher in criminals, with the probable exception of the bootleggers. The criminal offense groups are unanimously deficient in head length, head breadth, and head height. Head circumference is probably superior in murderers of the first degree and in versus public welfare offenders, and possibly in the fraudulent group. In four of the groups it is almost certainly lower than in the civilians. The breadth of the forehead is absolutely less in every criminal group except the bootleggers, but these deficiencies are statistically certain in but two groups (larceny and other sex). Facial breadth is insignificantly high in 8 of the 10 criminal groups. Four of the convict groups have assuredly longer total faces, and only in other sex offenders is the total face height deficient to a probably significant degree. On the other hand, the upper part of the face (from the root of the nose to the point on the gums between the upper middle front teeth) is invariably shorter in the criminals. This condition is probably due to older mean age and frequent loss of upper teeth, but it is perhaps associated also with the apparently more Negro physiognomy of the delinquents. Only two of the delinquent groups have certainly longer noses than the civilians and none have significantly shorter noses. Because the criminals are invariably older, it would be expected that all criminals should have longer noses, since nose length (or height) increases, supposedly, in middle age. The murderer groups have definitely broader noses than the civilians, and other groups all show insignificant increases of nasal breadth, with other sex offenders displaying the minimum nasal widening. Jaw breadth is definitely superior in five criminal groups and probably in one other. It is probably narrower in Negroid thieves and burglars than in college students. Ear measurements (taken by two observers with different techniques) are contradictory and yield no definite trends of difference. Shoulder breadth relative to stature is about the same in the criminals as in the college students, with the exception of the rapists, who are notably narrow-shouldered. But sitting height relative to stature is significantly higher in 8 of the 10 offense groups and probably higher in one other. The relation of head breadth to head length — the cephalic index — has no value as a criterion of distinction between criminal offense groups and Negroid college students. Only the robbers appear to present the probability of having slightly rounder heads than the students.

The breadth of the face relative to head breadth (cephalo-facial index) is in every criminal group significantly or probably higher than in the students. Elevation of this index is, on the whole, a primitive feature. The length-height and breadth-height indices of the skulls in the criminals are lower than those of civilians in each of the ten offense groups, and only in a few cases does the deficiency fail to attain statistical significance. Relative and absolute smallness of head height is an undubitably inferior anthropological character. The total face is longer relative to its breadth in second degree murderers and probably in thieves, but in other groups does not vary in any dependable measure from the average of the students. On the other hand, the upper face of the criminals is relatively shorter and broader in 9 of 10 offense groups, perhaps because of shortening of the face due to loss of upper teeth, or conceivably attributable to accentuation of the Negroid facial cast, in which the upper jaw and nose are short, but the lower jaw or mandible is absolutely deep. The crude indications are that the students have longer upper faces but shallower lower jaws than the criminals.

While the nasal index (relation of nose breadth to nose height) is usually very slightly higher in the criminals than in the civilians, no offense group shows a really significant deviation. The two observers disagree in the deviations of their subseries as to the proportions of the ear, so that the criminals cannot be said to differ from civilians in this character. In all 10 groups the breadth of forehead relative to total face breadth is inferior in the criminals and in 7 groups this difference is statistically certain. All of the criminal groups have wider foreheads relative to head breadth and these differences are statistically significant in 4 groups. Nine of the 10 offense groups have broader jaws relative to face breadth than have civilians, and in 5 groups the differences are certainly valid.

COMPARISON OF NEGRO CRIMINALS AND NEGRO CIVILIANS

Our civilian check sample of putatively pure Negroes who have not attended college is unfortunately limited to 31 men. The total Negro criminals are more than 6 years older, 10 pounds heavier, and insignificantly taller (1.17 cm.). The criminals also have definitely deeper chests and longer heads, as well as broader and probably longer faces. Further, the delinquents have greater sitting height absolutely and relatively to stature, broader faces relative to head breadth, narrower foreheads in comparison with their facial breadth, and narrower jaws relative to face breadth.

The pure Negro college students are also very few in number. They total only 47 men. Although the criminals are 8.65 years higher in average age and 9.5 pounds superior in average weight, they are insignificantly shorter than the students and probably narrower of shoulder. But the criminals have definitely broader chests. The criminal head length is inferior and the head breadth probably so. Deficiency in head height is present but uncertain. However, the delinquents have probably longer faces and broader jaws, although their noses are narrower. The criminal ear is probably shorter than the civilian ear. There is a strong suggestion that the criminals may have slightly rounder heads than the students. They certainly have proportionately narrower noses and broader jaws with reference to their face breadth.

SUMMARY OF METRIC AND INDICIAL DIFFERENCES BETWEEN
NEGRO AND NEGROID CRIMINALS AND CIVILIANS

We may now pool the results of metric and indicial comparisons of Negro and Negroid criminals, each with its two check samples of civilians — non-college and college.

The only unanimous findings in all comparisons of measurements are that the criminals average much older and considerably heavier. Both series of criminals are dubiously taller than the non-college civilians with whom they are compared respectively. The Negro criminals are probably shorter than college Negroes and the Negroid criminals are certainly shorter than Negroid collegians. Neither criminal series shows any difference in shoulder breadth from non-college civilians, but the Negro criminals are probably narrower-shouldered than Negro collegians, and the Negroid criminals are certainly inferior in this dimension to comparable students. Both criminal series exceed college civilians in chest depth; the criminal Negroes certainly surpass non-college civilians, and the criminal Negroids possibly excel their non-college check sample. In chest breadth Negro criminals do not differ from civilians, but Negroid criminals are definitely superior to both civilian classes. In sitting height the Negroes and Negroids of the criminal series exceed the non-college civilians, but the Negroid criminals are probably shorter than the Negroid college students. In head length both criminal groups are larger than non-college, and smaller than college, civilians. In head breadth both series of criminals are probably above the non-college civilians and probably below the students. There are no differences in head height and head circumference between the Negro criminals and civilians, but Negroid criminals are inferior in these dimensions to both groups of Negroid civilians.

Forehead breadth differences are confined to the Negroids, among whom the criminals exceed the non-college civilians and are probably inferior to the college students. Both criminal groups exceed non-college civilians in breadth of face. Neither the pure Negroes nor the Negroids differ from comparable students in this measurement. In the total height of the face (from the root of the nose to the base of the chin) Negro criminals are probably superior to both college and non-college civilians and probably to the collegians as well. The Negroid criminals excel the college students. In breadth of nose the Negroid criminals surpass college students but do not differ from non-college civilians; the pure Negro criminals fall below the students in this dimension. Both criminal groups probably exceed their college check samples in jaw breadth, but do not differ from the non-college civilians.

There is no difference between the criminals and the civilians in breadth of shoulder relative to stature. The Negro criminal series exceeds non-college civilians in relative sitting height and the Negroids also have a higher value of this index than the college students. The cephalic index, which expresses the breadth of the head as a percentage of the length, is of little importance in these comparisons. The criminal Negroes are possibly broader-headed than the college Negroes. In facial breadth as a percentage of head breadth the Negro criminals have higher means than the non-college Negroes and the criminal Negroids surpass the

Negroid collegians. The differences between head height indices are confined to the Negroids. The criminals fall markedly below both college and non-college Negroid civilians. In the facial index the Negroid criminals have lower means (implying shorter and broader faces) than non-college Negroids, and shorter, broader upper faces than the college students. The relation of forehead to face breadth is depressed in the Negro criminals when compared with non-college civilians and in Negroid criminals as contrasted with Negroid college students. Both criminal groups have wider jaws relative to face breadth than have college students, but the pure Negroes are surpassed by Negro non-college civilians in this measurement.

In most anthropometric features the criminal Negroes and Negroids are closer to the non-college civilians than to the college students. In every comparison the added age of the criminals tends to give them a distinct advantage in weight and in chest measurements. However, this would not be the case if the criminals were notably inferior in physique and in bodily strength to the civilians. Most of our White criminals are inferior to White civilians in weight and height quite irrespective of age differences. There is really no evidence whatsoever that the full-blooded Negro criminals are physically inferior to the full-blooded Negro civilians who have not attended college, but there are slight indications that the college Negroes rather excel the delinquents in head measurements, stature, shoulder breadth, and a few other characters. Similarly, the Negroid criminals do not fall below the level of non-college Negroids except in head measurements, and in most other features are physically superior to them. But with the exception of weight, chest diameters, and facial length, the Negroid criminals certainly represent a group which is below the physical standard of Negroid college students.

On the whole, these data suggest that Negro and Negroid

criminals have to be compared with distinctly upper class civilian samples of the same racial composition before they can be shown to manifest any marked physical inferiority. In other words, it can scarcely be claimed that the criminals of African descent (like Old American Whites) represent the biological dregs of their population. They certainly are not the finest physical specimens, but it seems probable that their bodily characteristics could be duplicated in many samples of law-abiding, respectable, but underprivileged Negroes and Negroids. In this connection it is interesting to note that the more or less pure Negroes of criminal habit, on the whole, differ less from the Negro civilians than is the case with the mixed Negroids. I think that lack of opportunity and sheer ignorance and primitiveness are much more important factors in Negro and Negroid criminality than they are among the Whites. Here and there we encounter suggestions that Negro and Negroid criminals show more pronounced Negroidal features than do comparable non-criminals, but certainly a generalization to this effect would be erroneous. As an instance to the contrary, it may be pointed out that criminal Negroes are probably less platyrrhine or broad-nosed than are college Negroes.

The analysis of the morphological features of Negro and Negroid criminals as contrasted with civilians has not yet been completed and hence must be omitted here Frankly, I hardly expect the comparisons to turn up general differences between the criminals and civilians which will be of any great significance. Nor have the sociological data been worked out. Of course it is perfectly useless to compare college students in marital state, education, occupation, et cetera, with criminals. The differences can be predicted, since they are dependent largely upon the different sociological categories of the groups.

COMPARISON OF CRIMINALS WITH CIVIL INSANE

NEGROES

For comparison with our series of 776 sane Negro criminals we have a sample of 71 insane civilian Negroes from North Carolina. The criminals average nearly 4 years younger than the civil insane (criminals 29.85 years, insane 33.75 years) and are nearly 7 pounds heavier (criminals 152.7 pounds, insane 145.8 pounds). The size superiority of the sane criminals is in most dimensions overwhelming. It will be simpler to mention those measurements in which the criminals do not certainly exceed the civilians. These include shoulder breadth, chest breadth, sitting height, head length, face breadth, nose breadth, and ear dimensions. In several of these criminal superiority is probable. In no case do the insane surpass the criminals by more than fractions of a millimeter.

The sane criminals also diverge widely from the insane civilians in indices, which are expressions of proportions. The criminals have significantly more brachycephalic or relatively broader heads, of which the height is greater relative to length and breadth. The face breadth of the criminals bears a reduced relation to total head breadth, and is relatively longer and narrower, both as a whole and in its upper segment. The nose of the criminal is longer and narrower, his forehead wider in comparison with his face, and his jaws broader relative to face breadth.

It is clear that the abysmal physical inferiority which we have found in the insane Whites is encountered also in insane Negroes. In the White groups also the sane criminals are much larger and appear to be biologically superior to the insane, whether civil or criminal, but the differences are not perhaps so marked, because White criminals quite clearly are selected more largely from biological inferiors than are Negro criminals.

NEGROIDS

We have 325 civil insane Negroids to compare with our large series of 3325 sane criminals. Again in this comparison the size superiority of the sane criminals over the insane civilians is overwhelming. Although the criminals are nearly 4 years younger in average age, they are more than 6 pounds heavier in mean weight. The criminals fall significantly below the insane only in head length and ear length. They definitely surpass the insane in all other measurements except shoulder breadth, head breadth, face breadth, and ear breadth.

Indicially the criminals are relatively broader-headed, have narrower faces relative to head breadth, higher heads relative to head length and head breadth, proportionately narrower and longer upper and total faces, proportionately far longer and narrower noses, relatively longer and narrower ears, broader foreheads relative to face breadth, and wider jaws relative to face breadth.

The Negro and Negroid criminals differ from their respective check samples of the civil insane in virtually the same measurements and proportions. Thus both sane criminal groups are younger, but heavier, taller, have shorter heads, more brachycephalic and higher heads both relatively and absolutely, absolutely longer and relatively narrower faces, proportionately longer and narrower noses, wider foreheads relative to face breadth and wider jaws relative to the same dimension. The differences in the two comparisons are negligible.

Since the insane civilian Negroids and Negroes seem to represent samples drawn from quite different anthropological types of population than those which produce the criminals, it is worth while to examine the observations of the soft parts in order to ascertain whether any consistent differences between the two pairs are evident there.

NEGROID SANE CRIMINALS AND NEGROID CIVIL INSANE

MOSAIC OF METRIC DIFFERENCES

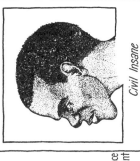

Criminal

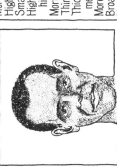

Civil Insane

Criminal

Civil Insane

CRIMINALS

Shorter, broader, higher heads
Lighter skin color
More woolly, less frizzly hair
Higher, wider and more sloping
    foreheads
Thicker eyebrows
Longer, narrower faces and noses
Shorter ears
Less pronounced antihelices
Less rolled helices
Slightly lighter eyes
Less pigmented sclerae
More inner eyefolds
Higher eye-openings
Smaller brow ridges
Higher, narrower nasal roots,
    higher bridges
More downward inclined septa
Thinner nasal tips
Thicker integumental and
    membranous lips
More pronounced lip seams
Broader jaws, less chin prominence
More pointed chins, more prominant
    malars and jaw angles
Fuller cheeks, more wrinkles
More prognathism

OBSERVATIONS ON NEGROES — CRIMINAL AND INSANE CIVILIANS

Comparison of the observations of civil insane Negroes and Negroids with the total criminal series of Negroes and Negroids is complicated by the fact that all of the insane were observed by a single anthropologist in North Carolina, whereas the large criminal series come from ten states and represent the combined data of two observers. Thus differences may be enhanced by possible state peculiarities of the insane and by any idiosyncrasies of morphological judgment which are due to the unbalanced personal equations. The data, taken at their face value, indicate that the insane Negroes are completely homogeneous in the possession of dark brown skin color and scanty beard and body hair — as compared with the far greater variability of the criminals. In fact, all of the pigmentation records suggest in these Negro insane a complete unanimity of the expression of full Negro features in hair and pigmentation. All of the Negro features of nose — such as low broad root and bridge, and concave profile — are fully expressed in the insane Negroes and, in general, the records show an extraordinarily small deviation from classical Negro racial characters. The anthropologist who collected these data was, I think, rather inclined to inflexibility in morphological judgments and saw things as either "black" or "white," or, in certain observations, overwhelmingly "medium." Thus the civil insane Negroids differ from the criminal Negroids in much the same way as noted in the case of the pure Negro comparison. The civil insane are much more homogeneous in morphological characters and express to a fuller extent typical Negro development.

When the Negroid civil insane and the Negro civil insane, both studied by one observer, are compared in morphological characters, the mixed bloods show in most features the extended range of variability and occasional convergence upon the racial features of Whites which would be expected. I therefore am of the opinion that before any final judgment can be passed upon morphological differences between the respective sane Negro and Negroid criminal series and civil insane of the corresponding series, it will be necessary to segregate the North Carolina series of criminals of these antecedents and compare them with the insane observed in that state. It would certainly be foolish to depend upon comparisons which involve both the possibility of exaggeration of difference due to personal equation and the influence of disparate distribution of types of Negroes which may be more or less specialized within the several states. The clear indications of the comparative series, as analyzed to this point, are that both Negro and Negroid insane civilians surpass corresponding sane criminal series in the development of features which are racially characteristic of the Negro.

This reservation does not apply to the measurements, except in a much lesser degree. There can be no doubt that the criminal metric superiorities over the insane are generally valid. The only dubious point is the extent to which North Carolina insane Negroes and Negroids may be specialized and thus incomparable with criminal groups drawn from ten states. The resolution of these difficulties will have to await the exhaustive working out of the Negro and Negroid data, which will be published in the third of the large monographs of this series. The present summary of the Negro and Negroid material is only preliminary, partial, and, in some measure, tentative.

SUMMARY OF NEGRO AND NEGROID CRIMINAL ANTHROPOLOGY

The study of Negro criminality in the United States offers an excellent opportunity for the testing of the Lombrosian hypothesis that criminals represent a class of men who not only retain many primitive physical characters such as are more commonly encountered in savages, but who also manifest types of behavior which may be called atavistic or reversionary. Of course it is absurd to assume that actions which are regarded as crimes today are accounted virtuous deeds among savages. There are very few savage societies, if any, in which one may rape and murder with impunity, nor is thieving regarded with leniency and toleration among most primitive peoples. Yet Cesare Lombroso was by no means the crack-brained theorist that he is often represented to be in the works of evangelical penologists who have never read the great Italian. There is nothing irrational in the assumption that many of the acts which modern societies arbitrarily consider criminal fall within the normal range of respectable and even meritorious behavior in simpler peoples. For example, there is no intrinsic evil in the home manufacture of corn whiskey, nor even in the purveying of it to thirsty customers. It is not very difficult to understand the confusion which may arise in the minds of ignorant Tennessee mountaineers when they discover that Sargent York is made a national hero and awarded the Congressional Medal of Honor for machine-gunning and capturing a couple of hundred of Germans, who have done him no wrong, whereas they are sentenced to prison for life because they have taken a successful pot-shot at a member of some family which has been at war with their own for several generations. Lombroso was not a fool when he suggested that there are in modern societies a considerable number of persons who are too ignorant and too stupid to understand the complicated and highly artificial codes of behavior, the infraction of which may be punishable by imprisonment. A large part of modern civilized populations is in precisely this state of befuddlement. Sometimes we call these confused in- dividuals morons.

Now if you take a race of persons which, for one reason

or another, has remained in a primitive state of culture in its own chosen habitat, and forcibly transplant it into a new environment and a complex alien civilization, you may reasonably expect that race to carry over its own patterns of behavior into its new surroundings and, if savage behavior is criminal behavior, to become a criminalistic race. The Negro was first brought to the New World as a slave and treated like a domestic animal. He was permitted only a very limited participation in European culture. Subsequently he was turned loose to fend for himself in an industrialized society, with very little tuition and encouragement and without any efficacious cultural tradition to assist him. Further, he has encountered more opposition in his efforts to adjust himself to American civilization than he suffered as a slave.

Under these circumstances, if there is such a phenomenon as atavistic behavior in modern society, and if there is inherent in any race a propensity for certain types of crimes, these potential realities ought to be brought out into the open in the case of the American Negro. So we find that the Negro and the Negroid are prone to murder and to steal but are relatively low in other forms of criminal activity, and perhaps we jump to the conclusion that Negroes confine their antisocial behavior to these categories either because they are little more than savages or because they manifest thereby an inherent Negro racial tendency.

Now it is perfectly true that both our Negroes and our Negroids commit somewhat more of first degree murder and considerably more of second degree murder than any of the White racial types delimited by the sorting of physical characteristics. On the other hand, Negroes and Negroids are convicted of rape in proportionately fewer numbers than any of our nine White racial types, with the exception of the Predominantly Nordic. They are committed for sex offenses other than rape in a smaller percentage of cases than is found in any White racial type with the exception of the Pure Nordic — an essentially asexual type to all appearances. Both the East Baltic and the Pure Nordic types surpass the pure Negroes in burglary and larceny, and the Negroid mixed group also falls below the Keltic, Alpine, and Predominantly Nordic racial types in this category of offense. It may then be stated that perhaps the type of crime which is most characteristically Negro is homicide.

When we divided up our large series of Negroidal criminals into a supposedly pure Negro group and a definitely mixed Negroid group, on the basis of the full expression of Negro physical characters or the admixture of morphological features ordinarily associated with Whites or Indians, we found that less than one-fifth of the colored criminals could be reckoned as apparently full-blooded Negroes. The Negroes and Negroids were discovered to be anthropometrically distinct as groups, apart from the morphological features which were used as a basis of separation. The pure Negroes were, among other features, slightly longer-headed, considerably shorter, and somewhat lighter in average weight. However, it was found that the sociological differences between these two groups were very slight indeed. In particular, they displayed virtually no offense differences, with the exception of a slight superiority on the part of the mixed Negroids in the more sophisticated offenses against property. Occupational differences were also very slight, although the men with perceptible or suspected White blood were a trifle more amply represented in the callings which require better education. More definite was the superiority of the Negroid or mixed group in educational qualifications, although by no means great.

We came to the conclusion that lack of sociological differentiation between the two groups was in part due to the fact that, on the basis of physical criteria, even the Negroid or mulatto group was, on the whole, overwhelmingly African in descent and included very few individuals with a preponderance of White blood. But, more important than this, it seemed that the regimentation of Negroes and Negroids alike into a very few occupations of low economic status, irrespective of education, body build, and natural inclinations, had the accessory result of limiting their choice of antisocial activity. In other words, it seemed that the repressive effect of social and economic discrimination against Negroes and Negroids may be, to a great extent, the cause of their concentration upon relatively few categories of crime. The comparatively low rate of sex offenses among these groups may be due in part to lack of repressions among a naturally lusty race; it may be partially attributable to a tendency on the part of White officers of justice to disregard sex crimes among Negroes unless they involve White persons also; it may be the result of the illegal brutalities which are customarily inflicted upon any colored person who is suspected of a sex offense against a White.

Since, for one reason or another, the social and economic differentiation of Negroes and Negroids has been severely restricted, it is rather astonishing to find, nevertheless, that the various categories of offenders are physically almost as distinctive, one from another, as was the case among the Whites, unhampered by racial discrimination. In the case of the Negroes and Negroids the anthropological differentiation of offense groups is much more marked than their sociological diversity. This fact suggests that, within the iron wall of social and economic limitation of Negro activities, built and maintained by Whites, criminological selection of physical blends for specific offenses has been at work. However, since the different states studied in this survey often contribute disproportionate quotas to the various offense groups, it is possible that the physical differentiation of prisoners convicted of certain categories of crimes may be exaggerated by the inclusion of an excessive number of men from the same state. This possibility would certainly have to be considered if the existence of local state types of Negroids and Negroes were demonstrated. In the case of the Old American Whites, such state types were physically so distinctive that it was necessary to apply a correction for state sampling before a final appraisal of the criminological significance of physical differences between offense groups could be made. In this preliminary analysis of the Negro and Negroid material no allowance has been made for state sampling. Ultimately it may be necessary to carry out the vast additional statistical labor which this process involves, but hitherto I have proceeded upon the assumption that the diversification of ethnic strains in the Negroes and Negroids of the several states is not sufficient to necessitate such a procedure. The irregular and unpredictable amount of White admixture with Negroes in each state would tend to prevent the development of stabilized local physical types, and the recent extensive Negro migrations would also obscure and adulterate such types, even if they have, in fact, developed.

Nevertheless, in one particular case, the versus public welfare offenders, a group heavily overloaded with Texans, the physical differentiae of both Negroes and Negroids from total criminals are so similar to those found among the Old American Whites of this same criminal category, also crowded with Texans, that one has to consider the extraordinary possibility of a local state physical type which cuts across racial lines and expresses itself in convergent manifestations in Negroes, Negroids, and Whites, alike.

The offense group differences within the two large series of African descent, Negro and Negroid, do not suggest that the amount of White admixture particularly influences choice of crime, except possibly in fraudulent criminals, who seem, on the whole, to carry a little more White blood than some other offense groups. The ordinary offense group distinctions which have been demonstrated in Whites seem to obtain to a large extent in Negroes and Negroids. Murderers are older, larger, and apparently physically superior to criminals in general, and to an even greater extent this generalization holds true in the case of fraudulent criminals and liquor offenders. Thieves and burglars are younger and undersized; robbers younger and inclined to weedy builds, rapists again older, but smaller and rather shrivelled. But there are a great many metrical and morphological peculiarities of the head and face in the various offense groups that are not easily explicable on the basis of racial composition, and which cannot be interpreted in any straightforward manner as indicative of biological superiority or inferiority. At present, I can offer no satisfactory explanation of the fact that bootleggers persistently have broad noses and short faces with flaring jaw angles, while rapists monotonously display narrow foreheads and elongated, pinched noses. It is well nigh incredible that these features should manifest themselves alike in the Whites, Negroes, and Negroids of these offense categories, but they in fact do.

The breakdown of body build correlation with nature of offense and with other sociological phenomena in these colored criminals enhances the difficulty of explaining offense group differences in physique. Purely constitutional factors seem to be in abeyance as contrasted with morphological variations in physiognomic features and differences of the proportions of head and face, which may be associated in some obscure way with temperament and mentality and are certainly due to the idiosyncrasies of individual and familial inheritance. The natural correlations of body build with nature of crime are repressed when the choice of occupation in its natural relation to constitution is denied, as in persons who live under the social stigma of being "Negroes."

Negro and Negroid criminals do not exhibit the unequivocal biological inferiority to civilians which is manifested in the case of Old American Whites. Indeed, in some respects, the criminals appear to be more strongly built and to possess more vigorous physiques than their law-abiding relatives. These strictures are most nearly accurate in the case of the comparison of criminals with non-college Negroes and Negroids. In North Carolina, at any rate, if one collects a sample of ordinary Negro working men who have had no particular educational advantages, the physical features of that civilian group will not distinguish them as a bigger, better nourished class than criminals. The criminals do indeed manifest some inferiorities of measurements of the brain case and some general evidences of evolutionary rigidity. When the delinquents are compared with college students, the former are found to be of smaller stature and the diminution in head measurements is marked. Presumably, or possibly, the smaller head sizes of the criminals may be associated with their indubitably inferior intelligence. In these comparisons again one wonders to what extent the geographical limitation of the civilian check sample to two states may serve to confuse the issue as to the significance of physical differences between the antisocial and the law-abiding.

However, when we proceed to the comparison of the sane Negro and Negroid criminals with racially similar but insane civilians, we find the same vast metric inferiority on the part of the mentally diseased as was manifest in the case of Whites. Further, the insane seemed to be morphologically more homogeneous and more typical in their physical expressions of Negro racial features. Here again, it is possible that the restriction of the insane civil sample to North Carolina may be a disturbing factor in the comparison. On the presumption that the differences are criminologically valid, we should have to conclude that mental defect and mental disease are much more closely correlated with biological inferiority in Negroes and in Negroids than is delinquency. This would be fully in accord with our findings upon Whites, among whom, however, the sane criminals are definitely below the physical standards of sane civilians.

It is rather difficult to avoid the conclusion that a depressed physical and social environment determines Negro and Negroid delinquency to a much greater extent than it does in the case of Whites. This may be due to the probability that, however wretched the environment of the White may be, that of the Negro and of the Negroid is, on the average, considerably worse. On the other hand, it is possible that Negroes and Negroids racially are more susceptible to criminalistic infection, so that antisocial behavior is likely to manifest itself more commonly than in Whites in individuals who are not obviously stunted, undernourished, and of a generally inferior constitutional and biological endowment.

CHAPTER XI

THE ANTHROPOLOGY OF CRIME

HUMAN evolution and cultural progress are blocked by man's insistence upon a status "a little lower than the angels" instead of a little higher than the apes. We have perversely refused to learn from organic evolution that animal behavior arises from the organism itself and that progress and improvement in behavior can be effected permanently only by raising the quality of that organism. Instead of applying the data, principles, and laws of organic evolution to the problem of improving man's biological status and thereby rendering possible a superior level of behavior, we have been misled into the imbecilic assumption that culture, an inanimate thing consisting of humanly manipulated matter and disembodied ideas, evolves by itself ever onward and upward, and that all man has to do is to grease the wheels and ride. It has taken more than two generations to eradicate nonsensical theories of social evolution and they are still implicit in the ways, methods, and thinking of social scientists and educators, and of those who labor or plunder in the murky half-world of government.

Religion combined with ethics, a once bright light which seemed destined to illuminate the pathway of mankind, has faded to the glimmer of a guttering taper, not because of its faulty standards of conduct, not because of the inherent improbability of an existing and guiding Creator, not even because of the unreality of man's alleged immortal soul, but merely because man has fatuously believed in a spiritual salvation and regeneration conceived and nurtured in organic corruption. You may plaster the degenerate human organism with lofty ideals of individual and social conduct, but they simply do not stick. The corruptible cannot "put on incorruption."

So the humble student of man attempts to investigate the relationship between the organism and its conduct in the most flagrant category of social pathology, on the supposition that here, if anywhere, the crude associations between the deteriorated body and vicious behavior should be demonstrable. This research was begun partly through idle scientific curiosity, partly through dissatisfaction with the futile and almost childish attempts of Lombroso to establish a tenable hypothesis by essentially unscientific methods, even more largely from disgust with the sanctimonious statistical deviousness of Goring, who succeeded in obfuscating the entire subject of the relation of organism to behavior and in misleading a whole generation of simple criminologists. No Messianic promptings to the discovery of a method of regenerating criminals actuated this research, nor any vain aspirations to facilitate the hopeless task of the overworked and under-brained police.

Some 15,000 sub-adult and adult male incarcerated offenders in ten states were examined in this study. These were compared with a sizable sample of the lowlier civilian population — national or racial groups of criminals with corresponding groups of civilians, insane offenders with the identical category of the relatively inoffensive civilian insane. Wherever sufficiently large groups of criminals were available for study an effort was made to compare the various offense subgroups of individuals with the total series of which they form a part, both in sociological and in physical characteristics. Back of this procedure was the seemingly logical assumption that, if prisoners differ biologically and sociologically from law-abiding citizens of similar origin, they ought also to differ among themselves in accordance with the types of crimes they commit.

In the gathering of the data, no effort was spared to utilize the best standardized and most searching anthropometric techniques known to the director of the survey, and the sociological data were restricted to such facts as seemed to be objective and capable of authentication from the institutional records.[1]

Whatever may have been the shortcomings of the data collected, they were statistically reduced by the use of the most nearly perfect and efficient mechanical appartus hitherto devised.[2] When the first trial tabulations of data amassed in this anthropological survey began to issue from the machines, I regarded them with some surprise, no little suspicion, and even with a limited credulity — I suppose because I too had been infected with the Aristotelian dogma of the separation of mind from body and of the general dissociation of human conduct from the gross anatomy of the human organism. I set about the task of minimizing and paring away differences like any anti-Lombrosian zealot, not because of any emotional bias against the existence of such differences, but because of the fear of mistaking copper pyrites or some other base metal for gold. I scrutinized techniques of field observation and made lavish and even extravagant allowances for the human errors and deviations of judgment which are called personal equation. When it

[1] In this preview of the results of a somewhat extensive survey, I have omitted entirely the material dealing with more than 2000 inmates of Massachusetts county jails, with the gathering of which the survey began under the auspices of the Massachusetts State Department of Mental Diseases. The anthropometric data on these county jail prisoners were collected during the period when the Division of the Examination of Prisoners under Dr. Winfred Overholser was simultaneously gathering extensive sociological and psychiatric information on the same jail populations. However, the jail populations shift so rapidly that a subsequent matching of records yielded less than 900 individuals who had been studied by the separate anthropological and socio-psychological staffs. This material, already tabulated, will enable us to penetrate much further into the socio-physical relationships of individuals. It will be published jointly by Dr. Overholser and myself, as a part of the third technical volume dealing with the results of this survey.

[2] These machines were furnished to our laboratory, sometimes at a rental below cost and sometimes entirely gratuitously, by the International Business Machines Company, to whom I am eternally indebted for disinterested scientific assistance.

became apparent that differences between criminals of the various offense groups were enhanced by the development of local state physical types, not equally distributed in the crime categories, I tore the Old American series to pieces and reanalyzed it by states (at the cost of an additional year of labor), and then devised and applied a formula whereby differences due to this confusing factor might be eliminated from general criminological consideration. Statistical safeguards for the insurance of valid results, not dependent upon the accidents of findings in small samples, were rigorously applied to residual differences, which were further subjected to the criticism of logic and of general anthropological significance. Many positive findings were rejected because of suspected flaws in technique, many others because of inadequate statistical evidence, not a few because they seemed irrational, illogical, and meaningless. If I had abode by the Biblical adage "If thine eye offend thee pluck it out," even the visual equipment of Argus would have left me blind as a bat at the end of this investigation. But still I was left with a mountain of positive anthropological differences between various classes of criminals and with a veritable cordillera of deviations between criminals and civilians. Fortified therewith, I venture to say with David, "Let the righteous smite me, it shall be a kindness; and let him reprove me, it shall be an excellent oil, which shall not break my head." A friendly though adverse critic has warned me "to look out for squalls" and I have every confidence that many will squall and that right loudly. I await these squallings with equanimity.

I will not enter here into a dreary recapitulation of the manifold physical and sociological differences which distinguish various types of offenders one from another and which separate criminal sheep from civilian goats. The bare fact of a few millimeters of independent and residual differences in nose length between crazy criminals and de-mented civilians entertains me as meagerly as you. We are interested only, if at all, in the broad human significance of combinations of such differences, which, taken singly, are trivial and meaningless.

Old American criminals, classified according to type of offense, differ profoundly from each other in groups, and quite as widely in anthropological features as in sociological characteristics. Some — usually those convicted of crimes of violence against persons — are comparatively large and brutish, presumably equipped with a moderate to excessive amount of sheer animal vigor, and generally ignorant and, without doubt, dull-witted. Sex offenders include among the rapists no few of full-bodied and probably over-sexed ruffians, but also, and especially in the other sex category, a majority of shrivelled runts, perverted in body as in mind, and manifesting the drooling lasciviousness of senile decay. Thieves and burglars tend to be sneaky little constitutional inferiors, either physically stunted or malnourished, or both. Their physiques and sociological status suggest inability to succeed even in the humbler law-abiding pursuits, in spite of moderate schooling. Robbers lean to several variants of the wiry, narrow, hard-bitten tough, not notably under-sized, not necessarily unintelligent, and often fairly well educated. They do not create the mass impression of excessive stupidity nor of abysmal economic incompetence. Forgers and fraudulent criminals are somewhat above the general level of criminal physique although well below that of comparable civilians. They are well educated as criminals go, and probably more inferior to ordinary small business men in honesty than in intelligence. Versus public welfare offenders, usually bootleggers, are in the Old American series a group of bulky, mostly rural, thugs; ignorant, but apparently not altogether lacking in a low practical shrewdness and economic capability. Each of these offense groups shows its craniometric and physiognomic differentiae from the total Old American criminal series of which it is a part, mostly conformable to its generalized type of physique, but often explicable only as the product of some selected racial blend.

Special studies of the relationship of body build to crime and of alleged occupations of criminals to physique and to general sociological status suggest that the type of a criminal's offense is the resultant of several selective forces or agencies. In the first instance rural or urban residence is determined to some extent by the ethnic and economic tradition of the immediate or remote ancestors of the delinquent. Some stocks are preferentially agriculturalists and pioneers, presumably less gregarious and more adventurous than the sedentary town dwellers and tradesmen. Rural residence puts a premium upon physical hardihood and restricts the choice of crime. Countrymen are prone to violence against persons, partly because of their physical equipment and partly because rustic life affords few opportunities for acquisitive offense. In general, one must rape, murder, or behave. Moonshining or bootlegging may be illegal avocations of the criminally ambitious, but there is little to steal save livestock, and sternly repressive measures of an informal nature, involving ropes and limbs of trees, are traditional and effective deterrents to horse stealing and cattle rustling. The American countryman has always been a vigorous defender of his own property rights. A by-product of rustic lawlessness is the rural bandit, who used to hold up trains and now specializes upon country banks and post offices. Selection for muscular vigor and for general physical toughness in rural occupations tends to shift those of inferior strength into the towns and cities, as well, perhaps, as certain endowed with ambition and unusual capability.

In the city, physique is the primary basis of selection among the lower occupational levels, whereas education (with its implications of higher intelligence) probably is a stronger determinant of status in the upper walks of economic life. In any case, there is a much greater diversification of criminal opportunity than in the country, and it is here that the weedy delinquent gets his chance. It is still possible to murder and to rape, and in addition there are excellent pickings for the racketeer, the fraudulent criminal, the pay roll robber, and every other sort of antisocial vulture. Even here it is a remarkable fact that tall, thin men tend to murder and to rob, tall heavy men to kill and to commit forgery and fraud, undersized thin men to steal and to burglarize, short heavy men to assault, to rape, and to commit other sex crimes, whereas men of mediocre body build tend to break the law without obvious discrimination or preference. Extremes of body build incline to specialize in crime, doubtless impelled by some mysterious constitutional proclivity.

One set of consistent contrasts rears itself in a solid, unbroken, and towering front. The putatively law-abiding citizen, however humble his social and economic status, is larger, superior in physique and in most anthropological characters, so far as judgments of quality can be made, to the White criminal of comparable ethnic and racial origin and drawn from approximately similar occupational levels. In metric and morphological features of the head and face the differences between criminals and civilians suggest more strongly lack of adaptability in the criminal organism than straightforward size diminution. On the whole, the biological superiority of the civilian to the delinquent is quite as certain as his sociological superiority. There are objectivity and substantiality in measured physical differences which are usually lacking to the appraisals of sociological phenomena. It is easier to measure a head than to estimate civic virtue, more simple to obtain lung capacity than capacity for civilization.

In the study of native born criminals of foreign parentage and of foreign born, it is necessary to separate the subjects into paired groups of the same nationality — the one American born, the other of European nativity. Thus we are forced to consider numerous small ethnic groups, each from several different points of view. We must know to what extent the first American generation of any nationality differs from the foreign born in distribution of criminal offenses and in general sociological status. Then we must ascertain how the Irish-American criminals, or any other New American criminal group, differ from the foreign born of that nationality also incarcerated in this country. We are thus involved in the question of the extent and significance of bodily changes in the children of immigrants, which is a vast subject, quite apart from its criminological implications. Then, finally, we have to compare both first generation American and alien born criminals of each nationality with the corresponding civilians. All in all, this results in a bewildering hash of comparisons, with many contrasted pairs frequently showing contradictory differences in this or that detail, partly because of ethnic individuality and partly because of variability in the size and adequacy of samples. However, out of this welter of differences there emerge sufficiently clear cut results.

The first generation American criminals, who tend to be substantially younger than the foreign born of the same stock, are almost invariably better educated and enjoy, when at liberty, a superior economic status. In spite of this fact, they are more persistently criminalistic than the foreign born, as measured by proportions of previous convictions. In general, the sociological shift from one criminal generation to another is more marked in the stock of recent immigration than in such groups as British, Irish, French Canadian, and Teutonic. Indeed, some of these latter groups show comparatively little improvement of sociological status in the first generation criminal Americans. There is a very strong trend of the American born criminals away from the simple and cruder offenses of personal violence toward the more lucrative pursuits of robbery, forgery and fraud, burglary and larceny. A notable exception to this generalization is the Italian-American group, which not only persists in an apparently traditional propensity for crimes against persons, but even exceeds the alien group in homicide. Of course, national differences in choice of offense and probably in proportional criminal activity are easily determinable from our records and quite as easily and much more fully from records of the United States Census. Such facts, though available, are not usually discussed or emphasized, because they arouse the animosities of large groups of respectable persons who are thus unpleasantly distinguished by their participation in an ethnic descent which commits an excessive amount of this or that crime. Since, on the whole, the majority of individuals of any ethnic descent are worthy citizens and it is only the inferior elements within each national group who are responsible for its crimes, it is expedient to soft-pedal national descent and to emphasize rather the nature of the biological and sociological selection which determines criminality in every ethnic stock. The exclusion of immigrants, of whatever nationality, would probably diminish the proportions of crimes of personal violence, but there would still be plenty of such crimes committed by our Old Americans, our colored population, and those somewhat aberrant descendants of recent immigrant stocks who have not followed the New American fashion of turning to acquisitive offenses. It is of little use to close the tent flap when the camel has already become a mother several times, inside.

The New Americans, born of alien parentage, display changes in bodily form which are virtually identical with those observed in the offspring of law-abiding immigrants and also in the rising generation of Old American ancestry. These are generally in the direction of increased stature and restricted head, face, and body breadths. It may be doubted that these coltish physical trends are a biological improvement. When the criminals, either the first generation American, or alien, are compared with civilians of the same stocks, they display, as do Old Americans, marked inferiorities of body dimensions, as well as morphological and metric differences of head and face which are sometimes suggestive of retarded development, sometimes of the retention of primitive features, and often of conservatism which may be described as evolutionary rigidity or a failure to conform to modern trends of physical change. The evidence that the criminals are derived from the baser biological stuff of their various ethnic stocks seems to me to be conclusive, although it might be argued that they come from families which are the anthropological victims of environmental depression.

First generation criminals seem to adhere more closely than first generation civilians to the squat, broad-faced types which are often characteristic of the foreign born emigrant from Europe, and are usually modified toward linearity or vertical stretching in the American born children of European parentage. This retention of a possibly stunted alien physique is also exaggerated in foreign born criminals of some stocks in comparison with the civilians of the same origin. These trends of difference strongly suggest that criminals are offspring of those elements in any ethnic or racial group which are conservative rather than progressive, rigid rather than adaptive in an anthropological sense. It seems possible that such biological inadaptability, such phylogenetic conservatism, is responsible for the association of primitive morphological features with retarded culture in modern savages.

When we study criminals by offense, by body build, or by occupation, all within the same ethnic and parentage group, suggestions of variation in racial composition keep cropping out, but they are usually ambiguous and confusing. But when large samples of White criminals of all sorts of ethnic and parentage derivation are pooled and sorted into so-called "racial types," on the basis of physical and presumably hereditary criteria, more than a semblance of order emerges from a relative chaos. These racial sortings involve the selection of individuals having like combinations of pigmentation, head form, and sometimes nose form, within each arbitrarily delimited group. The constituent individuals of a racial type then prove to possess many other morphological and metric uniformities, in addition to those which were used as sorting criteria. But much more important than the successful delimitation of comparatively homogeneous physical types is the association of those several types with marked variations in occupational status, educational attainment, and, above all, with nature of offense. Of course no racial type is addicted exclusively to any one kind of crime, but the regressions of these racial groups upon nature of offense are far more clear cut and unequivocal than those displayed by national groups, and they perhaps even supervene those displayed by body build groups. In a few cases, however, the individuals comprised within a specific national descent, either because of the peculiarity of the biological blend or because of a deep-rooted national tradition, are almost if not quite as distinct criminologically as are our selected races.

An expected concomitant of these racio-sociological correlates is that the purer racial types should show the most clear cut criminological and general sociological proclivities. This expectation is abundantly realized. Such secondary and frankly composite racial types as the Nordic Alpine and the Nordic Mediterranean show mixed sociological propensities and regressions, by no means inexplicable in the light of the dominant influences, in one or another case, of the two or more racial strains of which they are blends. But in the more nearly pure racial types the behavioristic differences are revealed in all of their nakedness. Whether on this basis one race is to be preferred above another would seem to depend upon a choice between evils: murder, rape, and other manifestations of violence against persons, or depredations of property.

When racial types of respectable civilians are sorted out by the same criteria which have been applied to the criminals, some of the racial types are found to be disproportionately high among the delinquents as compared with the civilians and *vice versa*. Here again it seems hardly worth while to worry the troublesome matter of the comparative amounts of crimes committed by these several racial types, since the dregs of every one of them are criminalistic and there are plenty of dregs in each. But it should be noted that, when you select racial types among criminals and civilians, utilizing the same physical criteria of head form, pigmentation, et cetera, you find yourself with groups which, apart from the common sorting combinations of physical features, are quite markedly diverse in many anthropological characters. Racial type for racial type, the criminals are quite as undersized and morphologically "down at the heels," when compared even with civilians of humble status, as when the antisocial and prosocial series are compared by state groups, by national groups, or on any other basis of selection.

The study of the insane, criminal and civil, each compared with appropriate national groups of sane civilians and sane criminals, and each with the other, is a complicated business. Diagnoses of mental disease are often so deplorably vague and fuzzy that in our samples, at any rate, it is hardly possible to differentiate anthropologically the patients afflicted with the various categories of insanity. Wherever our series were sufficiently large, however, there were strong indications that Dementia praecox patients, and also mental deficients, constitute anthropological and sociological groups distinct from the total insane. There is little doubt that ampler series in which strictly uniform criteria of mental diagnosis are assured will yield clear cut anthropological differences between the various disease groups.

If one considers in order sane civilians, sane criminals, insane civilians, and insane criminals, he finds that each succeeding group tends to manifest greater ignorance, lowlier occupational status, and more depressing evidence of all-around worthlessness. The same hierarchy of degeneration is evidenced in physical characteristics. The lower class civilian population is anthropologically fair to middling; the sane criminals are vastly inferior, the insane civilians considerably worse than sane criminals, and the insane criminals worst of all. It would be a rash person who would venture to assert that these parallelisms of increasing inferiority in sociological and anthropological characters are fortuitous and unrelated. The specific criminal proclivities found in certain races and nationalities among the sane prisoners are carried over, to a great extent, into the offenses committed by insane criminals of the same ethnic or racial origin. There are, however, some instances in which the insane of a nationality are distinguished by a different type of offense from that in which the sane are preeminent.

The uniformities of metric and morphological deviations which the insane criminals of any given nationality and parentage display when they are compared with insane civilians of the same stocks are very impressive. They suggest that within those segments of the population which are predisposed to insanity there is a special anthropological selection for criminalistic behavior. If you collect a sample of the law-abiding adult male population, you will almost invariably find it to be of older mean age than a large sample of incarcerated criminals of the same ethnic origin. The reason for this is that crime is primarily a manifestation of youth. Probably for the same reason the civil insane are usually older than comparable samples of the criminal insane. But the criminal insane in turn tend to be older than the sane criminals and the civil insane than the sane civilians, apparently because the age incidence of insanity, contrary to that of criminality, is, on the whole, late. There are some curious indications that insane criminals vary from insane civilians of the same stock along the lines of the so-called physical modernization in which first generation Americans differ from foreign born of the same stock. Yet there are also some uniformities of difference between all insane and all civilians. As a tentative hypothesis I suggest that the constitutional organic elements which make for antisocial behavior are different from those which predispose to mental disease, and that the combination of the two in the same individuals is the resultant of a very special anthropological selection. In other words, criminality and insanity are separate and not necessarily related manifestations of inferior human organisms.

There is, however, really potent evidence of certain racial predispositions to insanity, and especially to insanity combined with criminality. This comes out most clearly in the comparative dearth of blonds in both insane series and in their virtual absence among the criminal insane, together with the great prevalence in the latter of individuals having very narrow, long heads and faces. The disproportionate representation of racial types among the criminal and civil insane, respectively, in Massachusetts points toward the possibility that the Keltic and Dinaric races are especially susceptible to the simultaneous infection of criminalism and mental disease. But over and beyond that fact there is an excess of very dark pigmentation in the insane criminals, whether they are long-headed such as the Keltic, or round-headed like the Alpine race and the Dinaric race.

The study of crime among the Negroes of the United States is fraught with unusual difficulties and perplexities for several reasons. The first of these is that the American population classified as Negro presents a range of physical variation all the way from the approximately full-blooded African to persons who are predominantly White. Further, the Negro, even in an unmixed state, is not a single race, but a great division of mankind which includes a number of distinct races. Again, the mixtures with Whites have been confined to no single White race or nationality, but have been fairly promiscuous, and a great deal of intermarriage with the American Indian has also taken place. Consequently, there is an extraordinary variety of Negro and Negroid types, concerning the exact racial and ethnic composition of which it is almost impossible to secure reliable information. The second reason for the difficulty of studying crime in American Negroes is that all of these physically heterogeneous millions who are labelled "Negro" have been subjected alike to social and economic oppression and, indeed, have not been able to call even their bodies their own for as much as three-quarters of a century. Consequently, they have had very restricted opportunities for the expression of individual ability in the direction of cultural advance. Similarly, there has been a lack of the social and economic diversification which facilitates variation in anti-social behavior. If the White population be considered a comparatively still and sluggish stream in which the scum floats and the heavy sediment settles to the bottom, the Negro population is a pool in which there has been a continual stirring and churning such that the better and the worse biological and sociological elements have had very little chance to settle and to separate. Further, this fluid Negro body is rigidly enclosed within the water-tight container of racial prejudice, and all sorts of White sewage have been dumped into it.

Under these circumstances, it is not at all surprising that a division of our Negro material into two main groups on the basis of racial physical criteria — the approximately full-blooded Negro and the Negroid group of all degrees of White admixture — yields series which, although anthropometrically and morphologically distinct, are not sociologically well differentiated. If you put a sprinkling of law-abiding and biologically sound citizens in jail with a majority of hardened criminals and subject them to the same regimen and offer them the same meager opportunities for individual expression and advancement, it might be very difficult after a few years to separate them from the criminals on the basis of behavior or by any sociological criteria, because there is so little social mobility in jail. Some of these law-abiding jail inmates might be corrupted to the extent of behaving like the real criminals, and the others would have almost no opportunity to assert their sociological superiority.

Thus there is almost no difference in the distribution of kinds of criminal offenses between Negroids and Negroes; both commit a great deal of homicide, are parsimonious in sex offenses, perpetrate a modest amount of robbery and much less forgery and fraud, do extremely little in the way of liquor offenses, and heap up a preponderating bulk of plain stealing, and breaking and entering. Those Negroids with perceptible increments of White blood are to some slight extent favored socially, and this should be reflected in their general sociological status, but it is scarcely discernible in occupational categories, and not too marked even in educational attainment. Nevertheless, in both of these African criminal series the various main offense groups are well differentiated in anthropological characters. As in the Old American Whites, murderers tend to be bigger and brawnier, thieves and burglars smaller and physically less well endowed, bootleggers bulky, square-jawed, thick-necked, and broad-faced. Incredible as it may sound, some of the offense proclivities which are associated with various types of physique seem to cut right across racial lines and to manifest themselves in Negroes and Negroids, as in Whites. A few of the anthropological offense differences in the subgroups of the Negroid series seem to be correlated with greater or lesser amounts of White blood, but, on the whole, degree of mixture apparently has very little to do with offense.

The criminological ambiguities which seem assignable to the rigid social and economic strait-jacket in which the Negro is confined carry over to confuse the anthropological differences between both Negro and Negroid criminals and civilians. Forced to utilize college students as well as non-college men for comparison with the colored delinquents, we have kept the two classes of civilians separate in the respective checking of Negroes with Negroes and Negroids with Negroids. It then transpires that the criminals of both categories are not unequivocally inferior in physique to the humbler non-college civilians, but only to the collegians, and, in their case, the criminal inferiority is restricted to stature and some few other metric features. So it appears that, as far as we can judge from our incomplete study of this group of materials, Negro criminals are not so markedly and strictly selected from poor colored trash as are the socially more favored Whites from poor White trash. Yet when sane Negro and Negroid criminals are compared with their corresponding classes of insane civilians, the anthropometric inferiority of the insane is as clear as in the case of Whites. There is also evident a marked tendency for the insane of both Negro and Negroid civilian series to show a fuller expression of Negro racial features than the criminals, but this difference may be exaggerated by the localized character of our Negro insane series, which was gathered in but one state.

Certainly Negroes and Negroids have a sounder environmental alibi for their criminality than have Whites, yet I am confident that a further examination of the data and more complete materials will validate the evidence of biological inferiority of the Negro criminal to his civilian brother, which is somewhat equivocally indicated at this point.

It is now high time to summarize our conclusions on the etiology of crime which have arisen from these tedious but perhaps not unprofitable studies. In the first place, crime is neither an exclusively biological phenomenon nor yet purely a sociological phenomenon. Any organism exists by virtue of its environment and when there is no organism there is no environment. The organism and its environment are inseparable and interaction between the two is continuous. The one cannot be abstracted from the other by any artificial process of logic.

I have argued elsewhere that man has become man mainly because of his ability to manipulate and to control his physical environment to an extent unshared by any lower animal. He shows this superiority in adapting the environment to himself, rather than himself to it, because he possesses an inherently better and larger intelligence than any other animal. That this human intelligence has grown as more and more demands have been made upon it is possibly true, and it is even probable that the exercise of intelligence improves its quality. But the principal point which I wish to make is that man is the unique animal organism which has been able, comparatively speaking, to dominate and to control its environment. It is the weaker organism which is molded, distorted, and enslaved by environment, and which in the course of natural selection eventually succumbs to that environment, if it is adverse, and becomes extinct. It succumbs not so much because the environment is harsh and unfavorable, as because it is an inferior organism and has lost its power of adaptation. Flawed and weakened structures snap under strains. In the recent New England hurricane I watched young and strongly rooted trees bend double under the force of the terrific wind pressure, whereas some of the older trees went down like ninepins. But most of these older trees were rotten and many of them had had their roots weakened by the digging up of streets, the leaking of gas mains, and other environmental adversities.

So I think that inherently inferior organisms are, for the most part, those which succumb to the adversities or temptations of their social environment and fall into antisocial behavior, and that it is impossible to improve and correct environment to a point at which these flawed and degenerate human beings will be able to succeed in honest social competition. The bad organism sullies a good environment and transforms it into one which is evil. Of course, I should by no means argue that man should cease to attempt to ameliorate his social environment, but, when he entirely neglects the improvement of his own organism, he condemns his environmental efforts to futility.

That racial background of inheritance which determines our skin color, our hair form, and numerous anatomical and physiological features, may also in some vague and general way influence mental and temperamental characteristics, emotional sets, and so on. But race does not make the human animal criminalistic. All existing races have survived through scores of thousands of years the vicissitudes of natural and social selection and are mentally and physically sound at the core. But race undoubtedly influences choice of crime in those organic inferiors which are all too numerous within each racial group. It is the individual and familial inheritance which produce the deteriorated organism which cannot withstand environmental adversity. When a whole race is environmentally depressed, either because of coercion by other races or through inability to cope with the environment to which it has become adapted, we need not expect it to proliferate in antisocial or criminal behavior. Crime is not rampant in savage and retarded human societies. Crime flourishes rather in rich cultures where production is varied and abundant, so that constitutional inferiors are coddled and fostered, inevitably to bite the hands which have fed them.

I am frequently asked about the practical utility of the findings which have flowed from this investigation of the anthropological and sociological characteristics of criminals. Because of the formerly wide use of the Bertillon anthropometric method of criminal identification and because of the popularity of the Lombrosian conception of criminal types, people imagine that an anthropological study of crime is designed to invent new methods of "spotting" and catching potential or actual delinquents. I am not particularly interested in either of these ends. The police and the Federal Bureau of Criminal Identification are moderately efficient in apprehending criminals. Plenty of criminals are caught, but unfortunately most of them are eventually let go again to resume their predatory activities against society. I have been at considerable pains in this investigation to demonstrate the mathematical and biological impossibility of establishing criminal types exclusively devoted to some particular kind of offense, by seeking for intricate combinations of morphological or metric peculiarities. It is indeed possible, even in our present deplorable ignorance of human biology, to catalogue and to describe anatomical indications of organic inferiority and to predict that the more numerous and accentuated these are in any individual the more surely he is to be of low mentality and worthless character. But I do not anticipate that we shall soon be able to predict from the anthropology of the individual who shows signs of degeneration and inferiority what particular form of criminality or other antisocial behavior his organism may produce. There is a much better chance of diagnosing from the individual physique the type of mental disease which he is liable to develop, as soon as psychiatrists can clarify their diagnoses of mental disease, because the mind is in itself a part of the organism, whereas social conduct is merely a manifestation of that organism.

I do think that, in the near future, it will be possible to separate the incorrigible offenders from those possibly reclaimable, on the basis of their respective degrees of physical and mental inferiority. For there are many grades of constitutional inferiority, and it is to be presumed that the less severely flawed specimens are more amenable to environmental treatment and may be propped and patched into some semblance of social innocuousness.

It may be well to state quite bluntly here that I have not spent the greater part of twelve years in studying criminals from any humanitarian zeal for the rehabilitation of offenders, or from any deep interest in the treatment of incarcerated felons. Such motives are laudable and the efforts of those who engage in criminological work are usually disinterested and sometimes efficacious. More power to their elbows! I wish to disabuse everyone of the idea that the function of the general human biologist is that of the family physician — to comfort or to cure individual patients. The anthropologist studies the adult male incarcerated felon as the medical research scientist would study the manifestations of cancer in its advanced stages, so that he may obtain an accurate knowledge of the most pronounced, far-reaching, and exaggerated effects of the disease. I have selected the criminal for study principally because the extreme outrageousness of criminal conduct makes the delinquent a most suitable subject for an exploration of the relation between the quality of the organism and its behavior. No scientific criminologist or penologist, however optimistic he may be of the good effects of a favorable environment and of education and moral suasion, has any particular hope of rehabilitating hardened adult criminals *en bloc.* Crime prevention is centered upon the treatment of juveniles and when it gets to be really scientific, it will have to start earlier still and concern itself with familial heredity.

However, I have not fooled around with the study of criminals for so long without developing a few notions as to possible improvements of our penal system. They may well be unloaded here and I care not who kicks them about or what becomes of them after I am rid of them. As a primary measure, I think that first offenders ought to be segregated absolutely from recidivists, and carefully studied as to their constitutional endowment and social potentialities. Those who seem to be in any sense reclaimable should be carefully reeducated and taught some vocation, or given an opportunity while in prison to improve their skill in whatever law-abiding occupation they may have chosen and practised in civilian life. This, of course, is nothing at all new.

Either the United States government, or possibly the various state governments, should expropriate some very considerable tract of desirable land — a sizable slab of some state with good natural resources — and establish there a reservation for permanent occupation by paroled delinquents. Such a reservation would have its frontiers closed and would be under the supervision of federal or other officers. But within the reservation, I should allow these former delinquents to be almost completely self-governing. Government aid would be at first necessary for building and for establishing industries, but outside capital could be called in. Each paroled delinquent would be given the opportunity to work out a career within this protected area. The population would carry on its own form of government, electing its officials from its own numbers. Married men on parole should be allowed to bring in their wives and families and settle them there. While optimum eugenic considerations would demand that none of these delinquents raise offspring, it seems probable that the processes of genetic selection and recombination would produce from these partially criminalistic stocks a good many useful and capable citizens, and even a few of outstanding ability. If the inhabitants of such a territory were allowed to run their own affairs, it is possible that in the course of time they would run them very well, since the more able individuals would rise to the positions of leadership. I should be particularly optimistic about the ability of such a society to develop its own effective means of keeping public order and preventing crime, because criminals are not lenient to criminality when their own ox is gored. Emigrants from prison into such a reservation should be kept there permanently. I am rather inclined to believe that in a generation or two some of these penal reservations might develop into such prosperous and progressive areas that the inhabitants would be unwilling to receive new colonists from the jails. If natural selection were allowed to operate in such a society, it might work out its own salvation. It would, however, be quite essential to keep out extraneous politicians, criminologists, and uplifters.

You may say that this is a visionary and fantastic scheme — utterly impractical and nonsensical. It could not fail more completely than has our past and present penal system, and it would, at any rate, remove permanently from our midst a great number of our criminals and of our constitutional inferiors. I do not make this proposal as the net constructive result of my criminological investigation; I shall come to that presently. I merely throw out this superfluous pup for anyone to adopt, but doubtless someone will tie a can to his tail.

Of course I think that habitual criminals who are hopeless constitutional inferiors should be permanently incarcerated and, on no account, should be allowed to breed. Nevertheless, they should be treated humanely, and, if they are to be kept alive, should be allowed some opportunity for freedom and profitable occupation within their own severely restricted area.

It has been obvious for a long time to really scientifically-minded criminologists that the only purely environmental, non-biological means of crime prevention which has the slightest prospect of success is the training, supervision, and education of children from depressed areas and inferior stocks prior to the onset of delinquency. If we are to insist upon concentrating all of our efforts toward crime prevention along environmental lines, we must develop the mechanism and personnel of our system of juvenile supervision and juvenile courts to the highest possible extent without allowing parsimony or politics to interfere with its workings. But the root of the whole matter, in my opinion, is human biology. We must improve inheritance in order to make environmental amelioration effective.

I may now, at length, confess that to the biological anthropologist the entire question of crime and the criminal bulks very small indeed in comparison with the enormous problem of checking the degenerative trends in human evolution which are producing millions of animals of our species inferior in mind and in body. I deem human deterioration to be ultimately responsible not only for crime, but for the evils of war, the oppression of the populace by totalitarian states, and for all of the social cataclysms which are rocking the world and under which civilization is tottering. That man, with all of his pride of intellect, all of his success in manipulating environment and building up complex civilizations, with all of his boasted science, should be completely impotent to control human behavior and prevent wholesale outbreaks of savagery by entire nations is the most sardonic practical joke perpetrated by organic evolution.

The incredible truth is that man has sought to remedy human ills by tinkering with his mind, by drugging his body, by shuffling his institutions, by trying every sort of government, by killing or enslaving his fellow men, and by the emotional flagellation of various kinds of religion, but he has perversely refused to recognize that the human organism itself, by its qualitative variations, is the source both of human evil and of human good. Knowing that he is a human animal solely by virtue of physical human inheritance, just as any other animal belongs to his own species because he inherits the organism of that species, man has nevertheless neglected almost completely the study of human heredity. In the plant and animal world he has experimented and found ways of getting desired qualities by breeding and selection. But with unbelievable stupidity he has refused to admit the self-evident truth that the nature of his own behavior varies principally with the hereditary endowment of his own organism. Faced for centuries with the most blatantly obvious structural-functional relations, those of physical constitution to disease, the medical profession has obstinately turned away and occupied itself exclusively with diseases, microörganisms, pharmacology, hygiene, immunology, and everything except man himself. If those Martians whose fictitious attacks have recently terrorized the child minds of a nation did in fact exist, they might write the epitaph of man: "He was a physician who would not heal himself."

The salvaging of civilization and the resolution of man's desperate social and international difficulties must await the application of knowledge to be gained from a new program of research. Up to now, all of our unintelligent energies have been bent upon an unsuccessful treatment of symptoms which have been mistaken for causes. It may not be too late to acquire this vital knowledge, although the convulsions of civilization are alarmingly like death throes. This appallingly necessitous program can be outlined simply, but its full accomplishment and application will require the labors of more than one human generation. The first phase involves nothing difficult except the overcoming of the lethargy and stubborn resistance of those who will have to do the work. It is nothing more than the relating of disease, whether mental or physical, to the varying anatomical types of the human organism. The many medical specialties must relinquish their fatal habit of wearing blinders which prevent them from seeing anything except their own specific problems of pathology. They must intercorrelate their findings and relate them to the forgotten total organism. I am afraid that they will even have to utilize the services of the physical anthropologist, because he is the only human biologist who has bothered with the morphology and anatomy of man as an evolving animal rather than as a potential patient. He is at present also almost the only specialist who is accustomed to the scientific statistical analysis of intricate masses of data pertaining to great series of human beings.

I confidently predict that it will be a comparatively easy and short matter to determine the correlations of human body types with disease. At the same time it is equally necessary, and even more necessary, to relate gross anatomical structure to physiological and mental variation in the large mass of the so-called "normal" human beings — those who are not ill, or who, in blissful ignorance of the fact that they are ill, nevertheless go on functioning and living as if they were well. Since the individual behavior of the human being is indissolubly connected with the quality of his organism and its healthy functioning, the study of human conduct must not be divorced from the simultaneous attack of anthropology, medicine, and psychology upon the individual. The sociologist, or, if you prefer, the social anthropologist, is wholly indispensable in this cooperative effort. For our ultimate purpose is to improve human behavior through the study of the organism which produces behavior.

Intelligent and intensive work should yield in a decade

a fairly detailed and accurate knowledge of the associations of manifold human types of structure with the normal variations of physiological function, with pathological susceptibilities and immunities, with mental range and capacity, and with patterns of social behavior. We should then have learned what types of human beings are worthless and irreclaimable, and what types are superior and capable of biological and educational improvement.

But the practical application of such knowledge is dependent upon our ability to control and to predict the nature of the human organism as determined by its heredity. Without waiting for the results of studies of constitution in relation to disease, mentality, and behavior, we must begin at once to fill that vast and shameful hiatus in our knowledge of man — human genetics. The acquisition of the necessary data will be time-consuming and costly, but not at all impossible. We must begin by thorough scientific examinations of couples about to be married, and follow them and their children through life, observing, measuring, and analyzing, offering as compensation to these voluntary guinea pigs free medical care and other tangible advantages. By the time we shall have secured exact data upon physico-psycho-sociological correlates from the study of constitution in all of its broader implications, it is possible that the human geneticists will be able to furnish us with more than an inkling of the manner whereby desirable and undesirable human combinations are produced through the mechanism of heredity. If nature can evolve better and more complicated animal organisms through the blind processes of trial and error, natural selection, and fortuitous variation, surely man with his comparatively high animal intelligence, with the transmitted cultural knowledge of thousands of years, and with a purpose hardened by the realization that the fate of his own species is at stake, can learn the mechanism of human heredity. We can direct and control the progress of human evolution by breeding better types and by the ruthless elimination of inferior types, if only we are willing to found and to practise a science of human genetics. With sound and progressively evolving human organisms in the majority of our species, problems of human behavior

will be minimized, and there will be improved educability. Crime can be eradicated, war can be forgotten.

The theory of democratic government is noble and the practise of it offers the greatest opportunities for human happiness, if only the mass of the human individuals within the democracy is sound in body and in mind, and consequently social and to some extent unselfish in behavior. Progressive biological deterioration of the people leads inevitably to anarchy and dictatorships. More than ever, in the light of recent events, we have come to pin all of our faith for the future of civilization and of man on democracy. Like Noah we have builded an ark, the rains have come, and the deluge is upon us. Do we hope to take refuge in that ark of democracy, with our sons and our sons' wives, and survive the flood? We can succeed in this hope only if we leave out some of the noxious animals who are boring from within and making that ark dangerously leaky. So it behooves us to learn our human parasitology and human entomology, to practise an artificial and scientific selection with intelligence, if we wish to save our skins.

INDEX

INDEX